TEACHER EDUCATION AND NATIONAL EDUCATION POLICY 2020

VOLUME TWO

About the Editors

Professor P.K. Sahoo, hailing from Asureswar, Cuttack, Odisha, is a distinguished Educationist and Teacher Educator in India. Professor Sahoo has previously served as the Vice-Chancellor and Dean of the Faculty of Arts at the University of Allahabad, Allahabad. Presently, he is engaged as an ICSSR Senior Fellow in Education, leading a project focused on Developing a Blended Learning Package on Education for Sustainable Development. Additionally, Professor Sahoo holds the position of Lok Pal at UPRT Open University, Prayagraj. Professor P.K. Sahoo has held various significant roles throughout his career, including Chairperson of Digital Education in Social Sciences at the University of Allahabad. He has been an active participant in shaping educational policies, serving as Hon'ble Member of the Northern Regional Committee, NCTE from 2012 to 2019, and has been Hon'ble Member of the Teacher Education Standing Committee of UGC, New Delhi. His expertise has contributed to the formulation of the National Education Policy 2020 particularly in the domain of Teacher Education. With over three and a half decades of teaching experience, Professor Sahoo has held administrative positions, such as Head of the Education Department, Director of the Institute of Correspondence Courses at the University of Allahabad, and Director of Academics at Kota Open University, Kota and prior to this he taught at Institute of Education, Centre of Excellence at Devi Ahilya Vishwavidyalay, Indore over a decade. He began his research journey as a UGC Junior Research Fellow at the Centre of Advanced Study in Education, M.S. University of Baroda, and later served as a Research Associate. Professor Sahoo's contributions extend beyond academia; he has been actively involved in national and international level professional activities, collaborating with various institutions, universities, and government bodies. He is renowned for his pioneering contribution to Open and Distance Learning in India and across Asian countries, as well as for his work in Future Studies in Education, Management, and Teacher Education. With a notable publication record, including 10 books and over 100 research papers in many international and national journals, Professor Sahoo has also mentored numerous scholars, guiding 29 Ph.D. students, one post-doctoral project, and 25 M.Phil. students. He has led more than 20 research projects sponsored by prestigious organizations such as UGC, IGNOU, ISRO, NIEPA, MHRD, and NIOS. His academic contributions have been recognized internationally, receiving awards for paper presentations at conferences in countries such as the UK, China, Hong Kong, Thailand, Malaysia, the Philippines, Nepal, Pakistan, and Vietnam. He played a pivotal role as the coordinator of the MOOCs Programme in Education and has contributed significantly to the development of e-PG Pathshala modules in Education in collaboration with CIET, NCERT, which are accessible to students on SWAYAM. Furthermore, Professor Sahoo served as the President of the Indian Association of Teacher Educators (IATE) and has been the recipient of numerous national and international awards, showcasing his dedication and excellence in the field of education.

Dr. B.C. Das is Assistant Professor of Education, Department of Education, Ravenshaw University, Cuttack, Odisha. He has also served Faculty of Education, Banasthali University, Rajasthan, Rani Bhagyawati Devi Women's PG College, Bijnor and has been the Programme In-charge of IGNOU B.Ed. Programme Study Centre. He has owned the distinction of being a National Research Fellow of the Ministry of Tribal Affairs, Government of India at University of Allahabad. His teaching and research interest zeroes-in-on teaching skills, constructivist and digital pedagogy, tribal education, development education and education for sustainable development. Dr. Das is currently engaged with his research focus on Development Education and Empowerment of Tribal Communities which may be recognized as pioneering effort in India. Dr. Das has published seven reference and textbooks: Tribal Education: Trends and Future Scenario; Education for Tribals: Participation and Effectiveness; co-edited four volumes: *Professionalism in Teacher Education: Contemporary Perspectives; Quality in Higher Education: Issues and Practices; Quality Education in India*: Vol. 1; *Problems and Prospects; Quality Education in India*: Vol. 2; *Inputs and Initiatives*; Lead Author of the Textbook titled *Critical Understanding of ICT*; published more than 50 research papers and undertaken three research projects; guided M.Phil. and Ph.D. research students; and innovated K-4 Learning Transaction Model for teaching practice. Recently he has completed a TPACK based Research Project funded under PMMMNMTT, Government of India. Dr. Das has been elevated to the prestigious position of Hon'ble Member of NCTE (ERC), New Delhi.

TEACHER EDUCATION
AND
NATIONAL EDUCATION POLICY 2020

VOLUME TWO
Research and Quality Assurance

Edited by

P.K. Sahoo

B.C. Das

CONCEPT PUBLISHING COMPANY PVT. LTD.

NEW DELHI - 110 059

ISBN: 978-93-6344-587-1 (Set)
ISBN: 978-93-6344-083-8 (Vol. 1)
ISBN: 978-93-6344-700-4 (Vol. 2)

First Published 2025

Published and Printed by

Concept Since 1974

Concept Publishing Company Pvt. Ltd.
A/15-16, Commercial Block, Mohan Garden
New Delhi-110059 (India)
T: +91-11-41101460
E: publishing@conceptpub.com, *W*: www.conceptpub.com

Cataloging in Publication--Courtesy: D.K. Agencies (P) Ltd. <docinfo@dkagencies.com>

Teacher education and national education policy 2020 / edited by P.K. Sahoo, B.C. Das.
volumes cm
Includes bibliographical references and index.
Contents: volume 1. Development and technology integration -- volume 2. Research and quality assurance.
ISBN 9789363445871 (set)
ISBN 9789363440838 (vol. 1)
ISBN 9789363447004 (vol. 2)

1. Teachers--Training of--India. 2. Curriculum change--India. 3. Educational technology--India. 4. Teachers--Professional ethics--India. 5. Teachers--Training of--Government policy--India. I. Sahoo, P. K., editor. II. Das, B. C., Dr., editor.

LCC LB1727.I5T43 2025 | DDC 370.71154 23

Dedicated to

Professor M.B. Buch

Father of Teacher Education and Research in India

Preface

Teacher Education remains at centre stage in catering education for sustainable development as the priority of the global society. Quality education with emphasis on equity, inclusiveness and excellence is to be ensured for every child in the knowledge society. Blending indigenous knowledge base with modern technology in the socio-cultural milieu of every human being can lead the path of self-reliance. While generalised discipline oriented knowledge system helps us to generate universal understanding of natural and behavioural phenomena, the understanding of life world and its worth is deeply rooted in grassroots level life experiences. Therefore, education for life is imperative and its future must integrate the context specific experiences with universal understanding. The multiple realities concerning meaningfulness of individual and social life must be reflected in the curricular experiences. Teachers' role in promoting such experiences is to be valued duly in the preparatory teacher development programmes and in various kinds of professional development practices as well.

The National Education Policy, 2020 (NEP 2020), emphasises on the basic principle of "teachers as the heart of the learning processes". It spells about their preparation, professional development, and positive working environments. It also focuses on encouraging innovation through autonomy, good governance and empowerment indicating professionalism in teaching. Professionally competent teachers can do justice to the emerging concept of holistic education for a multidisciplinary world, with due emphasis on conceptual clarity, creative inquiry process, critical thinking and practice of morals and constitutional values (NEP 2020). Teachers' role is not just restricted to transaction of teaching activities inside the classroom, rather, they must have respect for the local context in all curriculum and pedagogy. Teachers' respect for equity and inclusion must be reflected in the whole school environment. Such principles have a lot of bearing for reforms in school curriculum as well as for teacher development programmes. Restructuring of school system has also implications for reforms in teacher education curriculum. Development rooted in NCF-2005 and NCFTE-2009 took a long path for bringing structural changes in Teacher Education. As per recommendations of Justice Verma Commission Report, 2012 and NCTE Guidelines, 2014 & 2019, integrated teacher education programme in composite higher education institutions has been a component of higher education institutions. The emphasis on professional skill development programme in the form of internship and longer duration exposure to teaching-learning practices in real school situation is a significant deviation from traditional teacher training practices. In this respect, the discourse on quality in teacher education and school education draw major attention of the stakeholders of the school system. Even, such debate is extended to the relationship between teacher inputs and teaching-learning process at higher education level. These issues have been discussed elaborately in these volumes through the contributions of reputed scholars, experts and the researchers in the field of education in the country.

The theoretical discussions on education, teaching, learning and assessment with multidisciplinary perspective of teacher education have been corroborated in the form of conceptual papers in these volumes. The write-ups reflect on compositeness, continuity and contemporary expressions on teacher education system in India and abroad. Moreover, the efforts on curriculum reforms in teacher education and its practices, even though it is a recent phenomenon, reveal openness of the system in Indian context. Teacher education programmes for pre-service teachers and in-service teachers in a wider framework of operation draw special attention of regulatory bodies and governance of the institutions. The Indian experiences of multiplicity and newness in teacher education talk about inclusiveness of teacher education. The system caters to the diversified professional needs of teachers of different stages of school system. Effort on innovative practices in teacher education is related to different institutional factors. The emergence of privatisation and unplanned growth of teacher education institutions in the country have a lot of negative bearing on professional orientation and innovations in teacher education. The empirical evidences on curricular practices of teacher education reveal multiplicity and variations in different practices in institutional context. The phenomena of technology use and technology integration in education are of a recent origin. Teacher education system has dual position in this regard.

The foremost requirement is to make teachers competent in suitable integration of pedagogy, content and technology in meeting the curricular objectives of school system. There have been integrated efforts to link teacher education programmes with online platforms, open distance learning programmes and blended learning approach. Some such disconnected efforts must be placed in the form of consortium for generation of e-resources, integration of technology inputs with innovative pedagogic principles and promotion of online education for teachers. The role of national level, state level and local level bodies in education for promotion of academic excellence and resource generation like NCERT, CIET, IGNOU, NIOS, EMRCs, SCERTs, SIEMATs, IASEs, CTEs, DIETs, etc. is very much meaningful in this regard. The chapters devoted to innovations, quality upgradation and technology integration in school education and teacher education ponder on different issues and practices concerning technology orientation of teachers. The nature of research in education, particularly in the context of teacher education needs a different orientation. The traditional approach of theory practice divide and dominance of generalised knowledge orientation of behavioural science in education are found obsolete to educational reforms, particularly, in the context of teacher development practices in the ground reality.

The teachers need to be oriented towards educational action based reforms through research. Their participation to interlink hands on reflective practices in education with broad- based knowledge framework must be encouraged through teacher empowerment programmes in decentralised form. The Schools of Education at university level must explore the quality enhancement oriented institutional possibilities on different aspects of education.

Professionalism is considered as the core of teacher development programmes. The globalised world has generated complexities in the role of teachers in current educational setup. Various issues have been raised about teachers' morals in the context of life in the ground reality and perception of a universal view of professional ethics. The teachers' position in quest of universal mission with critical reflection on day-to-day professional practices is very much significant in the current scenario. There is little scope for centralised code of conduct approach in generation of discourse on professional ethics among teachers, especially in the context of autonomous role of teachers and learners in teaching-learning process.

The discussions on different areas of professional ethics become more significant, when teacher is placed in the centre of school system, as per NEP, 2020. The concept of autonomy with accountability needs to be addressed in the form of dialogues among teachers at institutional level as well as in different forums of teachers through suitable networking. This will pave the way for promoting deep involvement of teachers in evolving professionalism in teaching. Thus, professionalism in teaching will be very much meaningful with inclusive perspective. As a whole, the experiences shared by the eminent scholars on different dimensions of professionalism in teacher education, policy orientation and reforms in teacher education curriculum, quality issues and technology integration research and development of professional ethics of teachers shall contribute meaningfully to development of contemporary knowledge on teacher education among teachers, students and scholars of education.

P.K. Sahoo
B.C. Das

Acknowledgements

We take immense pride in receiving the guidance of revered mentors Professor Y.P. Agarwal, former Emeritus Professor of Education, Kurukshetra University, Professor Murmur Mukhopadhyay, Chairman, ETMA Society and former Director, NIEPA, New Delhi and cooperation of senior colleagues. Professor R. Govinda, former Vice-Chancellor, NUEPA, New Delhi, Professor Mohan B. Menon, former Deputy Vice-Chancellor of Wawasan Open University, Penang, Malaysia and Chairperson DISHA Global Trust, Cochin, Professor D.N. Sansanwal, former Director, IOE, DAVV, Indore, Professor Santosh Panda, former Chairperson, NCTE and Professor S.S. Jena, former Chairperson, NIOS as source on inspiration for this outcome. Contributors were specifically urged to prepare write-ups on various themes covered in this volume. The list of authors encompasses a wide spectrum of young researchers, seasoned academicians, and experts in the field of education across the nation. We extend our heartfelt gratitude to each one of them.

Our sincere thanks go to esteemed colleagues Professor Shyam B. Menon, founding Vice-Chancellor of AUD, Delhi, and Professor Mohd. Miyan, President of IATE and former Vice-Chancellor of MANUU, Hyderabad, for their unwavering moral support and encouragement that could bring forth these volumes on Teacher Education, enriched with contemporary insights, policy perspectives, and research on the implementation of new guidelines for Teacher Education in India. We are deeply thankful to the most distinguished professors of education in the country for their generous contributions. Special acknowledgment is due to Professor M.S. Lalitha, Former Vice-Chancellor and Dean of the School of Education, Pondicherry Central University; Professor D.R. Goel, UGC Emeritus Professor, M.S. University of Baroda; Professor N.K. Dash, former Director of the School of Education, IGNOU, New Delhi; Professor A. Muthumanickam, Former Dean of the School of Education, M.K. University, Madurai; Professor Sunil Behari Mohanty, President of AIAER, Puducherry; Professor S.C. Panigrahi, CASE, MSU Baroda; and Professor Sushma Sharma, DDUGU Gorakhpur, for their invaluable contributions to these volumes.

The authors express their gratitude to senior colleagues from the University of Allahabad, including Professor Dhananjai Yadav, Head of the Education Department, and Professor Vidya Aggarwal and Professor Usha Mishra, former Heads of the Education Department, for their insightful write-ups. The editors owe a debt of gratitude to the young contributors from various universities and colleges, including Professor Sujeet Kumar from GGD Central University, Bilaspur; Professor Gyanendra Kumar Rout from IGNTU, Amarkantak; Dr. Ashok Dansana and Dr. Praveen Bobby Binjha from NCERT, New Delhi and formerly with Ravenshaw University, Cuttack; Dr. Meenakshi Biswal from Basanta Women's College, BHU, Varanasi; Professor Namita Sahoo from K.P. Training College, AU; Dr. Rama Gupta from JTGDC, AU; Dr. B.S. Gupta from CMPDC, AU; Dr. Surendra Kumar from UPRTOU; Dr. Subhash Chandra from DN PG College, Gorakhpur; Dr. Hemant Mistry from MSU, Baroda; and Dr. Prerna Mandhyan from D.S. College, Katihar.

We also acknowledge the contributions of promising scholars from the University of Allahabad and Ravenshaw University, including Dr. Priyanka Sharma, Dr. Chandan Prasad, Smt. Manju Kumari, Dr. Brijesh Kumar, Dr. Ashok Kumar, Dr. Uzma Khanam, Ms. Usha Devi, Shri Bijay Kumar Das, Shri Gulsan Behera, and

Ms. Debajani Sahoo, for their research-based articles on emerging areas of Teacher Education. Special recognition is extended to Dr. Priyanka Sharma for her consistent cooperation in word processing and editing tasks.

Our heartfelt gratitude goes to Shri Ashok Kumar Mittal, Managing Director of Concept Publishing Co. Pvt. Ltd., New Delhi, for timely publishing these volumes for our target stakeholders.

P.K. Sahoo
B.C. Das

Contents

SECTION II
Curriculum Reforms in Teacher Education

SECTION III
Technology Integrated Teacher Education

VOLUME 2

SECTION IV
Research Innovation in Teacher Education

SECTION V
Professional Development of Teachers

SECTION VI
Quality Assurance in Teacher Education

Introduction

P.K. Sahoo

Professionalism in teaching and Teacher Education has been a significant discourse in the era of globalization and liberalization. The imperative of cultivating high-quality human resources in teaching, equipped with professional knowledge, skills, and ethics, holds paramount importance in the education policy frameworks of both developed and developing nations. The core principle of the National Education Policy, 2020 underscores the pivotal role of teachers and faculty as the cornerstone of the learning process. It emphasizes the necessity for their rigorous recruitment, preparation, continuous professional development, positive work environment, and assured service conditions, advocating for a "light but tight" oversight and regulatory system to uphold the integrity and transparency of the educational system.

Teacher Education is valued in the context of quality professional education within the organized service sector, playing a crucial role in shaping the future of children and, consequently, the nation as a whole (NEP 2020). Furthermore, contribution of education to sustainable development, guided by principles of equity and inclusion, stands as a central agenda in global development discourse. Enhancing educational inputs is contingent upon strengthening the quality of teacher inputs. Effective teaching and learning practices hinge on the professional knowledge, attitude, and skills of teachers. Consequently, teacher development programmes, starting from the preparatory stage, are meticulously designed to address curriculum design, implementation, and assessment, adhering to guidelines and standards set by statutory bodies in Teacher Education and other educational authorities at national and state levels.

Recent years have witnessed a heightened emphasis on the professional development of in-service teachers, often encouraged on a voluntary basis. Centralized efforts are being made to disseminate knowledge and facilitate skill development exercises for teachers and other school functionaries, albeit within limited scopes. The growing concern for the teaching profession is further accentuated by the influence of liberal economies and private management in school and Teacher Education sectors, which have elevated expectations from teachers and accentuated their role in market-oriented endeavours within a globalized society.

Teachers' roles and responsibilities, *vis-à-vis* students, parents, communities, governance systems, and the broader global landscape, are undergoing a re-evaluation compared to the latter part of the last century. The Teacher Education community, particularly researchers and experts in the field of education, are compelled to explore various avenues for fostering professionalism among teachers in alignment with educational objectives and sustainable development goals. This book endeavours to shed light on new perspectives and avenues for the professional development of teachers, encompassing both theoretical frameworks and practical applications of Teacher Education, with a specific focus on the Indian context. It incorporates contributions from seasoned experts, leading teacher educators, and emerging researchers across different volumes, with Volume 1 focusing on "Development and Technology Integration", progressing to Volume 2 on "Research and Quality Assurance".

There are six sections in these volumes, viz.

I. New Perspectives in Teacher Education,
II. Curriculum Reforms in Teacher Education,
III. Technology Integrated Teacher Education,

IV. Research and Innovation in Teacher Education,
V. Professional Development of Teachers, and
VI. Quality Assurance in Teacher Education.

The first section of Volume 1 delves into the presentation of a conceptual framework for teaching and Teacher Education from a fresh perspective. While the conventional approach to fostering professional ethics, knowledge, and skills among teachers remains prevalent in pedagogical discussions, the incorporation of open distance learning methods and blended learning systems into Teacher Education practices is gaining traction. **Professor Shyam Menon's** article critiques the National Education Policy (NEP) of 2020 within the context of Teacher Education, particularly relevant in India's market economy landscape. Professor Menon evaluates the trajectory of Teacher Education, examining three key national education policy documents in India. His analysis reveals a lack of sustained commitment to instigating reforms aimed at future directions. He highlights the intricate role of the National Council for Teacher Education (NCTE), particularly concerning initial Teacher Education programmes governed by statutory provisions. It appears that continuous professional development programmes may fall outside the purview of the NCTE. Professor Menon advocates for structural reforms, emphasizing the critical integration of preparatory Teacher Education programmes with ongoing professional development initiatives under the dynamic leadership of university education departments. He expresses concerns about the growing influence of market-oriented approaches in school education, suggesting a potential dilution of focus on quality education, particularly regarding social inclusion and equitable access.

The chapter on Teaching and Professional Development of Teachers by **Professor P.K. Sahoo** focuses on conceptual analysis of teaching with different perspectives. Accordingly, different perspectives of teacher development have been discussed at length in this chapter.Different approaches of development of competencies, teaching skills and multiple models of teaching among student teachers and working teachers have been discussed. This chapter consolidates the participatory approach, ICT based information processing models and holistic framework of teacher development in real school situation. The integration of theoretical understanding, stakeholders expectations, training objectives, teachers and students aptitudes and abilities and skilful human interaction in conducive learning environment and feedback mechanism have been highlighted for continuous development of teachers in real school situation. **Professor N.K. Dash** has thrown light on the conceptualisation of teaching by taking into consideration different factors such as transaction and indirect engagement of teacher, learning outcome orientation, planned and unplanned activities of teachers. Professor Dash elucidated the relationship between different concepts like teaching and learning, teaching and instruction, teaching and training, teaching and indoctrination. He has extended the discussion on emerging concept of teaching in the era of open learning society and information and communication technology. He has aptly sited the view of Professor S.B. Menon that didactic teaching is the segment that is largely amenable to online and digital forms of transaction. It is to be extended to interaction between teacher and learner as well as to peer interactions for development of analytical and other intellectual skills through deconstructive approach. Professor Dash has focused on creating a hybrid model of teaching or blended learning approach through combination of digital learning and face-to-face teaching.

Education must be linked with core values of human life and societal system. The issues are, of course, context specific in nature. Keeping in view emerging issues of education, Teacher Education need to be restructured and reoriented with a larger scope of multistage schooling. Many such issues have been focused well by **Professor D.R. Goel** in his write up "Education in Quest of Identity: Role of Teacher Education" has raised concern about Teacher Education's identity. He has alarmed that, "soul of education is being killed through ruthless expansion and privatisation leading to marketization of education". Professor Goel has listed various issues in detail concerning digitalisation, peace and health. He has also listed a number of capacity building programmes in the context of Teacher Education and has given a number of suggestions for strengthening teachers professional development. Different themes concerning teachers' personality development, digitalisation in education, development of technology competencies and reorganisation of professional bodies in Teacher Education have been elaborated through the write up of Professor Goel.

Constructivist paradigm of teacher development has been proliferated in different policy documents like NCF 2005, NCFTE 2009 and NEP 2020. **Dr. Biswajit Behera** a pioneer has thrown light on humanistic teacher development practices in an inclusive setting. He emphasises on the collaboration roles of teachers and learners in constructive classrooms having a shift from teaching for teaching sake to teaching for learning sake. Thus, Teacher Education programmes must gear up for incorporating reflective collaborative and constructive practice in teacher preparation. To him, learners should involve themselves in talk, dialogue, public reasoning and shared problem-solving. Classroom environment is counterproductive to learning. Therefore, teachers should illustrate collaboration between and among the teachers and students.

The emphasis on education for teachers in Higher Education Institutions (HEIs) has been duly projected in NEP 2020. **Professor S.B. Mohanty** has made a comparative study of provisions for Teacher Education for HEI teachers in different developed countries of the world. He has highlighted the major attributes of teaching-learning system of HEIs as per NEP 2020, such as inclusive curriculum, flexibility, learner support and learning resources, community engagement and projects. The role of e-learning platforms for continuous professional development of HEI teachers occupies key position in teacher development. The on-going practices for Teacher Education through different schemes of UGC like HRDC programmes and Mahamana Madan Mohan Malviya Mission for Teacher Education need to be revamped with online blended learning approach and promotion of original contribution of resource persons in such programmes. There is a need for strengthening the quality inputs of online programmes for teachers of HEIs. In this context, the Inter University Consortium for Teacher Education (IUCTE) may be redesigned as National Centre for Teachers Excellence for Higher Education (NCTEHE) and treat HRDCs as regional centres for teachers' excellence for higher education. The Centre must develop appropriate learning materials for the mentors as well for newly-recruited teachers of HEIs.

The Second Section of the book has a wide coverage of issues concerning structure and process of Teacher Education curriculum in India. Curricular perspectives of Teacher Education have been discussed in the context of National Curriculum Framework (2005) National Curriculum Framework for Teacher Education (2009), Justice Verma Commission Report (2012) and NCTE Curriculum Guidelines 2014 as referred in NEP 2020. This has highlighted indigenous knowledge based curriculum at school stage. Mother tongue has been considered as basic medium of instruction to school children. The principles of plurality, multilingualism, cultural diversity and Indianness have been the major focus of curriculum. Accordingly, Teacher Education is to be geared towards such transformation. In his chapter on Gandhian Perspective of School Curriculum **Professor P.K. Sahoo** has made a review of national system of education as proposed by Gandhiji, while throwing light on the provisions of NEP 2020. **Dr. Akha K. Mao's** chapter on "Policy Conscious Teachers and Their Perception Towards Teacher Education Programme" reveals, worth reforming conclusion that "Teacher Education institutions should be embedded in universities as they provide more conducive and democratic environment for academics, scholars and practitioners not only engage with their parent disciplines but also carry a continuous intellectual dialogue across disciplines." In addition to the academic perspective the author has focused on collective participation of teachers to carry out reformation in education through "carrying forward a pollicised intellectual intervention with the system."

The essence of Teacher Education curriculum lies on making teacher development practices relevant to school system and development of professional quality of teachers. Several initiatives have been made during last decade to bring reform on structural and process dimensions of Teacher Education Curriculum. A major emphasis have been laid on bringing Teacher Education to the fold of higher education and provision for integrated Teacher Education programme (ITEP) with general education at undergraduate and postgraduate level. Pedagogic principle based practices in real school situations has been integral part of Teacher Education curriculum for elementary and secondary level Teacher Education programmes respectively. Similarly, master's degree programme in education has changed its focus to preparation of teacher educators with required competencies to deal with Teacher Education programmes.Internship practices at school level and Teacher Education institution level have been incorporated with emphasis on encouraging hands on experience based teacher training. A detailed discussion has been done on reforms in Teacher Education Curriculum by **Dr. B.C. Das** and **Professor Namita Sahoo** in their chapter titled "Reshaping Teacher Education Curriculum" especially in the context of NCTE guidelines and NEP 2020. They have portrayed the global vision as well as national level priorities of Teacher Education. They talk about the educational goals and shifting role of higher education institutions.

The programme evaluation study on integrated B.Ed. Programme of Central universities, as per NCTE Guidelines (2014) have been conducted by **Professor P.K. Sahoo** and **Dr. Priyanka Sharma** at all India level. In their study, Sahoo and Sharma have explored favourable perception of Arts and Science background student teachers on perspectives in education, curriculum and pedagogic studies, practicum and school internship components of Teacher Education curriculum. Similarly, in their chapter on the students and teacher educators' perception of M.Ed. programme, Sahoo and Sharma have found positive opinion of the stakeholders about new curriculum structure and implementation. The

Teacher Educators, of course, were comparatively less enthusiastic about reforms concerning M.Ed. programme's structure and its implementation strategies.

School internship practices have been considered as on integral component of Teacher Education curriculum. School internship builds a sound base to develop inclusive understanding of professional skills and its application in real School Situation with sustained involvement of would be teachers and mentors. **Professor P.K. Sahoo** and **Dr. Ashok Kumar** in their chapter on School Internship have deliberated on different empirical evidences regarding school internship practices in Teacher Education Institutions of India. Encouraging experiences were revealed regarding such practices. However, the private institutions did not take such programme as seriously in comparison to that of their government (aided) counterparts. Moreover, the lacunae concerning academic programme management and mentoring were very much prevalent in implementation of school internship practices. Linkage of theory and practice and *vice versa* could not be established well through school internship.

A good curriculum with proper implementation emphasises on stakeholders' involvement in it at different stages. In Teacher Education curriculum especially in Open Distance Learning (ODL) system learner autonomy is considered as the key feature. Hence, student teachers of ODL system are expected to get priorities in decision making in curriculum design, implementation and evaluation. There may be variations in students' involvement in the context of background factors like gender, locale and discipline. The research evidences gathered by **Professor P.K. Sahoo and Dr. Chandan Prasad** revealed that different components of ODL mode Teacher Education had significant effect on student teachers' decision making in different components of curriculum. Students' involvement was very high in curriculum transaction and assessment and evaluation components and low in teacher support system and curriculum design components. There was significant interaction of locale and ODL components on student teachers involvement in ODL mode Teacher Education programme.

Section Three of the book is devoted to Technology Integrated Teaching Learning and Teacher Education. Quality enhancement in Teacher Education is mainly linked with technology use and integration. The digital India campaign has gone into the ground level functioning of school education. This is high time to focus on development of technology competency among teachers for making teaching flexible, learner friendly and constructive in nature. On quality enhancements of Teacher Education several initiatives have been made at institutional level for promotion of blended learning approach. Of late, NEP 2020 has highlighted promotion of blended learning technology at different stages of education. At Teacher Education stage technology integration aims at developing competencies of teachers in pedagogy, course content and technology applications to achieve the objectives of curriculum. In this context Dr. B.C. Das and his colleagues have reported about their experiments on effectiveness of TPACK based internship practices at B.Ed. level. They have elaborated on the competency development of pre-service teachers using such package. **Professor A. Muthumanickum** has made a conceptual analysis of Blended Learning in Teacher Education highlighting its role in process and product of teaching learning system. He has focused on integration of offline and online learning in education. Different approaches of blended learning like instructor led e-learning facilitated e-learning and self-paced e-learning have been discussed in detail. The role of teachers in blended learning in the context of development of competencies, creation of learning environment, exploring learning needs, research competencies and evaluation strategies are considered key components of blended learning approach. He also talked about appropriate management of technology in Teacher Education programmes. **Dr. Sujeet Kumar** has highlighted the key features of hybrid model of teaching-learning through traditional face-to-face mode and advanced digital technology at school stage. He has presented how traditional face-to-face mode teaching has been replaced by smart classroom activities and virtual learning environment in Teacher Education.

Several efforts have been made to promote e-learning opportunities for teacher development. The SWAYAM portal has been devoted to MOOCs at higher education stage. Professor P.K. Sahoo *et al.* have focused on their experiences of developing e-PG Pathshala Programme in Education and its operationalization. The authors have found that majority of learners of MOOC course in education appreciated its quality and utility. This was noticed that the course was very useful in enhancing professional understanding of students. The students were motivated to join in more numbers of MOOC courses in the field of education.

As stated above technological skills, pedagogic competencies and Content Knowledge mastery must be well knitted for development of professionalism among teachers. **Dr. B.C. Das and B.K. Das** have done an analysis of the status of Technological Pedagogical and Content Knowledge in Teacher Education curriculum of different Teacher Education institutions of Odisha. Most of the student-teachers of integrated B.Ed. programme reported that they had minimum knowledge of Teacher Education system. They have highlighted on quality improvement with technology inputs in Teacher Education programme has a better scope in four-year integrated B.Ed. programme. The chapter on a study of uses of ICT by doctoral research scholars by **Professor P.K. Sahoo** and **Dr. Uzma Khanam** revealed no significant effect of faculty background on ICT use in different stages of research. However, there was significant effect of gender on use of ICT in research. The women scholars had an edge over their men counterparts on use of ICT in different stages of research. As a whole, the research scholars made optimum use of ICT in different stages of research.

Section IV of the book as included in Volume 2 deals with research and innovation in Teacher Education. Research in Teacher Education is one of the major areas of educational research. Teacher education research highlights different practices aiming at professional development of in-service and pre-service teachers. Of late, there has been emphasis on strengthening the base of teacher research. This section includes empirical studies concerning teacher development practices. Most of them belong to evaluation research category. Current researches on Teacher Education system have focused on study of perception/attitude of stakeholders about the outcome of different kinds of currently introduced pre-service and in-service Teacher Education programmes. Such programmes aim at development of professional competencies in different areas like personality development through *yoga* practices, computer education, decision making, action research etc. Teacher research has gained momentum as a tool for professional development of teachers. In this context, research competencies among working teachers need to be identified with top priority. There is a need to encourage context specific in-depth teacher research studies leading to development of research competencies among working teachers. Of late, there have been efforts by the teacher educators to emphasise on process based competencies of teachers. In their chapter **Dr. B.C. Das** and his team have focused on a study of application of K-4 learning model in pre-service teacher development practices.

In his article on developing research potential of elementary teachers through action research, **Professor Dhananjai Yadav** highlights the effectiveness of action research module as experimented over school teachers. The study found significant effect of action research module on improving research skills of elementary school teachers. **Professor Vidya Agarwal** and **Professor Sushma Pandey** conducted an extensive study on impact of teacher training programmes on teaching learning environment and student achievement at elementary level. They noticed that teachers are not using training experience in natural classroom situations and teaching. This was also reported that use of appropriate teaching methods and techniques have significant effect on enhancement of achievement of learners.

A study conducted on effectiveness of online Teacher Education programme of National Institute of Open Schooling (NIOS) by **Professor P.K. Sahoo** revealed that there was positive impact of online programme on attitude of the in-service elementary teachers. The online programme was found more effective among rural area teachers, especially teachers with longer teaching experience. The teachers' attitude towards different components of online programme was found to be of very positive in nature.

Dr. Subhash Chandra and **Professor P.K. Sahoo** conducted a study on learning style of traditional mode and ODL mode student teachers. The article revealed significant association between the modes of Teacher Education and participatory learning style of student teachers. It was noticed that the open distance learning mode student teachers were of higher participatory category than that of their face-to-face mode counterparts. As a whole, the student teachers had adopted high competitive as well as high collaborative learning styles in their studies.

Dr. H.K. Mistry and **Professor S.C. Panigrahi** had conducted an extensive study of "Inclusion of Students with Disabilities in HEIs". The findings revealed a meagre (0.56%) enrolment of students with disabilities at higher education. Among them there was predominance of students with orthopaedic background. The vocational skills training facility was very poor among them. The authors have discussed about the role of teachers in tackling challenges of inclusive education at higher education stage.

The Fifth Section of the book is devoted to "Professional Development of Teachers". Professional ethics has been a matter of discussion for teachers in the context of globalisation and liberal economy. The standard code of conduct for teachers and standard framework of assessment of educational institutions include professional component in Teacher Education system. The NEP 2020 talks about teachers' accountability towards students, institution and teaching profession. It highlights that teachers must be grounded in Indian values, languages, knowledge, ethos and traditions, while also being well-versed in the latest advances in education and pedagogy. These points have been discussed in the context of development of disciplinary/multidisciplinary knowledge, pedagogic knowledge with hands on experiences and theoretical understanding and professional ethics. Professional ethics is related to welfare of learners, own personality, critical reflection on teaching-learning practices, building conducive learning environment and leadership for innovative practices. It also includes institutional growth and continuous pursuit for equity, excellence and sustainability in academic endeavours. Thus, professional ethics is understood as the nerve system of teaching profession. It is imperative to ponder upon applied ethics in teachers' personality and teaching functions. How ethics can be evolved through continuous collective dialogue among experienced teachers and the experts has been the major concern of teacher development. Different approaches of nurturing ethics with special reference to empowerment of teachers have been presented in the chapter written by **Professor P.K. Sahoo**. Different group-based collective participatory models of teaching ethics have been projected for development of ethics.

Since professional ethics is a relative concept, "encouragement must be given to working teachers for continuous professional development activities on ethical issues concerning development of self, appropriate decision making and ethical approaches on students' development, institutional practice and eco-friendly approach to teaching." On Teachers Professional Development: Emerging Issues, **Professor G.K. Rout** writes on reforms in subject matter teaching (standards, curriculum and pedagogy), equity concerning heterogeneous student population; nature of learners' assessment and its application; social organisation of schooling; and professionalization of teaching. He focuses on professional development models and the tasks ahead, "teachers' autonomy may be intensified by various circumstances surrounding collegial and institutional life, the norms underlying peer acceptance and admiration, and the fabric of relationship between teachers and administrators."

Dr. Rama Gupta highlights content competencies for professional development of teachers at primary school stage. She found significant association between teaching competencies and students achievement in Hindi language at primary stage. She suggested the in-service programme must cover both the concerns—"how to teach and what to teach to whom". In this respect, professional development programmes must be a continuous part of working language teachers' career. While different responsibilities of teachers can be attributed to committed behaviour of teachers, human resource development orientation to Teacher Education must be in the forefront of Teacher Education policies. These ideas have been proliferated in the chapter of **Professor Usha Mishra** and **Dr. Prerna Mandhyan**. They have done a conceptual analysis of accountability of pre-service Teacher Education programme in relation to teachers' quality and student outcomes. To them "teaching quality in practice constitutes a set of actions and activities that improve student outcomes." They focus on the approach for influencing human capital pool in the form of context—specific intervention through teaching. This chapter discusses in detail about multiple teacher evaluation criteria. The chapter on Professional Development of Teacher Educators, written by **Professor P.K. Sahoo** and **Dr. Brijesh Kumar**, highlights the relevance of empowerment of teacher educators to prepare better teachers. The institution-based professional development programme models have been discussed in detail. The authors have presented empirical evidences on needs prioritised by the teacher-educators of elementary and secondary education on different areas, such as professional development, discipline, Teacher Education policy, research competencies and personality of teachers.

In her chapter on Inclusive Education and Development of Professional Ethics of Teachers, **Professor Minakshi Biswal** throws light on innovative teacher preparation model having input, process and output for development of professional ethics among teachers. Collaborative teaching and attitudinal change are considered as the training inputs, whereas the process is identified with strategies, methods and techniques. The outputs are listed in the form of professional ethics as reflected in teachers' behaviour for effective inclusive education.

Section VI of the book is devoted to quality assurance in Teacher Education. Professional education for teachers must be of quality oriented nature. The NEP 2020 has focused on equity and excellence in education.The global society expects high quality output of teachers to be absorbed in the school system. Quality enhancement concept is directly linked with internal efforts of quality management of institutions with regard to curriculum design and curriculum transaction process. Participatory management for quality enhancements must be promoted through stakeholders' committed involvement in planning and decision making, execution, assessment and feedback functions of the system. Quality appraisal by external body is done according to centralised parameters applicable to professional institution programmes. The role of statutory bodies is very much significant in formation of assessment and accreditation norms, procedures of institutional evaluation, grading of institutional performances. In the Indian context, such responsibility is vested with the regulatory bodies like NCTE for Teacher Education Programmes. Issues involved in accreditation practices and quality assessment mechanisms in different contexts of Teacher Education system have been elaborated on different forums of Teacher Education. A new development is witnessed for quality appraisal of different issues concerning Teacher Education quality and technology intervention. Major reform is expected in promoting different professional institutions under one Umbrella of National Higher Education Regulatory Authority.

Professor Lalitha in her chapter on "Teacher Education towards Excellence focuses" on various challenges of Teacher Education like qualitative experience in school education, technological interventions in school curriculum and its transaction and global context of schooling in the current society. She has thrown light on various issues concerning quality of Teacher Education covering curricular objects, management of content and process, professional development of teachers and teacher educators and research output. She talks about shift from pedagogical content knowledge to technological pedagogical content knowledge of teachers. She also emphasises on the competencies of teacher educators to produce teachers with twenty-first century skills, there is a need for continuous professional development among teacher educators. This is very much in tune with NEP 2020. She highlights that research should be built into process dimension of Teacher Education. The teacher educators must be inspired to innovate, and execute differently practices even based on intuitive judgement for improving Teacher Education. The role of networking technology for sharing of research experiences among teacher educators must occupy top priority quality enhancements in Teacher Education System.

The community orientation in Teacher Education has been highlighted in NEP 2020. A study conducted by **Professor P.K. Sahoo** and **Dr. Surendra Kumar** on curricular practices of open distance learning mode B.Ed. programme revealed that community awareness programme is an essential component of Teacher Education. Such kind of awareness programmes are encouraged through project-based activities. These experiences reveal different practices being promoted through alternative forms of Teacher Education in the country.

Research has been conducted by **Dr. B.S. Gupta** on yogic activities in quality enhancement in primary education in the context of intelligence of boy and girl students. The study confirmed significant effect of yogic activities in enhancement of intelligence of students. **Dr. Ashok Dansana** and **Mr. Gulsan Behera** have written on Resource Management and Challenges in Teacher Education on the basis of an empirical study in Teacher Education Institutions of Odisha. They concluded that different kinds of resource supports are essential for successful functioning of Teacher Education programme at institutional level. They suggested that learning resources should be made more effective and amenable to all the student-teachers.

Inclusion is one of the Principles of National Education Policy, 2020. The chapter on Inclusive Teacher Education by **Dr. S.K. Panda** focuses on the characteristics of Inclusive Teacher Education as highlighted in different policy documents. Dr. Panda discusses at length on institutional provisions and suitable strategies for implementation of Inclusive Teacher Education Curriculum. He emphasised on improvement of teaching practices and school-based experiences of special education students.

Dr. Subhash Chandra and **Manju Kumari** have deliberated at length about open distance learning mode and its role in professional development of teachers. They have visualised the significance of technology facilitated open learning strategies with high coverage of student population and cost-effectiveness. **Dr. B.C. Das** and **Debajani Sahoo** in their chapter on Need Level Assessment of Research Competencies focused on the assessment of research competencies which encompassed five dimensions: research review, proposal writing, research methodology, ICT utilization, and research publication and ethics. Findings revealed no notable correlation between various research competencies and the gender of the scholars. Nonetheless, scholars articulated differing levels of requirement, with the majority expressing a desire for further competencies although the Ph.D. coursework is tailored to pinpoint and fulfil these competency gaps.

The conceptual analysis of various factors associated with Teacher Education in India has a lot of bearing on understanding the policy perspectives as well as research priorities in education. Such understanding can prepare a sound base for visualising the nature and scope of Teacher Education in the contemporary India. The experiences reveal that integration of technology with pedagogical principles can deal very well with multidisciplinary knowledge base, subject to development of appropriate professional competencies of teachers. In this context, research evidences presented in the book will act as a beacon of light for rejuvenation of Teacher Education in Indian Subcontinent. The complexities arising in the context of provision of quality Teacher Education as envisaged in NEP 2020 need to be tackled with proper understanding of contextual realities of the school system and appropriate decision making. Moreover, such phenomenon is to be understood in the context of pluralistic factors linked with socio-economic and political developments taking place at national level as well as global level. Hence, multiple strategies need to be evolved for teacher development programmes. The chapters contributed by the eminent scholars in the book will inspire teachers and researchers to explore different perspectives of Teacher Education and work accordingly. This is anticipated that the students of education, researchers, teachers and the policy makers of education will be benefited a lot from this compendium of two volumes.

List of Contributors

A. Muthumanickam has been Former Professor & Head and Dean, Faculty of Education, Madurai Kamaraj University, Madurai. Professor Muthumanickam is a distinguished Syndicate Member of Tamil Nadu Open University, Chennai. His areas of expertise are Teacher Education, Quality and Teacher Management Issues in Education.
Email: professormuthumanickam@gmail.com

Akha Kaihrii Mao is an Associate Professor in the School of Vocational Studies, Ambedkar University Delhi (AUD). Dr. Mao's areas of research interests are in Traditional and Indigenous System of Education among the Nagas, Teacher Education, History of Education, Sociology of Education and Vocational Education. **Email:** kaihriimao@gmail.com

Ashok Dansana is Associate Professor in NCERT, New Delhi and formerly with School of Education, Ravenshaw University, Cuttack. Dr. Dansana is a scholar of Sustainable Development in Education. His research and publication interests include Policy Perspectives in Teacher Education and Development issues in Education. **Email:** dansana.cie@gmail.com

Ashok Kumar has been UGC Research Fellow, Department of Education, University of Allahabad, Allahabad. Dr. Ashok Kumar is currently working as Assistant Professor in the field

of Teacher Education. His research interest includes Teacher Education Programmes and Curriculum Reforms.
Email: ashokllbau@gmail.com

B.C. Das is Assistant Professor in the Department of Education, Ravenshaw University, Cuttack. His areas of interest are Teacher Education, Educational Technology, Development Education and Empowerment of Tribes. He has recently completed a project on TPACK Experiment in Pre-service Practice Teaching Programme in Science and Social Science under PMMMNMTT, Government of India.
Email: dasbcbu@gmail.com

B.S. Gupta is Assistant Professor in the Department of Education, CMP Degree College, University of Allahabad, Prayagraj. Dr. Gupta's areas of research interest remain on Teacher Education, Yoga and Well-being Education.
Email: bsguptaedu@gmail.com

Bijay Kumar Das is Assistant Professor in Education at Dharanidhar University, Keonjhar, Odisha and formerly has been Project Assistant, School of Education, Ravenshaw University, Cuttack. His areas of interest are Teacher Education and Educational Technology. He is currently engaged in a research on blended learning in higher education.
Email: dasbijay12345@gmail.com

Biswajit Behera is Associate Professor, NCERT, New Delhi and formerly with the Department of Education, Central University of Punjab, Bathinda. Dr. Behera is a scholar of Constructivist Pedagogy. His research interest remains on Technology Integration in Constructivist Pedagogy.
Email: biswajit.b@ncert.nic.in

Brijesh Kumar has been UGC Junior Research Fellow in the Department of Education, University of Allahabad, Allahabad. Dr. Brijesh Kumar is currently an Assistant Professor in Teacher Education. His research interest includes professional development of teachers and quality management in education.
Email: bk34855@gmail.com

Chandan Prasad has been UGC Research Fellow in the Department of Education, University of Allahabad, Allahabad. Dr. Chandan Prasad is a scholar in the area of ODL Mode Teacher Education. His research interests are curriculum design and teacher education programmes in open universities. **Email:** cprasadald@gmail.com

D.R. Goel has been the Professor of Education and the Director of Centre of Advanced Studies in Education, The M.S.University of Baroda, Vadodara. Professor Goel has also been the Chairman of Western Regional Committee, NCTE, Bhopal. Professor Goel has been awarded UGC Emeritus Fellowship. Professor Goel has been significantly engaged in the field of Teacher Education and substantially contributed to teacher education researches and technology integration in education. **Email:** goel_d_r34@rediffmail.com

Debajani Sahoo is Assistant Professor in Teacher Education in Bhadrak Government College, Bhadrak, Odisha. She is currently engaged in a research work on Quality of Ph.D. Coursework in Education and Need level Research Competencies of Scholars. She has been a Gold Medalist in her postgraduate studies from Ravenshaw University, Cuttack. **Email:** debajanisahoo2000@gmail.com

Dhananjai Yadav is Professor of Education and Head in the Department of Education, University of Allahabad, Allahabad. His areas of research interest include Philosophy of Education, Teacher Education Policies and Practices, Science Education and ICT in Education. **Email:** dhananjaiyadevedu@gmail.com

Gulsan Behera has been a Postgraduate Scholar in School of Education, Ravenshaw University, Cuttack. His areas of interest are policies and practices in teacher education programmes and curriculum reforms. **Email:** gulsanbehera95@gmail.com

Gyanendra Kumar Rout is Professor in the Faculty of Education, Indira Gandhi National Tribal University, Amarkantak. Dr. Rout is a scholar of Curriculum Studies in Education.

His areas of interest include Curriculum Reforms in Teacher Education. **Email:** gkr75@yahoo.com

Hemendra S. Mistry has been ICSSR Postdoctoral Fellow in the Department of Education, Faculty of Education and Psychology, The Maharaja Sayajirao University of Baroda, Vadodara. Dr. Mistry keeps on his interest in Teacher Education issues and developments. **Email:** mistryhemendra@yahoo.com

M.S. Lalitha is Professor of Education and Former Vice-Chancellor of Pondicherry University, Puducherry. She has been Head and Dean in Faculty of Education, Pondicherry University. Professor Lalitha is an eminent expert in the field of Teacher Education. She has significantly contributed to the development of Teacher Education in the country.
Email: nandakumarlalitha02@gmail.com

Manju Kumari is Research Scholar, UGC-JRF, Department of Education, University of Allahabad, Allahabad. Dr. Manju Kumari is currently engaged as Assistant Professor in the field of Teacher Education. **Email:** manjucret10@rediffmail.com

Minakshi Biswal has been Associate Professor in the Department of Education, Vasanta College for Women, Banaras Hindu University, Varanasi. Dr. Biswal has been a scholar of value education. Her areas of interest include Teacher Education, Value and Peace Education. **Email:** sanima11@rediffmail.com

N.K. Das is Professor of Education in the School of Education, Indira Gandhi National Open University, New Delhi. He has been Director of the School of Education, IGNOU. Professor Das has been involved in the development of several courses under different programmes of School of Education like PGDHE, B.Ed., D.El.Ed., PGDET and M.A. (Education). He is currently the Programme Coordinator of M.A. (Education) Programme. **Email:** nkdas123@gmail.com

Namita Sahoo is Professor of Education in K.P. Training College, University of Allahabad, Allahabad. Dr. Sahoo is a scholar of Educational Media and Technology. Her areas of interest are

Educational Technology, Teacher Education and Social Science Education. **Email:** drnamitasahoo@gmail.com

P.K. Sahoo is the Former Vice-Chancellor of University of Allahabad. Professor Sahoo has been the Director, Institute of Correspondence and Continuing Education, University of Allahabad. He has been Head, Department of Education and Dean, Faculty of Arts, University of Allahabad, Allahabad. Professor Sahoo is the Former President of Indian Association of Teacher Educators. Currently Professor Sahoo is engaged in ICSSR research project focusing on Education for Sustainable Development. **Email:** pksahooald@rediffmail.com

Praveen Bobby Binjha is Associate Professor at CIET, NCERT, New Delhi and formerly with School of Education, Ravenshaw University, Cuttack. Her area of interest remains in constructivist and ICT integrated pedagogy.
Email: bobby452@gmail.com

Prerna Mandhyan has been D.Phil. Scholar in the Department of Education, University of Allahabad, Allahabad. Her research interest includes emerging issues and quality improvement practices in teacher education.
Email: prernamandhyan@gmail.com

Priyanka Sharma has been a Senior Research Fellow in the Department of Education, University of Allahabad, Allahabad. Her research interest includes Teacher Education Curriculum and Issues, Integrated Teacher Education Programmes and Education of Teacher Educators.
Email: priyankasharmaedu.au@gmail.com

Rama Gupta is Assistant Professor in the Department of Education, Jagat Taran Girls' P.G. College, University of Allahabad. Dr. Gupta is a scholar of Quality Management in Elementary Education. Her research areas of interest include Elementary Teacher Education and Management issues.
Email: ramagupta81@rediffmail.com

Shyam B. Menon is Professor of Education in CIE, University of Delhi. Professor Menon is Former Vice-Chancellor of

Ambedkar University Delhi (AUD). He has been Head and Dean, Faculty of Education, University of Delhi; Professor and Director, School of Education, Indira Gandhi National Open University (IGNOU); and Professor of Educational Technology and Head, Department of Evaluation, Research and Training, Central Institute of Educational Technology, National Council of Educational Research and Training.
Email: shyambmenon@gmail.com

S.C. Panigrahi is Professor of Education, Former Director of Centre of Advanced Studies in Education, Coordinator of UGC-CAS, Department of Education, Faculty of Education and Psychology, The Maharaja Sayajirao University of Baroda, Vadodara. Professor Panigrahi is a renowned expert in the field of Education of Deprived. He has been engaged in many research projects in his field of expertise.
Email: panigrahi24@gmail.com

S.K. Panda is Associate Professor in the Department of Education, University of Jammu, Jammu. Dr. Panda is an emerging scholar in the field of Teacher Education. His research interest includes equity, quality and inclusion issues in teacher education.
Email: drpanda77@gmail.com

Subhash Chandra is Assistant Professor in the Department of Teacher Education, Digvijay Nath PG College, Gorakhpur. Dr. Subhash Chandra has worked upon teacher preparation through ODL Mode. He keeps on his research interest on the learning styles of student-teacher and imperative issues in ODL Mode teacher education programmes.
Email: subhash84au@gmail.com

Sujeet Kumar is Professor in the Department of Education, Guru Ghasidas Vishwavidyalay, Bilaspur. Professor Sujeet Kumar is a well known scholar for his innovations in teaching and research. His areas of interest include Skill-based Teacher Education, Application of Constructivism in Teacher Education and Blended Learning Approach to Higher Education Delivery.
Email: sujeetmishraedu@gmail.com

Sunil Behari Mohanty has been Professor of Education and served as the Principal in the Institute of Advanced Studies in Education in Odisha. Dr. Mohanty has been the President, All India Association for Educational Research. He is the Founder of International Forum of Researchers in Education, Puducherry and the Editor of the Journal of AIAER.
Email: sunilmohanty@gmail.com

Sushma Pandey is Professor in the Department of Education, DDU Gorakhpur University, Gorakhpur. Her research interest includes Teacher Education Policies and Initiatives.
Email: pandeysushma94@gmail.com

Usha Devi has been a Postgraduate Scholar in the Department of Education, University of Allahabad. Her research interest includes Teacher Education and Development Issues.
Email: ushachaudhary798@gmail.com

Usha Mishra is Professor of Education and has been Head, in the Department of Education, University of Allahabad, Allahabad. Her research interest includes School Education and Teacher Education. **Email:** ushamishraau@gmail.com

Uzma Khanam has been a PG Scholar in the Department of Education, University of Allahabad, Allahabad. Her areas of research interest include ICT in Education Research, Teacher Education and Emerging Issues.

Vidya Agarwal has been Professor and Head in the Department of Education, University of Allahabad, Allahabad. Her major areas of interest remain Educational Administration and Management, Teacher Education and Quality Management issues. **Email:** profvidyaagarwal@yahoo.com

Section IV
RESEARCH INNOVATION IN TEACHER EDUCATION

20

Innovation in Teaching Practice

K-4 Learning Transaction Model

B.C. Das, P.B. Binjha, Ashok Dansana and *Bijay Kumar Das*

The study empowered the pre-service teachers to identify TPACK-based teaching competencies and adopt them in teaching practices up to optimum level. Such practices facilitated teaching learning processes of science and social science subject areas at secondary schools. Based on this experiment and feedback given by the practising student teachers, the project team innovated TPACK-based K-4 Learning Transaction Model with its unique features and practicability in the area of curriculum transaction. This chapter focused on development of K-4 Learning Transaction-based Teaching Practice in Science and Social Science. The outcomes of the study have potentials to initiate reforms in teacher preparation more learner friendly manner. The teacher education curriculum, especially during school internship practices must take a clue from the present project for innovations at institutional level. This report is of worth reference as a piece of research in teacher education. The teacher educators, curriculum designers, researchers, both in-service and would-be teachers shall be benefited by application of this innovated K-4 Learning Transaction Model.

Base of the Study

The investigators under a PMMMNMTT Project made interventions in enabling pre-service teachers to adopt technological pedagogical and content knowledge (TPACK) as a framework during school internship programme. The research team studied the effectiveness ofTPACK-based teaching practices in science and social sciences with references to learning achievement and mastery of competencies. The practitioners' (student-teachers) reaction was also studied as a parameter of success of the training programme. The experiment was spread over one full term of internship programme. The study was carried out with a sample of 40 pre-service teachers who taught in 4 CBSE schools of Cuttack city under internship programme with 341 students by adopting Solomon Four Group Design. Research tools used were Achievement Test; TPACK-based Competency Scale, Reaction Scale, Feedback Sheets and field notes. Data were analysed by using One-way ANOVA, post-hoc t-test and per cent and content analysis technique. The pedagogic principles like situated cognition, anchored instruction, contextualized discursion, disrupted collaboration and constructed manifestation were used to develop TPACK-based competencies among pre-service teachers. The pre-service teachers were exposed to theoretical background as well as skill-based demonstration on workshop mode prior to school internship. During TPACK-based teaching practices the investigators monitored the teaching activities, conducted group discussion sessions on daily experiences and motivated the subjects to prepare on the line of expected guidelines. There were continuous peer interactions on regular basis. Progressively, the pre-service teachers were monitored and assessed by the project team. The study indicated effectiveness of TPACK-based teaching practice with reference to teaching competencies and students' achievement. Solomon Four group design was adopted. The study empowered the pre-service teachers to identify TPACK-based teaching competencies and adopt them in teaching practices up to optimum level. Such practices facilitated teaching learning processes of science and social science subject areas at secondary schools. Based on this experiment and feedback given by the practising student teachers, the project team innovated TPACK-based K-4 Learning Transaction Model with its unique features and practicability in the area of curriculum transaction.

Rationale

Technological Pedagogical Content Knowledge (TPACK) has been proposed as a conceptual framework to describe the knowledge base teachers need for effective technology integration. The issue of what teachers need to know about technology for effective teaching has been the centre of intense debate in the recent past. Teaching with technology for a given content matter is complex and multidimensional. It requires understanding the representation and formulation of concepts using technologies; pedagogical techniques that utilize technologies in constructive ways to teach content; knowledge of what makes concepts difficult or easy to learn and how technology can help address these issues; knowledge and theories of epistemology; and an understanding of how technologies can be utilized to build on existing knowledge and to develop new or strengthen old epistemologies (Koehler *et al.*, 2007: 743).

We live in exponential circumstances where advancements have effectively changed the way we work and play. From mobile phones to sites, from YouTube recordings to multiplayer diversions innovation is essentially evolving. The eventual fate of innovation is all the more encouraging. It is of nothing unexpected that the progressing talk of innovation and its part in training takes significantly more prominent noteworthiness today. This brisk change in innovation can be a major change for teachers and managing bodies, as innovation winds up noticeably behind the times incredibly rapidly in presence. Notwithstanding this, billions of dollars and innumerable hours have been spent on equipment, planning, and preparing (Barron *et al.*, 2003; Cuban, Kirkpatrick and Peck, 2001; Bauer and Kenton, 2005; Frank and Zhao, 2003; Keengwe, Onchwari, and Wachira, 2008). A current audit of the examination and grant on innovation incorporation recognized educator learning as one of the key boundaries for powerful innovation coordination (Hew and Brush, 2007; Mishra and Koehler, 2006). Educators must know more than the specialized parts of innovation and must comprehend that innovation has affordances and requirements both for speaking to content and distinguishing apropos instructing approaches (Harris, Mishra, and Koehler, 2009). In the recent past, the TPACK structure consents that educating is an exceedingly complex type of issue chasing and critical thinking utilizing adaptable and incorporated learning (Glaser, 1984; Putnam and Borko, 2000; Shulman, 1986, 1987). Educators rehearse in a compound, a dynamic condition must incorporate information of understudy considering and learning, information of the topic and progressively, learning of innovation. Today, all people inside the educational framework have been over the top by the utilization of the web. The necessity for people to be required in innovative change and improvement is being educated, has come to the light. Presently, learning situations are being strengthened with innovation and adjustment in course content whereas the classroom administration requires that educators ought to have the vital information and aptitudes for the incorporation of innovative technologies in training. The need has emerged for educators to have a framework that gives the coordination of innovation in their specialties. The specialized capability and specialized proficiency are additionally required alongside digital technologies. Further, there is a prerequisite of knowledge and abilities on the most proficient method to utilize technologies that will give point-by-point teaching and learning (Kereluik, Mishra, and Koehler, 2010).

Objective

1. To innovate and validate TPACK-based K-4 Learning Transaction Model (K-4 LTM) for improvement in practice teaching in science and social science with reference to reaction of pre-service teachers.

Methodology

Based on the feedback given by the pre-service teachers the project team brought in innovation in two phases. The Project Team Innovated K-4 Instructional Design with following four stages within the framework of TPACK-5 guidelines developed by the project team. Further, this innovated K-4 instructional design-based on TPACK-5 components was presented for reaction of pre-service teachers.

The data related to reaction of pre-service teachers belonging to science and social science towards innovated TPACK-5 based K-4 lesson plans were collected through TPACK Reaction Scale by using a Google form.

The study adopted both quantitative and qualitative data analysis techniques.

Innovating TPACK-5-based 'K-4 Instructional Design'

Analysis of TPACK-5 Guidelines

The Guidelines for Development of TPACK-5 was designed by the project team by integration of following five pedagogical processes leading to holistic learning and teaching.

Five processes may be K-5:

1. Knowledge Tension
2. Knowledge Presentation/Extension
3. Knowledge Acquisition
4. Knowledge Collaboration
5. Knowledge Check/Assessment.

Knowledge Tension

(*Pedagogy involved: Situated cognition—consciously igniting cognition in learners' own observation, learning and skills*)

(i) Knowledge tension exists in learners on the verge of entering new experience.
(ii) The teacher may create conducive learning situation to mount tensions in learners' knowledge surface.
(iii) Learners' curiosity, interest, anxiety, need, and expectations get vibrant.
(iv) Arousing tensions in learner, teacher leads them to the releasing points and relates to new knowledge.
(v) For this teacher may show some tension mounting learning contents (multimedia files) and pose relevant previous knowledge-based questions.

Knowledge Presentation/Extension

(*Pedagogy involved: Anchored Instruction—integrating technology in learning approaches which place learning within meaningful and problem-solving context*)

(i) Learners are given exploring space to determine what they eager to learn (teacher uses lead question/demonstration followed by lead question).
(ii) Thus, with the help of learners the teacher determines the learning points that are major to master the topic.
(iii) Students may inquire the conceptual surface and depth through ***subject-specific tools*** facilitated by the teacher.
(iv) This facilitation may be followed by logical explanation/ problem solving along with context, illustrated examples brought in by the teacher or elicited from learners.
(v) Comprehensive questions can be posed (by both the teacher and students using W5—what, why, when, where, which).

Knowledge Acquisition

(*Pedagogy involved: Contextualized discursion—reflecting logically beyond the content and context*)

(i) Teacher creates a comprehensive mind map by using mind-mapping tool (online/offline).

(ii) Students pose relevant questions.

(iii) Thus, learners are put in a cognitive apprenticeship situation while acquiring the learning concepts, learning skills and overcoming learning difficulties.

(iv) The learners will use the learning skill of internalizing new concepts and building conceptual applications based upon known knowledge and demonstration.

(v) Going beyond the content/context for generalization.

Knowledge Collaboration

(*Pedagogy involved: Disrupted Collaboration—awakening the mind by posing questions begin with how, why and if, while contributing in group*)

(i) Learners will be in group learning situation (whole class group/small group as per content) and pose questions to group members, defending and debating logically.

(ii) The learners share new knowledge with peers, get learning space to relate and compare. New interpretation and finding manifest/concretize the learnt knowledge in daily life situation.

(iii) Accepting the valid ideas and avoiding the irrelevant ideas take place in the process of peer interaction and collaboration (idea, concept, opinion/fact).

(iv) In whole group discussion, teacher recognizes the valid ideas/arguments with supplementary reasons and consolidation.

(v) A consolidated board summary may be developed with the help of learners and teacher.

Knowledge Check Assessment

(*Pedagogy involved: Constructed Manifestation—interpreting and manifesting while linking the whole to learners' own experiences and applications*)

(i) Learners' new knowledge may be assessed by knowledge check containing a set of assessment questions (objective types using assessment tools preferably c-map) encouraging learners to check how much they have learnt.

(ii) Peer assessment may be encouraged by allowing learners to pose questions.

(iii) Learners may confirm their new knowledge by asking questions to teacher.

(iv) Learner may be assigned learning task relating their new experience and advancing multiple manifestation.

(v) Encouraging learners for further readings: essentials and suggested.

Phase-I Innovation

In Phase-I the Project Team innovated K-5 Instructional Design with following Five stages:

1. Knowledge tension—contextualization
2. Knowledge presentation—conceptualization
3. Knowledge acquisition—construction
4. Knowledge collaboration—sharing
5. Knowledge check—assessment.

These stages were again discussed by the project team and the pre-service science and social science teachers after practices in classroom situation. Again, these stages were discussed in comparison to existing TPACK-based instructional design and a four-stage instructional process was suggested for Phase-II innovation because of the following limitations:

The limitations of the practiced TPACK-based instructional design are found with

1. Time consuming.
2. Pedagogy processes are lengthy.
3. Contents used instructional design is found bulky.
4. Technologies used are found limited to Google images and videos only.

5. Assessment practices used are found traditional.

The feedback given for improvement in instructional design included:

1. Viable time duration.
2. Pedagogy processes needs to be operational in maximum four stages.
3. Contents need to be reduced.
4. More subject specific software needs to be used.
5. Both self-check and evaluation using peer-assessment, rubrics and ICT-based assessment practices need to be adopted.

Phase-II Innovation

Based on the feedback given by the pre-service teachers the Phase-II innovation brought in four stages of pedagogical processes while improving the Phase-I innovation.

In Phase-II the Project Team innovated K-4 Instructional Design with following four stages:

1. Knowledge tension—contextualization
2. Knowledge presentation—acquisition
3. Knowledge collaboration—extension
4. Knowledge check—assessment

The K-4 instructional design was used to evolve the lesson plans both in science and social science based on the discussions and feedback given by the pre-service science and social science teachers.

The pre-service teachers could be able to develop K-4 Instructional Design by using the following Revised TPACK-5-based Framework.

1. Knowledge tension—contextualization

TPACK-1

- *Constructivist Pedagogy involved:* Situated cognition—consciously igniting cognition in learners'own observation, learning and skills.
- *Technology integrated:* Used technology (multimedia files) to develop cognition in learners' own observation, learning and skills in science/social science.
- *Teaching-learning process:* Teacher mounts interest and tensions in existing knowledge of learners by facilitating a topic introductory video (TIV) followed by contextualization by learners drawing meaning out of it. Learning outcomes takes place alongside.

2. Knowledge presentation—acquisition

TPACK-2

- *Constructivist Pedagogy involved:* Anchored Instruction—integrating technology in learning approaches which place learning within meaningful and problem-solving context.
- *Technology integrated:* Used Free and Open-Source Software (FOSS) in facilitating learners' learning of basic concepts and principles in science/social science.
- *Teaching-learning process:* Teacher presents a sequence of activities followed by learner conceptualizes knowledge in a problem-solving context by reflecting logically. Learning outcomes takes place alongside.

TPACK-3

- *Constructivist Pedagogy involved:* Contextualized discursion—reflecting logically even beyond the content and context.
- *Technology integrated:* Used technology/subject-specific (science/social science) software in facilitating learners to reflect logically beyond the given content and context for understanding important theories in science/social science.

- *Teaching-learning process:* Teacher presents a sequence of activities followed by learner conceptualizes knowledge in a problem-solving context by reflecting logically even beyond the content and context. Learning outcomes takes place alongside.

3. Knowledge collaboration—extension

TPACK-4

- *Constructivist Pedagogy involved:* Disrupted Collaboration—awakening the mind by posing questions begin with how, why and if, while contributing in group.
- *Technology integrated:* Used technology (multimedia files)/subject-specific (science/social science) software in facilitating collaborative learning by posing questions begins with how, why and if, while contributing in group with reference to recent research and development in science/social science.
- *Teaching-learning process:* Teacher facilitates collaborative learning by placing learners in a group learning situation (small group discussion followed by whole group discussion). Each learner collaborates and contributes in respective small group followed by whole group as well extending the larger application of their learnt knowledge. Learner is given freedom to express in new ways, communicate in formal language and apply new learning in similar/different situations. Learning outcomes takes place alongside.

4. Knowledge check—assessment

TPACK-5

- *Constructivist Pedagogy involved:* Constructed Manifestation—interpreting and manifesting while linking the whole to learners' own experiences and applications.
- *Technology integrated:* Used assessment technology/software

to assess learners' performance and let them to interpret/solve/reflect linking the whole to their own experiences and applications with newer problems/phenomena/examples/experience in science/social science.

- *Teaching-learning process:* Teacher gives opportunity to learners' self-check of how much they have learnt and what needs to be learnt. This self-check can be done by Sentence prompt questions like, 1. The ideas I learnt today..................... 2. Further ideas I need to learn............................ Teacher facilitates outcome-based evaluation of learners by using peer assessment, rubrics or ICT supported Multiple-choice questions (MCQ), Drag and drop, Multiple responses, sequencing/ordering. Fill-in the blanks, one word or phrase, Select, Numeric, Linear scaling and so on.

Validating *TPACK-5-based 'K-4 Instructional Design'* for improvement in practice teaching in science with reference to reaction of pre-service teachers

The validation of *TPACK-5-based 'K-4 Instructional Design'* for improvement in practice teaching in science with reference to reaction of pre-service teachers has been presented in following Table and Figure.

Table 20.1: Reaction of Science Pre-service teachers towards the developed TPACK-5 used for K-4 Instructional Design

TPACK	Statement	Most useful	Useful	Average Useful	Not Useful	Never Useful	Total 100%
TPACK-1	Used technology (multimedia files) to develop cognition in learners' own observation, learning and skills in science/social science.	15 (60.00)	5 (20.00)	3 (12.00)	1 (4.00)	1 (4.00)	25 (100.00)

(Contd.)

TPACK	Statement	Most useful	Useful	Average Useful	Not Useful	Never Useful	Total 100%
TPACK-2	Used Free and Open-Source Software (FOSS) in facilitating learners' learning of basic concepts and principles in science/social science.	16 (64.00)	7 (28.00)	2 (8.00)	0 (0.00)	0 (0.00)	25 (100.00)
TPACK-3	Used technology/ subject-specific (science/social science) software in facilitating learners to reflect logically beyond the given content and context for understanding important theories in science/social science.	13 (52.00)	8 (32.00)	2 (8.00)	1 (4.00)	1 (4.00)	25 (100.00)
TPACK-4	Used technology (multimedia files)/subject-specific (science/ social science) software in facilitating collaborative learning by posing questions begin with how, why and if, while contributing in group with reference to recent research and development in science/social science.	12 (48.00)	8 (32.00)	3 (12.00)	2 (8.00)	0 (0.00)	25 (100.00)

(*Contd.*)

TPACK	Statement	Most useful	Useful	Average Useful	Not Useful	Never Useful	Total 100%
TPACK-5	Used assessment technology/ software to assess learners' performance and let them to interpret/solve/ reflect linking the whole to their own experiences and applications with newer problems/ phenomena/ examples/ experience in science/social science.	14 (56.00)	9 (36.00)	2 (8.00)	0 (0.00)	0 (0.00)	25 (100.00)

Numbers in the parentheses indicate percentage.

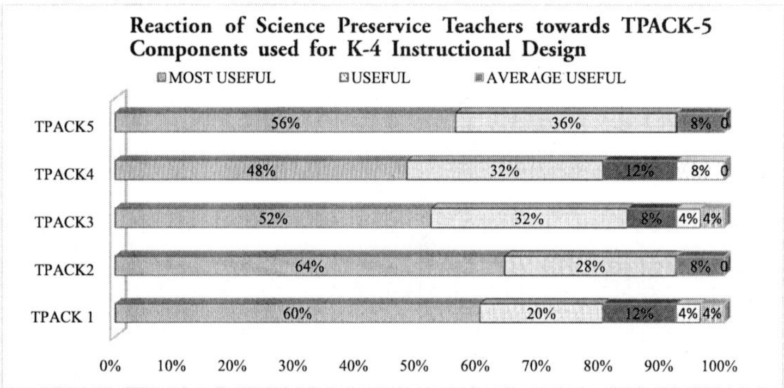

Fig. 20.1: Reaction towards TPACK-5 Components used for K-4 Instructional Design

- It is evident from the Table and Figure that the TPACK-1 component: 'Used technology (multimedia files) to develop cognition in learners' own observation, learning and skills in science' has been found favourable reaction from about 80 per cent science pre-service teachers belonging to 60 per cent in most useful category. An additional 12 per cent science pre-service teacher also reacted in average useful category. Only a negligible 8 per cent respondent reacted unfavourably.

- It is witnessed from the Table and Figure that in the TPACK-2 component: 'Used Free and Open-Source Software (FOSS) in facilitating learners' learning of basic concepts and principles in science' has been found favourable reaction from about 92 per cent science pre-service teachers belonging to 64 per cent in most useful category. Additional 8 per cent science pre-service teachers also reacted in average useful category. No respondents reacted unfavourably.
- It is reported from the Table and Figure that the TPACK-3 component: 'Used technology/subject-specific' (science) software in facilitating learners to reflect logically beyond the given content and context for understanding important theories in science' has been found favourable reaction from about 84 per cent science pre-service teachers belonging to 52 per cent in most useful category. Additional 8 per cent science pre-service teachers also reacted in average useful category. Only a negligible 8 per cent respondent reacted unfavourably.
- It is evident from the Table and Figure that the TPACK-4 component: 'Used technology' (multimedia files)/subject-specific (science/social science) software in facilitating collaborative learning by posing questions begin with how, why and if, while contributing in group with reference to recent research and development in science/social science' has been found favourable reaction from about 80 per cent science pre-service teachers belonging to 58 per cent in most useful category. Additional 12 per cent science pre-service teachers also reacted in average useful category. Only a negligible 8 per cent respondent reacted unfavourably.
- It is evident from the Table and Figure that the TPACK-5 component: 'Used assessment technology/software to assess learners' performance and let them to interpret/solve/reflect linking the whole to their own experiences and applications with newer problems/phenomena/examples/experience in science/social science' has been

found favourable reaction from about 92 per cent science pre-service teachers belonging to 56 per cent in most useful category. Additional 8 per cent science pre-service teachers also reacted in average useful category. No respondents reacted unfavourably.

Validating *TPACK-5-based 'K-4 Instructional Design'* for improvement in practice teaching in social science with reference to reaction of pre-service teachers

The validation of *TPACK-5-based 'K-4 Instructional Design'* for improvement in practice teaching in social science with reference to reaction of pre-service teachers has been presented in following Table and Figure.

Table 20.2: Reaction of Social science Pre-service teachers towards the developed TPACK-based K-5 lesson plans

TPACK	Statement	Most useful	Useful	Average Useful	Not Useful	Never Useful	Total 100%
TPACK-1	Used technology (multimedia files) to develop cognition in learners' own observation, lear-ning and skills in science/ social science.	14 (56.00)	8 (32.00)	2 (8.00)	1 (4.00)	0 (0.00)	25 (100.00)
TPACK-2	Used Free and Open-Source Software (FOSS) in facilitating learners' learning of basic concepts and principles in science/ social science.	12 (48.00)	9 (36.00)	3 (12.00)	1 (4.00)	0 (0.00)	25 (100.00)
TPACK-3	Used technology/ subject-specific (science/social science) software in facilitating learners to reflect logically beyond the given content and context for understanding important theories in science/social science.	15 (60.00)	7 (28.00)	2 (8.00)	1 (4.00)	0 (0.00)	25 (100.00)

(*Contd.*)

TPACK	Statement	Most useful	Useful	Average Useful	Not Useful	Never Useful	Total 100%
TPACK-4	Used technology (multimedia files)/ subject-specific (science/social science) software in facilitating collaborative learning by posing questions begin with how, why and if, while contributing in group with reference to recent research and development in science/social science.	12 (48.00)	9 (36.00)	3 (12.00)	1 (4.00)	0 (0.00)	25 (100.00)
TPACK-5	Used assessment technology/software to assess learners' performance and let them to interpret/ solve/reflect linking the whole to their own experiences and applications with newer problems/ phenomena/ examples/experience in science/social science.	13 (52.00)	7 (28.00)	3 (12.00)	1 (4.00)	1 (4.00)	25 (100.0)

Numbers in the parentheses indicate percentage.

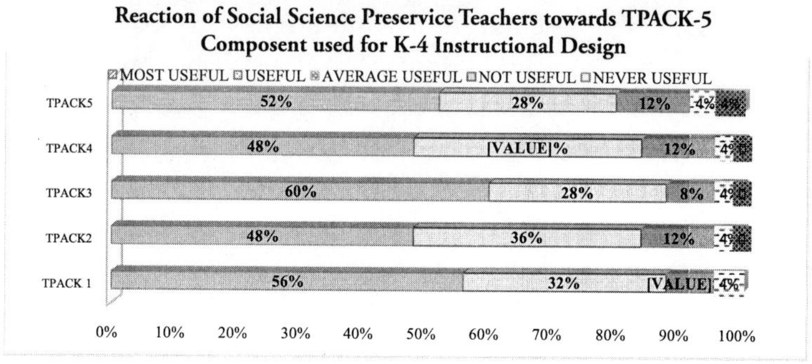

Fig. 20.2: Reaction towards TPACK-5 Components used for K-4 Instructional Design for Social Science

- It is evident from the Table and Figure that the TPACK-1 component: 'Used technology (multimedia files) to develop cognition in learners' own observation, learning and skills in science' has been found favourable reaction from about 88 per cent social science pre-service teachers belonging to 56 per cent in most useful category. Additional 8 per cent social science pre-service teachers also reacted in average useful category. Only a negligible 4 per cent respondent reacted unfavourably.
- It is witnessed from the Table and Figure that in the TPACK-2 component: 'Used Free and Open-Source Software (FOSS) in facilitating learners' learning of basic concepts and principles in social science' has been found favourable reaction from about 94 per cent social science pre-service teachers belonging to 64 per cent in most useful category. Additional 12 per cent social science pre-service teachers also reacted in average useful category. Only a negligible 4 per cent respondent reacted unfavourably.
- It is reported from the Table and Figure that the TPACK-3 component: 'Used technology/subject-specific (social science) software in facilitating learners to reflect logically beyond the given content and context for understanding important theories in social science' has been found favourable reaction from about 88 per cent social science pre-service teachers belonging to 60 per cent in most useful category. Additional 8 per cent social science pre-service teachers also reacted in average useful category. Only a negligible 4 per cent respondent reacted unfavourably.
- It is evident from the Table and Figure that the TPACK-4 component: 'Used technology (multimedia files)/subject-specific (social science) software in facilitating collaborative learning by posing questions begin with how, why and if, while contributing in group with reference to recent research and development in social science' has been found favourable reaction from about 84 per cent social science

pre-service teachers belonging to 58 per cent in most useful category. Additional 12 per cent social science pre-service teachers also reacted in average useful category. Only a negligible 4 per cent respondent reacted unfavourably.

- It is evident from the Table and Figure that the TPACK-5 component: 'Used assessment technology/software to assess learners' performance and let them to interpret/solve/reflect linking the whole to their own experiences and applications with newer problems/phenomena/examples/experience in science/social science' has been found favourable reaction from about 80 per cent science pre-service teachers belonging to 52 per cent in most useful category. Additional 12 per cent science pre-service teachers also reacted in average useful category. Only negligible 8 per cent respondents reacted unfavourably.

Conclusions and Implications of the Study

1. The study brought in an innovation in TPACK-based lesson plans on the basis of feedback given by the pre-service teachers and the teacher educators engaged in the process of experiment. This innovated instructional design is K-4 Learning Transaction Model based on TPACK guidelines developed by the project team. This innovated instructional design may be called as TPACK-based K-4 LTM. Similar innovations may be carried out by other researchers and teacher educators.
2. Further, the study revealed that 85.6 per cent science pre-service teachers and 84.8 per cent social science pre-service teachers responded their favourable reaction towards TPACK-based K-4 LTM. Hence, t can be suggested that this genre of TPACK-based K-4 LTM may be recognized for use in practice teaching organized by teacher education programmes at secondary and even elementary and higher secondary level. This model may be useful in day-to-day

real teaching at school level and even in education delivery at higher stage.

Innovative Feature of K-4 Learning Transaction Model

This model has four learning processes such as (1) Knowledge tension-contextualization, (2) Knowledge presentation-acquisition, (3) Knowledge collaboration-extension, (4) Knowledge check-evaluation.

Innovated pedagogical processes involved:
(Total Time—40 Minutes for a class)

1. **Knowledge tension—contextualization (7 minutes):** The student-teacher mounts interest and tensions in existing knowledge of learners.
   Used Pedagogy of Situated cognition—consciously igniting cognition in learners 'own observation, learning and skills. Used technology (multimedia files) to develop cognition in learners' own observation, learning and skills.
2. **Knowledge presentation—acquisition (13 minutes):** The student-teacher presents a sequence of activities followed by learner conceptualizes knowledge in a problem solving context by reflecting logically even beyond the content and context.
   Used Pedagogy of Anchored Instruction—integrating technology in learning approaches which placed learning within meaningful and problem-solving context. Used Free and Open Source Software (FOSS)/images in facilitating learners' learning of basic concepts and principles. Used Contextualized discursion-reflecting logically beyond the content and context. Used technology/subject-specific software/ images in facilitating learners to reflect logically beyond the given content and context for understanding important theories connected to the topic.
3. **Knowledge collaboration—extension (12 minutes):** The student-teacher facilitates collaborative learning by placing learners in a heterogeneous group learning situation.

Used Pedagogy of Disrupted Collaboration—awakening the mind by posing questions begin with how, why and if, while contributing in group. Used technology (multimedia files)/ subject-specific software/images in facilitating collaborative learning by posing questions begins with how, why and if, while contributing in group with reference to recent research and development connected to the topic.

4. **Knowledge check—assessment (8 minutes):** By using a Google Form the student-teacher gives opportunity to learners' self check of how much they have learnt and what needs to be learnt.

   Used Pedagogy of Constructed Manifestation—interpreting and manifesting while linking the whole to learners' own experiences and applications. Used assessment technology/ software to assess learners' performance and let them to interpret/solve/reflect linking the whole to their own experiences and applications with newer problems/phenomena/examples/ experience connected to the topic.

K-4 Learning Transaction Model in Science (Innovated Lesson Plan)

Name of the Student-teacher: Sujnani Panda (Under the Supervision of the Project Team)	
Class: VIII	**Date:**
Subject: Biological Science	**Period:** 5th
Topic: Asexual Reproduction	**Time:** 40 minutes

Learning Objectives

On completion of the lesson, the learners will be able to:

- Define asexual reproduction;
- List out different types of asexual reproduction;
- Differentiate between asexual and sexual reproduction;
- Explain the process of budding in hydra; and
- Illustrayte the process of binary fission in amoeba.

Teaching Learning Materials/Hardware and Software Used

- Animation showing budding in hydra
- Animated video of binary fission in amoeba (Augmented Reality) using AI App
- Flow Chart showing asexual reproduction
- **Hardware:** Laptop, Projector
- **Software:** Flickr, Animoto, C-map, AI App

Teaching-Learning Process	Expected Learning Outcomes
Knowledge tension—contextualization (7 minutes) The student-teacher mounts interest and tensions in existing knowledge of learners by facilitating a ***Topic introductory video (TIV) of** 4-5 minutes* related to **budding in hydra** which demonstrates **the steps of budding** followed by contextualization by learners drawing meaning out of it. 1. Have you ever seen the new offspring of plants? 2. How does this new offspring appear? 3. What do you mean by the term reproduction?	The learners are expected to— • Define the term reproduction. • Define sexual reproduction. • Elicit examples from own experience. • Articulate key differences between asexual and sexual reproduction. • Identify various forms of asexual reproduction, such as binary fission, budding, vegitative propagation, fragmentation etc. • Describe budding process in hydra using specific vocabulary. • Demonstrate binary fission in Amoeba in different steps and contexts.

(*Contd.*)

4. In how many ways living organisms can reproduce? 5. What is asexual reproduction? 6. Give examples of asexual reproduction.	
Knowledge presentation—acquisition (13 minutes) As a co-learner the student-teacher presents a sequence of activities followed by learners conceptualize knowledge in a problem-solving context by reflecting logically beyond the content and context. **Activity-1** 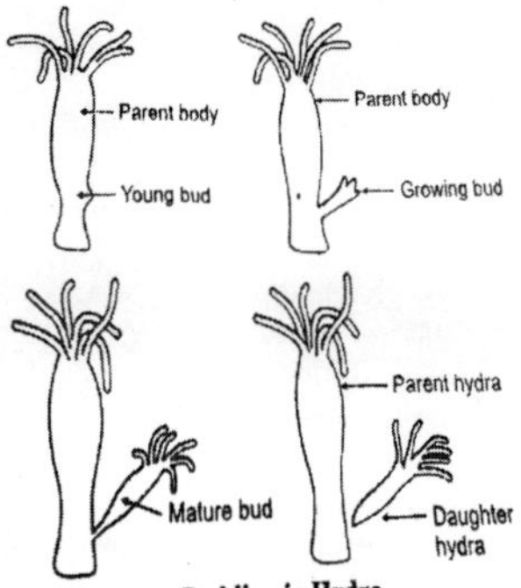 **Budding in Hydra** *Activity key-points* • Asexual reproduction involves one parent. • Hydra reproduces by budding.	• Explain the process of budding in hydra. • Define asexual reproduction. • Describe different types of asexual reproduction. • Draw the labelled diagram of budding in hydra. • Compare and contrast asexual and sexual reproduction in a structured manner, highlighting key differences and similarities in a tabular or diagramatic format. • Elicit examples of organisms that reproduce asexuality. • Explain each step of budding in hydra in detail from bud to its detachment from the parent organism.
Activity-2 Animated video and image on binary fission of amoeba is shown to the students. 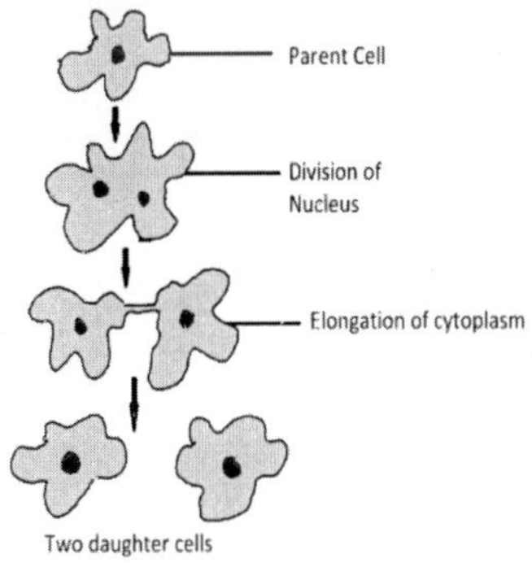 	• Define binary fission. • Explain binary fission in amoeba. • Describe nuclear and cytoplasmic division in the process of binary fission. • List out different types of asexual reproduction. • Draw the labelled diagram of binary fission in amoeba. • Explain the process of binary fission. • Explain each step involved in binary fission in Amoeba, including the reproduction of genetic maternal and division of the cell into two daughter cells. • Conduct simulated experiments on binary fission in Amoeba.

(*Contd.*)

Activity key-points • Asexual reproduction involves one parent. • Amoeba reproduces by binary fission. The learners will be encouraged to • Explain the process of binary fission. • Draw labelled diagram of binary fission in amoeba. • Relate the budding and binary fission as asexual reproduction.	
Knowledge collaboration—extension (12 minutes) The teaching learning will be facilitated through collaborative approach by engaging learners in group learning activities (small group discussion followed by whole group discussion). Learner's autonomy will be encouraged to express their understanding on related concept, reflect in written and oral, and apply the learnt concept in different context. Each group will be provided different images and videos showing the process of asexual reproduction and its modes of reproduction followed with various learning points to discuss. **Group A:** This group will be provided with different images of asexual reproduction. They will discuss asexual reproduction and its characteristics. **Group B:** Group B will discuss the process of budding in hydra.	• Elaborate the characteristics of asexual reproduction. • Discuss various modes of asexual reproduction. • Differentiate between sexual and asexual reproduction. • Develop concept map on asexual reproduction. • Relate the asexual reproduction with living world. • Create a presentation on how asexual reproduction is utilised in agriculture or bio-technology (cloning plants, propagating crops etc.). • Design a survey questions for farmers on asexual reproduction. • Create a project of poster showcasing various types of asexual reproduction. (including real life examples from natureand human application). • Develop digital animation that explains the budding process in hydra.
Group C: This group will discuss the process of binary fission. **Group D:** This group will be provided with flow charts showing the difference between asexual and sexual reproduction. **Within the group** the learners will discuss the assigned task and will draw key-points. Learners of each group will present key learning points of their group. There will be a contributing dialogue after each presentation. Multiple interpretation of the concept will be presented by the learners. The learners will understand the following key-points. • Describe the characteristics of asexual reproduction. • Explain the modes of asexual reproduction.	• Collaborating create a comprehensive definition of asexual reproduction and present in the class. • The small groups develop Venn diagrams or comparision chart that highlights the differences and similarities between asexual and sexual reproduction and present findings to class groupwise. • Group of students perform role play or a skit that demonstrates the process of binary fission in Amoeba with each student representing a different stage of the process.

(*Contd.*)

• In hydra new individuals develop from bud. • Amoeba reproduces by dividing itself into two. Learners will develop concept map on asexual reproduction and will develop a comprehensive concept map using c-map tool. Learners will be encouraged to explore and relate the asexual reproduction in living world.	

Knowledge check—assessment (8 minutes)

Self-Assessment by Sentence Prompt

By using a Google Form the student-teacher gives opportunity to learners' self-check of how much they have learnt and what needs to be learnt. Following self-check Sentence prompt questions will be self-checked by the learners.

1. The ideas I have learnt today..
2. Further ideas I need to learn..

Peer Assessment by Rubric

Students will be divided into two groups. Each group will ask five questions to other group. The peer groups will assess each group's performance with reference to given parameters and level of performance.

Assessment by Teacher

The student-teacher facilitates outcome-based assessment of learners by asking following knowledge, application, analysis and critical thinking-based questions.

1. Asexual reproduction involves fusion of gametes. (True/False)
2. Give examples of animals which reproduce by budding?
3. What is the mode of reproduction of Amoeba?
4. Why daughter cells are formed in binary fission?

Home Assignment

Teacher will assign homework linking to future learning.

Prepare a c-map of differences between sexual and asexual reproduction.

K-4 Learning Transaction Model in Social Science (Innovated Lesson Plan)

Name of the Student Teacher: Koyal Mohanty (Under the supervision of the Project team)	
Class: VIII	**Date:**
Subject: Geography	**Period:** 7th
Topic: Our Environment	**Time:** 40 minutes

Learning Objectives

On completion of the lesson, the learners will be able to:

- Define Environment;
- Describe the components of environment;
- Recognize changes those take place in environment;
- Distinguish between natural and human made environment; and
- Find out the reasons of changes in ecosystem from place to place.

Teaching Learning Materials/Hardware and Software Used

- News reports on environmental issues.
- Short documentary on natural disasters.
- Virtual tour on conservation of environment (Augmented Reality) using AI App.
- Concept map on environment using c-map tool.
- Projector and laptop.

Teaching Learning Process	Expected Learning Outcomes
Knowledge tension—contextualization (7 minutes) The interest and tensions in existing knowledge of learners will be mounted by facilitating a ***Topic introductory video (TIV) of*** *4-5 minutes* related to '**Our Environment**' which demonstrates **the concept and types of our environment** followed with contextualization by learners drawing meaning out of it. 1. Where do you live? 2. What do you call the surroundings around you?	The learners are expected to— • Relate the topic with their day-to-day life experiences. • Define environment. • Relate the natural and man-made components of environment. • Discuss various elements that make up the environment, such as air, water, land and living organisms. • Classify components of environment into biotic and abiotic factors.

(*Contd.*)

3. What are the components in our environment? 4. Are all these components important for life sustaining? 5. What will happen, if all these components get destroyed?	• Identify the causes of changing environment. • Predict the impact of environmental changes on local echo systems.
Knowledge presentation—acquisition (13 minutes) The sequence of concept activities followed by learner conceptualizes knowledge in a problem solving context by reflecting logically even beyond the content and context. **Activity-1** As a co-learner the student teacher presents a video on environmental changes, distracts and conservation. Learners are expected to interact on— • How the environment changes due to various reasons? • How does the natural calamities take place? • How the natural eco-system must be conserved/ maintained by human beings? *Activity key-points* • Environmental changes due to natural and human made causes. • Natural causes are variation in climate of the earth, temperature, rainfall, light wind, changes in the sun, emissions from volcanoes, levels of carbon dioxide etc. • Human causes impacting on environmental changes are overpopulation, pollution, deforestation and burning of fossil fuels etc. • Climate change leads to natural calamities. • Reducing pollution and over use of natural resources can be helpful in maintaining a balanced eco-system. **Activity-2** The lead learners present news reports on importance of environment followed by question-answer session *Activity key-points* • The environment is our basic life support. • Environment must be conserved well in order to balance the eco system. The student teacher leads the learner to— • Explore the biotic and abiotic environment on the basis of their understanding. • Identify the components of environment. • Differentiate between natural and man-made environment or resources.	• Analyse reasons causing environmental changes. • Reflect on the factors leading to natural calamities. • Extend Critical reflections on conservation of natural eco-system. • Use real world examples and experiences to illustrate the impact of human activities on natural environment. • Analyse and compare different eco-systems by virtual tours/field visits. • Gather evidences from various sources to know how eco-systems change due to environmental factors, presenting their findings through group reports. • Explain environment as our basic life support. • Develop concerns on conservation of environment well in order to balance the eco-system. • Examine the biotic and abiotic environment with a new look about their relationship. • Differentiate between natural and man-made environment and resources. • Engage in peer discussions and debates to refine their understanding of the environment. • Create models or posters that showcase the interaction between biotic and abiotic environment.

(*Contd.*)

Knowledge collaboration—extension (12 minutes) Collaborative learning by placing learners in a learning situation (small group discussion followed by whole group discussion). Each small group will be provided different images and videos and will be assigned different learning points to discuss. Learner's autonomy will be encouraged to express their understanding on related concept, reflect in written and oral, and apply the learnt concept in different context. **Group-1:** Components of Environment. **Group-2:** Biotic and Abiotic Environment. **Group-3:** Differentiate between natural and man-made environment. **Within the groups** the learners will discuss key learning points. **In whole group** one lead learner of each group will present key learning points of their group. There will be a contributing dialogue after each presentation. The learners will understand the following essence of the dialogues. **Dialogue-I** Environment is our basic life support system. It provides the air we breathe, the water we drink, the food we eat and the land where we live through natural components like trees, rivers, mountains etc. Human beings make cars, industries; wells etc. and modify the natural environment. **Dialogue-II** The components of environment include natural resources, human-made resources and human as resources. **Dialogue-III** It is important to conserve the environment in order to conserve the natural resources and wildlife in our environment. The learning extension grounded with following reflections by the learners: • Ecosystem is a system formed by the interaction of all living organisms with each other. • Environment contains of four domains—Lithosphere, Atmosphere, Biosphere and Hydrosphere. • Barter system is a trade in which goods are exchanged without the use of money. • On 5 June every year, the world Environment Day is celebrated.	• Discuss the provided topics in groups. • Elaborate the components of environment. • Differentiate between natural and man-made environment. • Differentiate between biotic and abiotic environment. • Collaborate to investigate and present on different causes of environmental changes using real case experiences from various regions. • Participate in group discussion to explore the human activities and their impact on natural processes of environment. • Work together to create visual presentation highlighting differences between natural and human environment. • Participate in extension activities or virtual field visit to get deeper insights into the interconnections between different domains of environment. • Extend their analysis by conducting case studies of eco-systems in different regions, presenting findings using multi-media support. • Participate in community initiatives to observe and document changes in local eco-systems.

(*Contd.*)

Knowledge check—assessment (8 minutes)
Self-Assessment by Sentence Prompt
By using a Google Form the student-teacher gives opportunity to learners' self-check of how much they have learnt and what needs to be learnt. Following self-check sentence prompt questions will be self-checked by the learners.
1. The ideas I learnt today.................... ....
2. Further ideas I need to learn..
Peer Assessment by Rubric
Students will be divided into two groups. Each group will ask five questions to other group. The peer groups will assess each group's performance with reference to given parameters and level of performance.
Assessment by Teacher
The student-teacher facilitates outcomes-based assessment of learners by asking following knowledge, application, analysis and critical thinking-based questions.
1. Give examples of biotic and abiotic resources.
2. What are the natural and man-made resources you see around yourself?
3. List out some man-made activities that bring change to the environment.
4. What will be the consequences of human race if natural resources will be removed from environment?

Home Assignment
The Teacher will assign the homework linking to future learning.
Develop a concept map on 'Our Environment' using Concept Map Tool.

Acknowledgements

The authors acknowledge the valuable feedback from the senior experts Professor P.K. Sahoo, Professor Subhas Chandra Panda, Professor G.C. Nanda, Professor B.N. Panda, and Colleagues Professor Sudarshan Mishra, Professor Gyanendra Nath Tiwari, Professor Sujeet Kumar Misra, Profesor Lokanath Mishra, Dr. S.K. Rout, Dr. D.B. Tali, Dr. A.K. Mohanty and Dr. Gitanjali Mohanty and the concerned student-teachers 0of Department of Education, Ravenshaw University.

Funding

The authors acknowledge Professor. S.K. Bawa, Central University of Punjab and PMMMNMTT, Government of India.

REFERENCES

Airasian, P.W. & Walsh, M.E. (1997). "Cautions for Classroom Constructivists". *Education Digest, 62*(8): 62-69.

Archambault, L.M. & Barnett, J.H. (2010). "Revisiting Technological Pedagogical Content Knowledge: Exploring the TPACK Framework." *Computers & Education*, *55*: 1656-62.

Duffy, T.M. & Cunningham, D.J. (1996). "Constructivism: Implications for the Design and Delivery of Instruction". In D.H. Jonassen (Ed.), *Handbook of Research for Educational Communications and Technology*. NY: Macmillan Library Reference, USA.

Harish, J.B. & Hofer, M.J. (2011). "Technological Pedagogical and Content Knowledge (TPACK) in Action: A Descriptive Study of Secondary Teacher's Curriculum-based, Technology Related Instructional Planning". *Journal of Research on Technology in Education, 43*(3): 211-229.

Lee, M.H. & Tsai, C.C. (2010). "Exploring Teachers' Perceived Self Efficacy and Technological Pedagogical Content Knowledge with Respect to Educational Use of the World Wide Web". *Instructional Science: An International Journal of the Learning Sciences, 38*(1): 1-21.

Lim, C.P. & Chai, C.S. (2008). "Teachers' pedagogical belief and their planning and conduct of computer mediated classroom lessons". *British Journal of Educational Technology, 39*(5): 805-28.

Mishra, P. & Koehler, M.J. (2006). "Technological pedagogical content knowledge: A framework for teacher knowledge". *Teachers College Record, 108*(6): 1017-54

Shulman, L.S. (1986). "Those who understand: Knowledge growth in teaching". *Educational Researcher, 15*: 4-14.

Starkey, L. (2010). "Supporting the digitally able beginning teacher". *Teaching and Teacher Education: An International Journal of Research and Studies. 26*(7).

Tokmak, H.S., Surmeli, H. & Ozgelen, S. (2013). "Pre-service science Teachers perception of their TPACK development after creating digital stories". *International Journal of Environmental and Science Education, 9*: 247-64.

Tsai, P.S., Chai, C.S., Koh, J.H.L. & Yang, S.J.H. (2012). "Examining the relationships between in-service teachers' technology and non-technology related knowledge of TPACK". In B. Chang, S.C. Tan, T. Matsui, G. Biswas, L.H. Wong, T. Hirashima & W. Chen (Eds.), *Workshop Proceedings of the 20th International Conference on Computers in Education* (pp. 258-62). Singapore: Asia-Pacific Society for Computers in Education.

UNESCO (2003). *UNESCO Report: Information and Communication Technologies in Teacher Education—A planning Guide*. Division of Higher Education, UNESCO.

Webb, M. & Cox, M. (2004). "A Review of Pedagogy Related to Information and Communications Technology". *Technology, Pedagogy and Education, 13*(3): 235-86.

Wozney, L., Venkatesh, V. & Abrami, P. (2006). "Implementing Computer Technologies: Teachers' Perceptions and Practices". *Journal of Technology and Teacher Education, 14*: 173-207.

21

Developing Research Potential in Teachers through Action Research

Dhananjai Yadav

Constant acquisition of knowledge, skills and competencies are the important determinants for the growth of any profession. This is equally true to the field of teachers and teacher educators. Due to rapid changes in the academic and social world order the very demand and expectations form the system is changing. In order to make school system accountable and responsive, all the functionaries should have a critical eye on each and every change both at micro as well as at macro level. The system should have to evolve an indigenous mechanism amongst its stakeholders to respond to such changes through evidence based reflective and tenable wayouts. Keeping in view the above premise a study has been undertaken to find out the level of existing research potential amongst practicing elementary school teachers, perception of practicing school teachers about action research and the extent to which action research based practices contribute to the development of research potentials amongst practicing elementary school teachers. The study has been conducted on five *Parishadiya* Primary Schools of rural Allahabad. All the practicing teachers of target schools constitute the sample of the study. Pre-post-experimental design has been used. The subjects were exposed to a structured treatment module on Action Research. The data has been analyzed using t-test. It has been revealed that research potential can be significantly improved through Action Research based practices amongst practicing elementary school teachers' irrespective of gender, experience and academic background. Majority of teachers perceive that action research can contribute positively in improving existing teaching-learning practices and making them more responsive towards society at large.

In the Twenty first century there will be major focus on developing knowledge based society. Therefore, the system of education must be so designed as to develop critical and reflective learner, so that they can establish themselves as creator of knowledge. It will not only ensure the authentic addition to the body of knowledge but develop research aptitude among the learners. In this scenario, the teacher ought to have professionally equipped to analyze and develop the skill of learning to learn amongst learners. Learning based society can ensure knowledge based society. In order to ensure the above cherished target, teacher preparation programme must be designed with special focus on inculcating research potentials among teachers and teacher educator of all levels. For Dewey, reflective thinking 'impels to enquiry' through the search for knowledge beyond immediate, individual experience (Dewey, 1910:7). Teachers presented with problematic situations in the classroom look for solutions and collaborate with other people to develop an understanding of what they can do.

Rapid changes in the academic and social world order changes the expectations from the system as well. In order to make school accountable and responsive, all the functionaries should have a critical eye on each and every change both at micro as well as at macro level. The system should have to evolve an indigenous mechanism amongst its stakeholders to respond to such changes through evidence based reflective and tenable wayouts. In order to develop skill of learning, how to learn the serving teachers should also be equipped with analyzing the demands of school system both academic and professional. Since elementary education is the backbone of any education system and elementary school teachers can impart basic skills of enquiry and assessment among learners. This study has been conducted to know the status of awareness about skills of enquiry and research amongst serving elementary school teachers? Whether the research potential of serving elementary school teachers can be improved? Whether teachers can be motivated to undertake action research based projects? Whether orientation of elementary school teachers towards action research varies with respect to different background variables, e.g. gender, qualification, experience etc.? In order to get fact based answers to above questions, the present study is being undertaken with following objectives:

- To prepare a working module on basics of action research to orient serving teachers.
- To study the effectiveness of the module on action research.

Single group pre-test and post-test design of experimental study has been used to study the effectiveness of the module with hypothesis—"There is no significant difference in pre-test and post-test mean achievement scores of sample respondents." This hypothesis was tested for total achievement as well as in knowledge, comprehension and application levels of cognitive domain. The study was conducted on 20 teachers serving in five *Parishadiya* Primary Schools of Chaka Block of Prayagraj district. Since, it was an experimental study, all the serving teachers of sample schools were taken as sample respondents. The sample was heterogeneous comprising BTC trained, Special BTC and *Shiksha Mitra*, belonging to both genders, dwelling in rural and urban settings, and having a wide range of teaching experience.

A training module was developed by the researcher to acquaint the serving teachers on basics of research methodology so that the teachers can be oriented to identify different day-to-day problems in the management of teaching and learning, proceed scientifically to search for different reasons for the same and workout evidence based solutions to address these issues effectively. The module was transacted in a workshop mode by the researcher and his team. Progress of teachers had been monitored in formative as well as summative manner through achievement test. Self-structured achievement test was constructed to measure the status of awareness about action research in sample respondents in knowledge, comprehension and application components of cognitive domain of learning. The test had 50 items of objective type questions having 20 of knowledge, 20 of comprehension and 10 of application level. The effectiveness of module was judged by pre-test and post-test analysis using t-test.

Table 21.1: Showing comparison of Pre-Test and Post-Test Total Achievement Scores

Treatment	N	Mean (Total)	S.D.	Corre-lation	t-value	Significance
Pre-Test	20	12.05	3.486	+0.81	14.12	Significant at .01 level
Post-Test	20	21.20	4.774			

Since the value of t-ratio 14.12 is greater than the Table value of .01 at df 19, the hypothesis, "There is no significant difference between pre-test and post-test mean achievement scores" is rejected at .01 level of significance. Since post-test mean achievement score is greater than the pre-test mean score, it can be inferred that the module of action research contributes significantly to the overall achievement of sample respondents regarding different components of action research.

Table 21.2: Showing comparison of Pre-Test and Post-Test Achievement in Knowledge Domain

Treatment	N	Mean (Knowledge)	S.D.	Corre-lation	t-value	Significance
Pre-Test	20	7.15	1.98	+0.85	14.128	Significant at .01 level
Post-Test	20	11.75	2.61			

Since the value of t-ratio 14.128 is greater than the Table value of .01 at df 19, the hypothesis, "There is no significant difference between pre-test and post-test mean achievement scores in Knowledge domain" is rejected at .01 level of significance. Since post-test mean achievement score in knowledge domain is greater than the pre-test mean score, it can be inferred that the module of action research contributes significantly to the knowledge domain of achievement of sample respondents regarding different components of action research.

Table 21.3: Showing comparison of Pre-Test and Post-Test Achievement in Comprehension Domain

Treatment	N	Mean (Comprehension)	S.D.	Corre-lation	t-value	Significance
Pre-Test	20	3.95	1.43	+0.81	10.70	Significant at .01 level
Post-Test	20	6.70	1.89			

Since the value of t-ratio 10.70 is greater than the Table value of .01 at df 19, the hypothesis, "There is no significant difference between pre-test and post-test mean achievement scores in Comprehension domain" is rejected at .01 level of significance. Since post-test mean achievement score in comprehension domain is greater than the pre-test mean score, it can be inferred that the module of action research contributes significantly to the comprehension domain of achievement of sample respondents regarding different components of action research.

Table 21.4: Showing comparison of Pre-Test and Post-Test Achievement scores in Application Domain

Treatment	N	Mean (Application)	S.D.	Corre-lation	t-value	Significance
Pre-Test	20	0.95	0.887	+0.72	7.10	Significant at .01 level
Post-Test	20	2.75	1.551			

Since the value of t-ratio 7.10 is greater than the Table value of .01 at df 19, the hypothesis, "There is no significant difference between pre-test and post-test mean achievement scores in Application Domain" is rejected at .01 level of significance. Since post-test mean achievement score in application domain is greater than the pre-test mean score, it can be inferred from the above table that the module of action research contributes significantly to the application domain of achievement of sample respondents regarding different components of action research.

It can be concluded from above observations that research competencies among serving teachers that too at elementary level can be developed significantly and they can be made competent enough to identify different problems of teaching-learning and institutional management both of micro as well as macro nature on their own. They can also be motivated to search for tenable context specific solutions on their own. This is true for the working teachers of different cross-sections, i.e. gender, experience, qualifications, locality are no hindrance in developing the potentials of serving teachers. Many of the serving teachers are still coming out with innovative action research based projects on their own.

REFERENCES

Best, J.W. and James, V.K. (2007). *Research in Education*, Ninth Edition. New Delhi: Pearson Prentice Hall.

Garrett, Henry E. (2004). *Statistics in Psychology and Education.* Eleventh Indian Edition, Bombay: Paragon International Publication.

Guillford, J.P. (1979). *Psychometric Methods.* TMH Edition Reprint. New Delhi: Tata McGraw Hill Publishing Co. Ltd.

Vivienne Baumfield, Elaine Hall and Kate Wall (2013). *Action Research in Education.* SAGE Publications.

22

Impact of In-service Teacher Training Programmes on Teaching-Learning Environment and Students' Achievement

Vidya Agarwal and *Sushma Pandey*

India is a huge democratic country all over the world but is far from attaining universal enrolment of children of 6-11 years age though many Asia's Countries in similar position have already done so. To achieve this goal many efforts have been made including universalization of primary education and *Sarva Sikha Abhiyan* and Right to Education. India has made an impressive progress in elementary education sector. NPE 1986 also propagated decentralization approach in developing Primary Education in the country. National Policy on Education 1986 direction for greater decentralisation and local relevance in all educational endeavours, leading institutions have been established at each district for the purpose of in-service education of elementary school teachers. These District Institutes of Education and Training have been functioning since 1988 and are responsible for organizing pre-service and in-service courses for elementary school teachers and for the personnel working in non-formal and adult education. In-service Teacher education is essentially a continuation of pre-service programmes.

In other words, the two types of teacher education programmes can be visualised as necessary although different in their purpose and substance. The knowledge base has predominance over the practice component in a pre-service teacher education programme. This is because teacher has to gain a clear understanding of pedagogy and also the manner in which they operate in the field, and then practice these for confirming own understanding and gaining the initial level of skills. Teaching, being creative and individualistic, always requires periodic rejuvenation of teachers' attributes and upgrading of their technical knowledge. Even school teacher begins their teaching career with great enthusiasm, equipped with an initial amount of technical knowledge need positive feedback and continuous improvement. According to Gardner (1994), the most common form of in-service teacher education is that which provides an opportunity to teachers to update, refresh, improve and try out new knowledge and skills. Continuous in-service training programmes are organized for teachers of elementary level to update and prepare them for new challenges and changes in education.

Main Feature of the In-service Teacher Training Programme

Duration—One to Two Weeks

Objectives of the Training Programme

- To update teachers knowledge with latest pedagogy of concerned subject teaching.
- To remove difficulties faced by the teachers during teaching subject through discussion and interaction.
- To make aware of change in syllabus to the working teacher and prepare them for new.
- To provoke their knowledge and skill related to child centred Education.
- Develop skill for making Teaching-Learning Material and way of effective use related to the concerned subject.
- To develop competencies for conduction of project works, exercises, experiment and teaching through environment.

- Continuous assessment of student for all-round development.
- To develop competencies among teachers to make subject easy, joyful and understandable, develop skill to facilitate child to child learning.

Organization

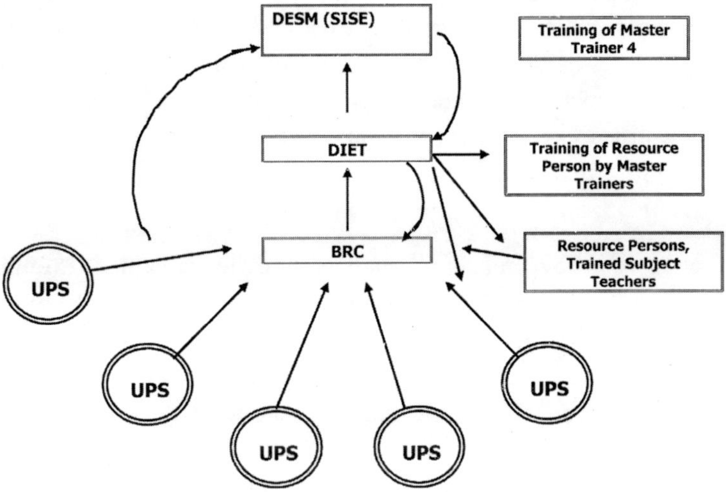

Part-1: Theoretical knowledge of the subjects. Skill teaching, Making, TLM, Discussion of Problems related teaching.

Part-2: Actual classroom teaching by the trainees in Teaching Class in nearest Government Upper Primary School, Observation by the trainers and providing feedback.

The demand for qualified and quality teachers has been continuously on the increase the world over. The 86th Amendment of the Constitution made elementary education a fundamental right. Teacher has greater responsibility of preparing children in school. So a powerful teacher education system is needed to prepare such competent teachers for elementary schools.

As per the recommendations after deliberations of Commonwealth countries, Quality Indicators for Teacher Education are:

- Curriculum Design and Planning
- Curriculum Transaction and Evaluation
- Research, Development and Extension
- Infrastructure and Learning Resources
- Student Support and Progression
- Organization and Management.

Taking into consideration the above indicators, a snapshot study has been taken to enquire the real utility of teacher education programmes organized by DIETs. Utility of all efforts depends on the use of experiences of training in the natural classroom situation. This study seeks to know the impact of training on the original classroom situation and students' achievement.

This study achieved the following objectives:

1. To study the use of teachers' knowledge gained through training programmes in their teaching.
2. To study the effect of Training on students' achievement level.
3. To study the Problems of teachers in using gained knowledgement into the classroom situations.
4. To identify some ways of making training programme more effective for the schools.

Hypotheses: In the context of above objectives, these hypothesis were framed:

- Teachers are not using training experience in natural classroom situations and teaching.
- There is no effect of teachers' training on student achievement.
- There are many problems and barriers faced by the teachers in using their gained knowledge into the natural classroom situation.

Research Design

The present study is primarily aimed on the study of the use and impact of In-service teacher training programmes organized by DIET in real classroom situation. To fulfil this objective, it was the need to go to the field and observe the real situations and practices going on. Researcher found **Descriptive Survey Research Design** to be the most suitable for this investigation.

Sample: Gorakhpur, Jhansi, Pratapgarh, Gaziabad and Aligarh districts were selected. The target groups were selected by using Stratified Random Sampling method.

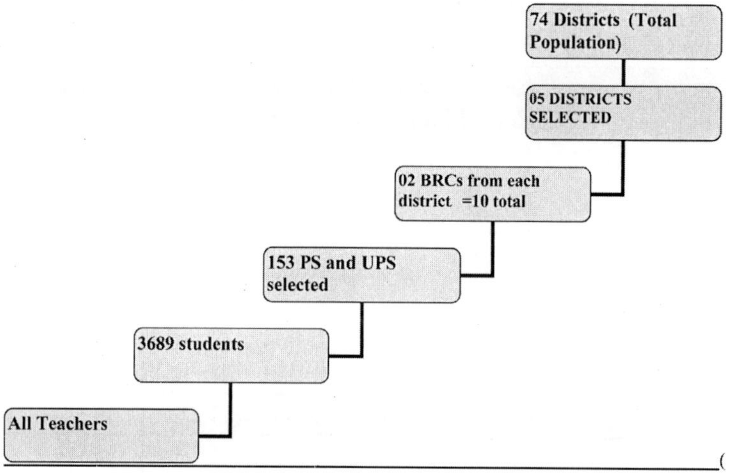

Source: The list obtained through B.S.A. offices of District.

Tools Prepared: Following tools were prepared by the researchers themselves:

1. Science Achievement Test (Standardized)
2. Math's Achievement Test (Standardized)
3. Classroom Observation Schedule.

Data were collected through Personal Survey by using Questionnaire, Checklist, Interviews, Observations and FGD.

Major Findings

Analysis, discussion and interpretation of the data collected through tools from Headmasters, Students and Teachers of *Parishadiya* schools of Uttar Pradesh lead to major findings.

Objective 1: To study the use of teachers' knowledge gained through training programmes in their teaching.

To fulfil this objective 2 classes per selected schools were observed with self-made Classroom Observation Schedule and Data collected was statistically treated to draw the results. Table 22.1 reflects the results.

Table 22.1: Teachers' activity during classroom teaching in Mathematics and Science

Sl. No.	Teachers' Activity in the classroom during teaching Maths and Science	Situation Found (%)	
		Yes	No
1.	While entering teacher gave attention towards sitting arrangement	30	70
2.	Teacher gave attention towards student's way of sitting	63	47
3.	Used Introductory question to avail attention of the students	40	60
4.	Started teaching with the use of Material-aid	29	71
5.	Teacher assessed students' gained knowledge with using teaching-aid	47	53
6.	Teacher gives full attention towards student's problem	64	36
7.	Teacher motivated students to answer the asked question	81	19
8.	Teacher gives full freedom to the students to ask the questions	72	28
9.	Teacher proceeded with using due examples	56	44
10.	Teacher is using classroom materials for teaching	25	75
11.	Teacher used pictures and models to clarify tough concepts	48	52

(*Contd.*)

Sl. No.	**Teachers' Activity in the classroom during teaching Maths and Science**	**Situation Found (%)**	
		Yes	**No**
12.	Important things have been written on the blackboard	80	20
13.	Teachers are probing various types of questions	73	27
14.	Teacher gave attention towards the answer given by the students	60	40
15.	Teacher gave opportunity to the student for self-learning by using material-aid	48	52
16.	Teacher directed the students to do the classroom work	80	20
17.	Teacher evaluated the classroom work done by the students	59	41
18.	Teacher suggested students to improve the work	80	20
19.	Teacher observed every activity of the students' very carefully	60	40
20.	Teacher suggested students to improve their achievement	23	77

Discussion

Table 22.1reflects the snapshot of the teaching-learning environment and teaching habits and teaching technique of the teachers of Mathematics and Science teaching in *Parishadiya* Primary Schools.

- 30 per cent of the teachers started their teaching with checking the sitting arrangements of the class. 63 per cent of the teachers checked the student's way of sitting and informed them to sit properly.
- Only 40 per cent of the class teachers asked introductory questions to avail the attention of the classroom. Rest of the teachers came to their topics directly.
- Only 29 per cent of the teachers used Teaching Learning Material in their teaching; only 47 per cent of the teachers assessed students gained knowledge with using teaching-

aid. Only 40 per cent of the teachers used pictures and models to clarify tough concepts.
- 64 per cent of the teachers paid full attention towards student's problem and motivated students to ask questions.
- 56 per cent of the subject teachers proceeded with using due examples. More than 25 per cent of the teachers used classroom materials for teaching. About 80 per cent of teachers used blackboard for writing important things.
- More than 60 per cent of the teachers found attentive towards the answer given by the students.
- 48 per cent of the teachers found giving opportunity to the student for self-learning by using material-aid.
- Above 70 per cent of the teachers instructed the students to do the class work but 59 per cent of the teachers evaluated the work.
- More than 60 per cent of the teachers observed every activity of the students very carefully during teaching.
- Merely 23 per cent of the teachers suggested students to improve their achievement.

Above finding reflects that only average 50 per cent of the teachers included some aspects of the gained knowledge in their teaching, but it is unsatisfactory that more than 50 per cent of the teachers do not use Teaching Learning Material and appropriate method of teaching in their classroom teaching. Thus, research hypothesis, "Teachers are not using training experience in natural classroom situations and teaching" is selected.

Objective 2: To study the effect of Training on students' achievement level.

To assess the effect of Teachers' teaching techniques and inclusion of Teaching Learning Material (TLM) on the student's achievement, Mathematics and Science achievement test was administered on the two groups of the students. Group-1, where teachers were found using appropriate teaching technique with TLM and Group-2, where teachers do not use gained knowledge.

Test administered were treated separately compared. Result drawn has been presented in Fig. 22.1A and Fig. 22.1B.

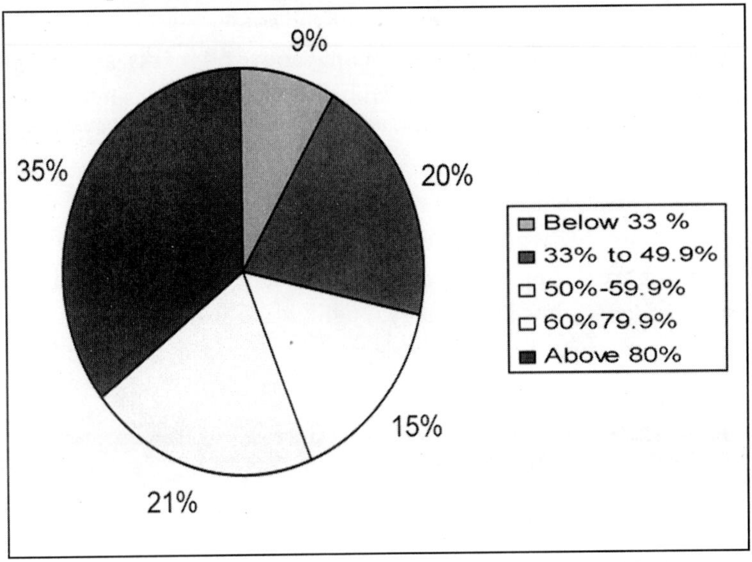

Fig. 22.1A: Achievements of Students where teachers use TLM.

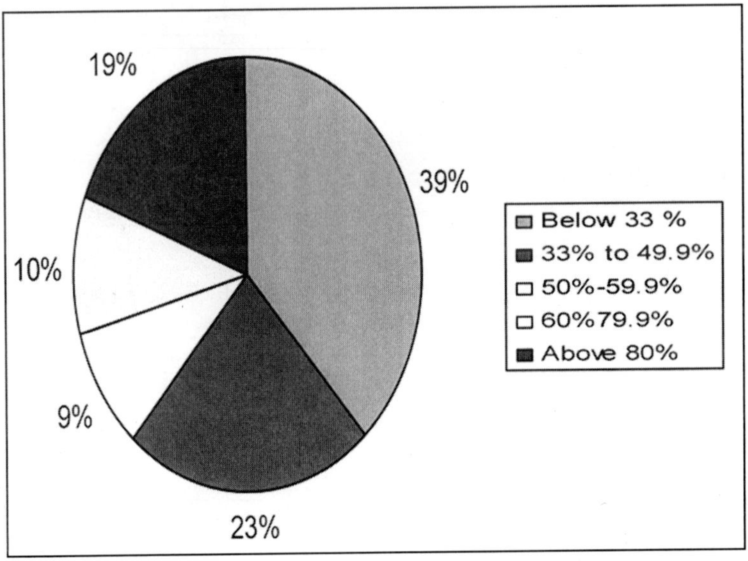

Fig. 22.1B: Achievements of Students where teachers do not use TLM.

Fig. 22.1A and 22.1B reflect scores of group where teacher used appropriate teaching methodology with Teaching Learning Material, more than 35 per cent of the students scored 80 marks and 21 per cent of the students scored above 60 marks, and merely 9 per cent of the students scored below passing marks, whereas in the group studied in traditional methods without TLM more than 39 per cent of the students failed and 23 per cent of the students scored below 50 per cent of marks. Its shows that the schools, where the teachers are using their training related knowledge in subject teaching are having students with better achievement and indicates that students who were usually taught with the use of TLM scored good marks because their concepts were very clear and it reflected in their achievement level.

Table 22.2: Significance difference in Mathematics achievement between two groups

Mean	Achievement of Student (A)	Achievement of Student (B)	C.R.(T)	Significant Level
	21.22	27.252		0.05 Level
Standard Deviation	4.995	2.876	10.79	0.01 level

Group (A): Teacher used traditional method not using new techniques.

Group (B): Teacher used gained knowledge through training in Teaching.

Table 22.3: Significance difference in Science achievement between two groups

Mean	Achievement of Student (A)	Achievement of Student (B)	C.R.(T)	Significant Level
	19.4000	34.5533		0.05 Level
Standard Deviation	8.62025	8.23525	10.97	0.01 level

Group (A): Teacher used traditional method not using new techniques.

Group (B): Teacher used gained knowledge through training in Teaching.

Tables 22.2 and 22.3 indicate the difference assessed between the achievements of students examined. C.R value 10.97 and 10.79 shows that there is a significance difference in achievement between the two groups' students in Science and Mathematics. It also highlights a clear difference and describes that the teachers using appropriate teaching technique and teaching habits affected the teaching-learning process positively and it makes the difficult and boring subjects so interesting and understandable which makes a remarkable effect on the achievement level. Thus, research hypothesis "There is no effect of teacher's training on student achievement" was rejected as it means that teachers' teaching technique and approprite teaching methodology affect positively students' achivement.

Objective 3: To study the Problems of teachers' in using gained knowledge into the classroom situations.

To identify the problem, Teacher Attitude Scale towards importance of teacher training in schools was administered on 320 teachers working in Upper Primary Schools of selected districts in Uttar Pradesh. The results drawn are represented in Table 22.4.

Table 22.4: Barrier in using gained knowledge in classroom teaching

Sl. No.	Problem related items	Agree in %
1.	Difficult to create suitable environment in school	75
2.	Having less time for using gained knowledge	90
3.	Creates problems in completing the course in time	100
4.	Less number of teachers according to the class	95
5.	Lack of Teaching learning material in school	65
6.	Improper management of TLM in school	87.5

(*Contd.*)

Sl. No.	Problem related items	Agree in %
7.	Irregularity of student's attendance	100
8.	Students' curiosity more in TLM less in subjects	72.5
9.	Less awareness of students towards education	77.5
10.	Lack of reading Material among students	50.25
11.	Extra duties for the teacher	100
12.	Students' less co-operation	65
13.	Students' low interest and attendance	70
14.	Parent's unawareness and less interest towards education	95
15.	Holding the responsibilities related to incentives and interventions of government	100

Discussion

More than 75 per cent of teachers responded positively that they are working in that environment in which there is no awareness to education exists among student and parents so it becomes a challenge for a teacher to build appropriate environment for teaching:

- 90 per cent of the teachers responded positively that periods divided are not very suitable for using gained knowledge. Most of the schools were having only one teacher who teaches more than one subject so it was difficult to manage all the classes per day.
- At this spot about the entire teacher came in one queue and reacted that teaching through the technique of training received, it will difficult to complete the courses in time.
- 95 per cent of the subject teachers at primary level are single teacher have to manage six classes per day, it becomes impossible to use gained knowledge in classroom situation.
- About 65 per cent of the teachers explained that most of the schools are not having proper teaching-learning materials.

87.5 per cent of the teachers reported that schools are having limited rooms so it is very difficult to manage TLM in schools.

- All the teachers assembled at this point and reacted that although many efforts have been made to increase students' attendance but the results are not satisfactory. Students' are irregular so this makes teachers' efforts false and mostly teachers were demoralized.
- 72.5 per cent of teachers accepted that when any matter is taught with the help of TLM most students do not pay attention towards content for which TLM is used and most of them become curious towards TLM.
- 77.5 per cent of the teachers accepted that mainly children of rural area do not have much awareness towards importance of education than it become a hard task to create anxiety and motivation to learn.
- 50.25 per cent of the teachers accepted that although students were provided book but they do not bring it daily or do not manage the reading materials properly so it becomes a tough task to give any exercise or class work with proper books or copies.
- Cent per cent teachers accepted that they are having extra work load. Pandey (2004) in her study found that extra duties, like Pulse-Polio, Makan Ganana, Jansankhya Ganana are over load works on primary school working teachers. All these duties affect school teaching-learning environment. Teacher cannot pay full attention towards teaching with these extra duties.
- About 65 per cent of teachers reported that most of the students do not pay more interest and attention towards education and their attendance in the schools. They are more interested in facilities and incentives provided to them.
- More than 95 per cent of the teachers reported that mostly rural parents are having less awareness towards education so they do not motivate their students for schooling, it

becomes a challenge for the teachers to create a effective environment for teaching and learning.

- At last we can conclude that there are many problems and barriers faced by the teachers in using their gained knowledge into the natural classroom situation.

Objective 4: To identify some ways of making training programme more effective for schools.

As per my knowledge these steps should be taken for making training programme more effective for the schools.

- *Training Programme officer should be appointed if possible* at District level having some administrative power. Training officers should be attached to Department of In-Service and Pre-Service Training Programme in DIETs and all teachers working in DIETs should be a part of his supervision team. *This Training Programme officer should be made fully responsible* for the better organization of every Training Programme organized by DIETs and also should bear the responsibilities to supervise the respective district Primary Schools and their teaching-learning environment.
- There should be at least one teacher in each Primary school, with deep subject and pedagogical knowledge because in most of the primary schools subject related teachers are not appointed, it affects the teaching-learning process of these important subjects.
- If administration wants to produce competent teacher with new glowing mind so our Training programmes should be more effective. Actual classroom teaching presentation should be provided. Teaching Presentation by the trainer should be added to programmes so that related subject teacher can easily observe the whole classroom interaction system as a whole and solve his/her problem themselves related to use of TLM, Communication skill, Teaching skill methods and principles.

- *A combined team from SCERT, SIEMAT, SIET and SISE can also visit once or twice in a year* accidentally to some school so that the real situation might visualized and Teacher attitude of taking the training duty but not using in classroom might change and it will create a pressure to maintain the standards.
- Continuous In-service training programme should be organized to update teachers with innovations so that they could be expertise competent motivated and having innovative mood continuously.
- Organization of Seminars and Workshops for the students and teachers will motivate teachers to update their knowledge in the required field.
- To activate students and teachers towards betterment of teaching-learning Process, subject related competition should be organized at District, State and National level. Best teachers and students in teaching and achievement could be awarded might motivate others to do better.
- To enhance subject knowledge and subject-specific pedagogical skills, teachers of these subjects should be motivated to do researches and research innovations for confidence and effectiveness in teaching.
- Elementary school teaching-learning programmes only could be improved when—
  - Teachers practice and continuous and comprehensive evaluation.
  - Teachers participate in action research in elementary classes.
- Laboratory facility as much as possible should be provided in Upper Primary Schools to facilitate teaching in Mathematics and Science.
- Separate subject teacher having good qualification and training should be appointed separately for Upper Primary Schools. Teachers already working in Primary school usually after a long experience of teaching in lower Primary school sometimes they never fit in set frame.

- Teachers should be prepared to correlated teaching and achievement with students' self-concept and interest.
- A special time bound teaching module for various subjects should be provided to the teachers continuously and the administration should take proper care of teaching of these special models to the teachers.
- Administrators must provide support systems by—
    - Facilitating appropriate Teaching-learning materials.
    - Encouraging special subject events.
    - Solving problems regarding subject teaching.
- *Continuous assessment and supervision should be done* by the DIETs Trainers, Training officers, coordinators of BRCs and Specialized inspection team to inspect teacher activities and give guidance towards related problems and this assessment should be in writing and should be added as minimum requirement for yearly increments of teachers.
- To provide motivation towards best effort, if it is possible, the teacher performing their duties at the excellent level should *be awarded at Blocks and District level per year* by giving awards *or one extra increment* might motivate other teacher to do their best.

REFERENCES

diethatta.nic.in/aboutd.htm retrieved on 02/12/13

dietthadlaskein.gov.in/aboutus.htm retrieved on 02/12/13

www.educationforallinindia.com retrieved on 02/12/13

www.dietbhopal.nic.in/bri.htm retrieved on 02/02/14

www.dieternakulam.org/retrieved on 02/11/13

www.nuepa.org/retrieved on 02/02/14

23

Attitude of Teacher Trainees towards Online Pre-service Teacher Education Programme of NIOS

P.K. Sahoo

Distance mode teacher education programmes gained ground in India during the year 1964, when Regional Colleges of Education introduced correspondence-*cum*-contact programmes for pre-service training of on the job teachers. In service Teacher education programmes through open distance mode were given priorities through New Policy on Education, 1986.The open universities as well as traditional universities promoted distance mode teacher education programmes, mostly for secondary school teachers. In-service education programmes through IGNOU-DPEP project were offered for professional development of elementary school teachers. However, National Institute of Open Schooling (NIOS) and Indira Gandhi National Open University (IGNOU) took lead in clearing the backlog of untrained elementary school teachers by offering Diploma in Elementary Education (D.El.Ed.) programmes in some of the states of the country within NCTE framework. Of late, NIOS introduced a massive project on on-line D.El.Ed. programme at national level for pre-service teacher education of untrained teachers serving in the elementary schools under Sarva Shiksha Abhiyan (SSA). Its aim is to provide alternative opportunity to on the job teachers to get pre-service education to qualify themselves for permanent absorption in the teaching job at elementary level. Distance mode teacher education programme makes use of distance media based education integrated with practical activities performed in own school under the supervision of mentor teachers and local level resource persons. Learners support services are organized through counselling sessions and workshops. Assignment and continuous monitoring practices promote formative evaluation in teacher development activities. NIOS introduced Online facilities in different languages for information system, study materials, learners support services and evaluation learners. The user student teachers avail such facilities at their workplace schools as well as study centres. The emphasis of such kind of teacher education programme remains on changing role of the teacher in the age of technology. The new role of the teacher is perceived as a learning facilitator, knowledge guide, knowledge navigator and co-learner with students. Workplace based professional education programme with the support of online based ODL programme provides great opportunity for integrating day-to-day teaching experiences for exploring meaning of pedagogic principles in their own cognitive framework and try to apply for further experiences in teaching. Moreover workplace based learning of teachers generate from their interaction with own students and colleagues. Teacher learns by giving students more options and responsibilities for their own learning. Teachers' ethical orientation towards learners' autonomy and their collaborative functions to generate knowledge strengthens the scope for teachers acquiring novel experiences from such environment. The ODL mode teacher's active participation in own learning process, in daily interaction sessions with the help of ICT networking and learning collaboratively with colleagues in own school and the participant teachers of ODL programme.

Senapati (2009) highlighted conductive learning environment for ICT supported, leaner centric approach. Its implications can be sited on the following points:

- Development and sustenance of motivation among participants.
- Making flexible work plan.
- Collaborative among participants.
- Continuous interaction among counsellors, tutors and resource persons with the participant teachers.
- Sharing of experiences in own studies and its linkage with routine activities in school.
- Open sharing of ideas among co-participants.
- Making optimum use of technology supported recourses along with other sources of learning provided by the ODL institution.
- Enabling working teachers to develop professional competencies through distance mode is a great challenge in terms of many contextual variables like subject area of teaching, locality and teaching experiences. A centralised programme success may be examined in different contextual background of the participant teachers.

Since, such innovative project has been in operation to bring in teacher education system at national level, it is worthwhile to explore how the key stakeholders appreciate such programme and what are their attitude towards different components of On-line Teacher Education. Several researches have been conducted in the area of distance mode teacher education like one significant study conducted by Sharma (2019) on a comprehensive evaluation of online programmes at IGNOU revealed that the course contents were easily down loadable (72%) and were supplanted by audio/video. They were motivating and thought provoking synchronous and asynchronous counselling. Around 56 per cent students attended virtual class. Besides virtual class, discussion forums, chat and SMS were the most popular communication modes. The learner respondents preferred to use laptop to access IGNOU-LMS platform. Three-fourth of the learners agreed that they required assistance of the instructors. The LMS were not sufficient for self-learning. Most of the instructors opined that learners could not write the assignments systematically and needed guidance of the counsellors.

Another study conducted in India by Singh (2018) on NIOS online education programme revealed the status of D.EI.Ed. project for teacher education. The study reported about successful integration of television and digital media for teacher training. The users appreciated the content covered in TV presentation. They insisted on re-telecast of the video programmes through YouTube. The feedbacks of the learners were encouraging with regard to the lectures delivered by the subject experts. However, least feedback was procured about the quality input of online materials and lectures. As a whole, the viewership of NIOS MOOCs programme were progressively increasing depending on their course requirement. As many as 1.25 lakh had subscribed to the NIOS MOOCs programme. Integration of YouTube with programme telecast helped the teacher trainees to a large extent.

So far no study has been conducted to study the teacher trainees experiences on different components of teacher education inputs of online programme of NIOS. Hence, the researches intended to conduct the present study with following objectives:

Objectives of the Study

1. To study the attitude of in-service teacher participants towards online Diploma in Elementary Education (D.EI.Ed.) programme of NIOS Component-wise.
2. To study the effect of student teachers subject background on their attitude towards online D.EI.Ed. programme of NIOS.
3. To study the effect of student teachers teaching experience on their attitude towards online D.EI.Ed. programme of NIOS.

Hypothesis of the Study

The hypotheses of the study were stated in null form:

1. There is no significant difference between Arts and Science teachers' mean attitude experience student mean attitude scores towards online D.EI.Ed programme component-wise.
2. There is no significant difference between more teaching experience and less teaching experience student teachers' mean attitude scores towards online D.EI.Ed. programme component-wise.
3. There is no significant difference between rural and urban area student teachers' mean attitude scores towards online D.EI.Ed. programme component-wise.

Methods and Procedures of the Study

The population or the study covered all the in-service elementary school teachers enrolled in on-line D.EI.Ed. programme offered by NIOS in Uttar Pradesh State, India. The sample of the study included 200 student teachers, 50 each from four study centres of Allahabad district of UP. The multistage sampling was used to identify four study centres of Allahabad district of UP. The multistage sampling was used to identify four study centres from each study centre, 50 respondents were picked up randomly. The sample teachers were in-service teachers having varied experiences of teaching in Arts 130 and Science 70. Teachers having more than 3 years of teaching experience were categorised as more experienced N=80 and Less experienced 120. 140 teachers were from rural area and 60 were from urban area. Attitude scale developed in Likert form was used for data collection by the researcher. The scale included positive and negative items with five alternatives. The attitude areas covered seven components of online teacher education programme, viz. Information system, online study materials, counselling session, e-learning, m-learning delivery mode, school based experiences and projects, workshop based experiences, assignment and evaluation of learners. There were 54 items in the scale. The content validity of the items were judged by the experts of ODL system. Data were analysed (component-wise) to test the null hypothesis with the help of 't' tests.

Analysis and Interpretation of Data

Data Analysis has been presented in the following points:

1. Effect of subject background of student teachers on attitude towards online D.EI.Ed. programme component-wise.
2. Effect of teaching experience of student teachers on attitude towards online D.EI.Ed. programme component-wise.
3. Effect of locale background of student teachers on attitude towards online D.EI.Ed. programme component-wise.

Table 23.1: Comparison of mean attitude scores of Arts and Science D.EI.Ed students towards online teacher education programme component-wise

Component	Arts		Science		't' value
	M	SD	M	SD	
Information system	4.34	0.40	4.53	0.38	3.80**
Online study materials	4.16	0.44	4.30	0.39	2.80**
Counselling sessions	4.20	0.40	4.03	0.54	2.40*
e-learning/in-learning, delivery mode	4.20	0.40	3.77	0.57	6.10**
School based experiences and project	3.87	0.64	4.09	0.56	2.70**
Workshop based experience	3.94	0.49	4.00	0.53	0.85 NS
Assignment and evaluation of learners	3.94	0.42	3.86	0.43	1.60 NS
	N=130		N=70		

Notes: **= Significant at 01 levels,*= significant at 0.05 levels, NS = Not Significant.

Table 23.1 indicates data on effect of teaching subject background on attitude of open distance D.EI.Ed. students towards online teacher education programme of NIOS in different areas, such as Information system, online study materials, counselling sessions, e-learning, m-learning delivery mode; based experience and projects, workshop based experiences, assignment and evaluation of learners.

The 't' test scores on comparison of mean attitude scores of Arts and Science group students component-wise reveal different results. The t-values indicated significant difference between mean attitude scores of Arts and Science group students at .01 level with df 198 on following areas.

E-learning, m-learning delivery modes and school based experiences and projects. On these aspects, the null hypothesis of no significant difference of mean attitude scores of Arts and Science groups rejected at .01 level. Since the obtained 't' values were found higher than the table values with df 198 was significant difference of mean attitude scores of Arts and Science group student teachers on counselling sessions at .05 level. Hence, the null hypothesis of no significant difference of mean attitude scores on counselling session of Arts and Science students was rejected.

Table 23.1 indicates that Arts and Science group student expressed positive attitude towards online teacher education programme, the science group students expressed very high positive attitude towards Information system whereas online study materials and school based experiences and project, the Arts group students expressed very high positive attitude towards counselling sessions and e-learning/m-learning delivery mode. In the case of rest of the components, viz. workshop based experiences and assignment and evaluation of learners. The attitudes of Arts and Science students were of high positive level. There was no significance with df 198 of these areas.

As a whole it can be commented that subject background had moderate effect on student attitude towards online teacher education programme offered by National Institute of Open Schooling.

Table 23.2: Comparison of mean attitude scores of more teaching experience and less teaching experience of D.EI.Ed. students towards online teacher education programme : component-wise

Component	Less teaching experience		More teaching experience		't' value
	M	SD	M	SD	
Information system	4.47	0.40	4.44	0.40	0.60 NS
Online study materials	4.19	0.44	4.20	0.44	2.80 NS
Counselling sessions	4.10	0.48	3.99	0.50	1.80 NS
e-learning/in-learning, delivery mode	3.85	0.62	3.76	0.68	1.10 NS
School based experiences and project	3.84	0.46	4.12	0.53	5.60*
Workshop based experience	3.91	0.46	3.98	0.45	1.40 NS
Assignment and evaluation of learners	3.79	0.40	3.97	0.40	3.60*
	N=120		N=80		

Notes: NS = Not Significant. *Significant at .01.

Table 23.2 indicates effect of teaching experience on attitude of D.EI.Ed. student towards online teacher education programme offered by NIOS on different components, viz. Information system, online study materials, counselling sessions, e-learning/m-learning delivery mode, school based experiences and projects, workshop based experiences. The 't' tests reveal that there was significant difference between mean attitude scores of less teacher experienced and more teaching experienced D.EI.Ed. student teachers.

On two components, viz. School based experiences and projects and assignment and evaluation of learners at .01 level with df 198. In these components longer teaching experience student teachers expressed very high positive attitude than that of their less teaching experience student teachers learning/m-learning delivery mode and school based experiences and projects. There were no significant differences between mean attitude scores of more teaching experience and less teaching experience student teachers, since the respective 't' values were not significant with df 198. Hence, the null hypothesis of no significant difference mean attitude scores of more teaching experience and less teaching experience mean attitude scores of mean attitude scores of more teaching experience and less teaching experience were not rejected. The results revealed that both the group student teachers expressed very high positive attitude towards these components.

As a whole, it can be commented that teaching experience of D.EI.Ed. student teachers exhorted low effect on their attitude towards online teacher education programme of NIOS.

Table 23.3: Comparison of mean attitude scores of rural and urban D.EI.Ed. students towards online teacher education programme: component-wise

Component	**Rural**		**Urban**		**'t' value**
	M	**SD**	**M**	**SD**	
Information system	4.50	0.41	4.21	0.49	4.10*
Online study materials	4.21	0.44	4.01	0.47	3.30*
Counselling sessions	3.92	0.64	3.98	0.46	0.85 NS
e-learning/in-learning, delivery mode	4.05	0.40	3.54	0.61	6.20*
School based experiences and project	4.01	0.53	4.02	0.54	0.14 NS
Workshop based experience	4.04	0.43	3.72	0.47	5.00*
Assignment and evaluation of learners	3.84	0.43	3.79	0.40	1.00 NS
	N=120		N=80		

Note: NS = Not Significant. *Significant at .01.

Table 23.3 reveals data about effect of locale on online teacher education programme of NIOS in different areas, such as Information system, online study materials, counselling sessions, e-learning/m-learning delivery mode, school based experiences and project workshop based experiences.

The 't' scores on comparison of mean attitude scores of rural and urban group student teachers component-wise reveal different results. The 't' test indicate significant differences between mean attitude score of rural and urban area. Student teachers at.01 level with df 198 on following areas:

1. Information system
2. Online study materials
3. E-learning and m-learning delivery mode
4. School based experiences and project
5. Workshop based experiences.

The null hypothesis of no significant difference of mean attitude scores of rural and urban group were rejected at .01 level. In other words it can be said that the rural and urban students differed on their attitude towards online teacher education programme on above components component-wise in favour of rural group of student teachers. The rural area student teachers' attitude towards information system online study materials, e-learning and m-learning delivery mode, school based experiences and project and workshop based experiences were found to be higher than that of urban student teachers counterparts. They expressed very high positive attitude towards online programme on these components. It indicates significant effect of locale on student teachers attitude towards online programme of teacher education.

Conclusion

Analysis of data revealed that the online D.El.Ed. programme students expressed high positive attitude towards different components of teacher education programme offered by the NIOS. There was moderate effect of background factors on students' attitude. The science group students' attitude towards Information system, online study materials, modes and school based experiences and projects was very high in comparison to their arts group counterparts indicating very high relevance of online programme to them. Arts group expressed very high positive attitude towards counselling sessions and e-learning delivery mode which might have met their special needs. Even through, teaching experience variable exhorted less effect on student attitude, it was noticed that high teaching experience student teachers very high positive attitude towards school based experiences and project and assignments and evaluation of learners through online programme. It revealed their favour towards practical orientation in training programme and facilities for formative evaluation. The study also indicated significant effect of locale background on student teachers' attitude. Rural students' higher positive attitude towards different components of online teacher education in comparison to their urban counterparts indicated more favourable status of the programme among them. It justifies the relevance of distance teacher education programme for teachers working in far flung rural area school, especially on the components of information system online study materials, e-learning, m-learning delivery mode school based experiences and workshop based experiences.

This study reveals effectiveness of online teacher education programme among the in-service elementary school teachers for meeting their professional requirements. More specifically, the programmes' success among rural area school teachers and high teaching experience school teachers have been reflected in their attitude towards the online teacher education programme of NIOS. There is more scope for improving the counselling activities and formative evaluation practices through e-learning mode to meet professional requirement of on the job elementary school teachers. The NIOS must evolve suitable strategies in the areas.

REFERENCES

Senapaty (2009). Professional Development of Teachers in a New paradigm of Technology Mediated Constructivist Learning, in DEP-SSA, IGNOU, New Delhi. (2009). *Technology Mediated Learning for Professional Development of Personnel at Elementary Education.*

Singh, G. (2018). *Blending Television with MOOCs: An Experiment in Elementary Teacher Education in India.*

Sharma, M. (2019). *A Comprehensive Evaluation of Online Programme of IGNOU.* Unpublished Ph.D. Thesis IGNOU, New Delhi.

Tran Thi Phuong, Ed. (2018). *Open Education in Human Resource Development in Asia's Period of Integrtation,* Vol. 2, Hanoi Bach Khoa Publication.

24

Learning Styles of B.Ed. Students in Regular and ODL Mode

Subhash Chandra and *P.K. Sahoo*

The concept of learning style was first presented by Rita Dunn in 1960. Learning style is similar to cognitive style, but is a more specific form of cognitive style. Grasha (1996) defines learning style as child's preferences in thinking and interaction with other children in different classroom environments and experiences. Learning styles are characteristic strengths and preferences of the learners for responding to the stimuli in environment and processing the information. It is a behavioural pattern developed for any new learning. Keefe (1979) defined the learning styles as *"the composite of characteristic cognitive, affective and physiological factors that serve as relatively stable indicators of how a learner perceives, interacts with, and responds to the learning environment."* Grasha & Reichmann identified 6 different learning styles: Independent, Avoidant, Collaborative, Dependent, Competitive and Participant.

Aragon, Johnson & Shaik (2002) state that online learning can be as effective as face-to-face learning in many respects, even though students have different learning style preferences. Learning style differences were found between face-to-face and online students, but these differences were not significantly apparent when students' success was controlled.

Johnson & Johnson (2006) study revealed that the college students are aware of their learning style and the conditions that facilitate their learning. Active learners of college expressed preference for face-to-face study groups rather than online study groups and for online quizzes rather than pencil-and-paper quizzes. Visual learners of college expressed preference for online quizzes rather than online study groups.

In the study by Hura (2007), results revealed that for the Accommodating learning style (LSI) there was one statistically significant result that indicated students in a face-to-face class prefer to study with a teacher. For the other three learning styles (Diverging, Converging and Assimilating), there were one or two statements that statistically indicated online students had a higher level of comfort or satisfaction than face-to-face students regarding computer work or usage.

In the study by Liu (2007), results revealed the significant statistical differences in many learning style subscales at post-test between experimental and control groups. At the end of the course, online students seemed to have a higher preference for peer interaction, competition, interaction with the instructor, details of the course materials, independence, authority, reading, direct experiences, and clear goal setting than their counterparts. No significant statistical differences were detected in learning performance between both groups.

Above study revealed the importance of comparative study of learning styles. It signified the need of study of comparative learning styles. Since there is scarcity of study related with learning styles teacher trainees of ODL mode as well as Regular mode. So researcher aimed to investigate the learning styles of Regular mode and ODL mode B.Ed. students.

Objectives of Study

Objective of the present study are:

1. To study the learning styles of B.Ed. Students of Traditional and Open University.
2. To study the association between learning styles and university types of B.Ed. students.
3. To study the association between gender and university types of B.Ed. students of different learning styles.
4. To study the association between subject area and university types of B.Ed. students of different learning styles.

Hypotheses of Study

The hypotheses of the study are stated in null form:

1. There is no significant association between learning styles and university types of B.Ed. students.
2. There is no significant association between gender and university types of B.Ed. students of different learning styles.
3. There is no significant association between subject area and university types of B.Ed. students of different learning styles.

Research Design

Survey research method was used in the present study.

Tools Used in the Study

Grasha-Reichmann Learning Style Scale (1996) was used to determine the Learning Style of learners of B.Ed. course. It was developed by Grasha-Reichmann (1996). What kinds of an interaction of the students are in with the teachers and their peer groups or friends are the learning style dimension of this inventory. It focuses more on students' preferences for the learning environment. The questionnaire is a 60 item self-evaluation inventory scored using a 5-point Likert scale.

Population and Sample

Population of the study consisted of all the second year B.Ed.

trainees enrolled in different programme study centres of open universities (IGNOU & UPRTOU) in Uttar Pradesh and all B.Ed. students studying in Allahabad University, Prayagraj (Allahabad), UP. 100 final year B.Ed. trainees (50 from IGNOU & 50 from UPRTOU) were selected by purposive sampling method. Similarly, 100 B.Ed. trainees were selected by purposive sampling method Allahabad University (50 from Kali Prasad Training College, Allahabad and 50 from Ewing Christian College, Allahabad).

Statistics used: χ^2-tests and percentage analysis were used for testing the null hypotheses and interpreting and analyzing the data of the study.

Data Collection

Data were collected from the sample respondents available in the programme study centres or in the colleges towards completions of second year programme.

Analysis and Interpretation of Data

Learning Styles of trainees were determined accordingly to GRLSS scale percentage analysis and χ^2-tests between learning styles and university types of B.Ed. students are represented in following Tables and Figures.

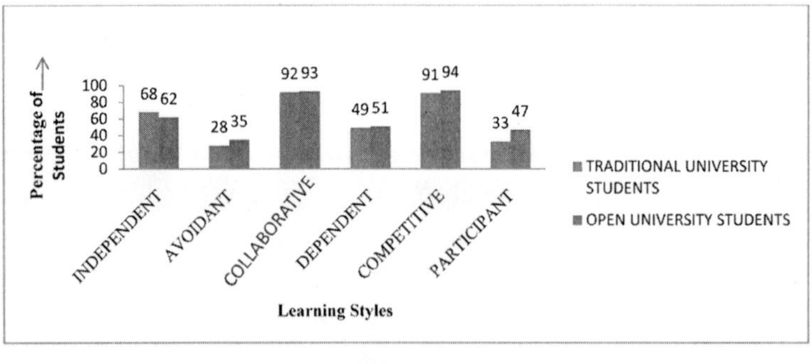

Fig. 24.1: Learning styles of Regular and ODL mode B.Ed. Students

It can be noticed from Table 23.1 that the calculated χ^2-values of independence between university type and learning styles (Independent, Avoidant, Collaborative, Dependent and Competitive) are found 0.79, 1.15, 0.07, 0.08 & 0.65 respectively. The obtained values were lesser than the Table value (3.84) at .05 level of significance with df:1 and (5.99) at .05 level of significance with df:2. Thus, the observed values were not found significant at .05 level. Hence, the learning styles (Independent, Avoidant, Collaborative, Dependent, Participant and Competitive) and university types of B.Ed. students are not significantly associated with each other.

Table 24.1: χ^2-test of independence between learning styles and University Type

Learning Styles	**University Type**	**Levels of Learning styles**			**Total**	**χ^2-value**
		High	**Mod-erate**	**Low**		
Independent Learning Styles	Traditional University	68	32	–	100	0.36 N.S. df=1
	Open University	62	40	–	100	
	Total	**130**	**72**	–	**200**	
Avoidant Learning Styles	Traditional University	28	66	06	100	1.15 N.S. df=2
	Open University	35	60	05	100	
	Total	**63**	**126**	**11**	**200**	
Collaborative Learning Styles	Traditional University	92	08	–	100	0.07 N.S. df=1
	Open University	93	07	–	100	
	Total	**185**	**15**	–	**200**	
Dependent Learning Styles	Traditional University	49	51	–	100	0.08 N.S. df=1
	Open University	51	49	–	100	
	Total	**100**	**100**	–	**200**	
Competitive Learning Styles	Traditional University	91	09	–	100	0.65 N.S. df=1
	Open University	94	06	–	100	
	Total	**185**	**15**	–	**200**	

(*Contd.*)

Learning Styles	University Type	Levels of Learning styles			Total	χ^2-value
		High	Mod-erate	Low		
Participant Learning Styles	Traditional University	33	67	-	100	4.08 * df=1
	Open University	47	53	-	100	
	Total	**80**	**120**	-	**200**	

Notes: * = Significant at .05 level; N.S. = Not Significant.

It can be noticed from Table 24.1 that the calculated χ^2-value of independence between university type and participant learning style are found 4.08. The obtained value was greater than the Table value (3.84) at .05 level of significance with df:1. Thus, the observed value was found significant at .05 level. Hence, the participant learning style and university types of B.Ed. Students are significantly associated with each other. Open University B.Ed. trainees are more participant than that of their traditional University counterparts.

Table 24.2: χ^2-test of independence between Gender and University Types of B.Ed. Students of different learning styles

Learning Styles	University Type	Gender		Total		χ^2-value
		Male	Female			
Independent Learning Styles	Traditional University	36 (52.9)	32 (47.1)	68	(100)	0.001 N.S.
	Open University	33 (53.2)	29 (46.8)	62	(100)	
	Total	**69**	**61**	**130**		
Avoidant	Traditional University	23 (82.1)	05 (17.9)	28	(100)	2.84 N.S.
	Open University	22 (62.9)	13 (37.1)	35	(100)	
	Total	**45**	**18**	**63**		
Collaborative	Traditional University	44 (47.8)	48 (52.2)	92	(100)	0.05 N.S.
	Open University	46 (49.5)	47 (50.5)	93	(100)	
	Total	**90**	**95**	**185**		

(*Contd.*)

Learning Styles	University Type	Gender		Total	χ^2-value
		Male	Female		
Dependent	Traditional University	27 (55.1)	22 (44.9)	49 (100)	0.17 N.S.
	Open University	26 (51.0)	25 (49.0)	51 (100)	
	Total	**53**	**47**	**100**	
Competitive	Traditional University	47 (51.6)	44 (48.4)	91 (100)	0.04 N.S.
	Open University	50 (53.2)	44 (46.8)	94 (100)	
	Total	**97**	**88**	**185**	
Participant	Traditional University	14 (42.4)	19 (57.6)	33 (100)	0.15 N.S.
	Open University	22 (46.8)	25 (53.2)	47 (100)	
	Total	**36**	**44**	**80**	

N.S. = Not Significant.

Note: Figures in Parentheses indicate percentages.

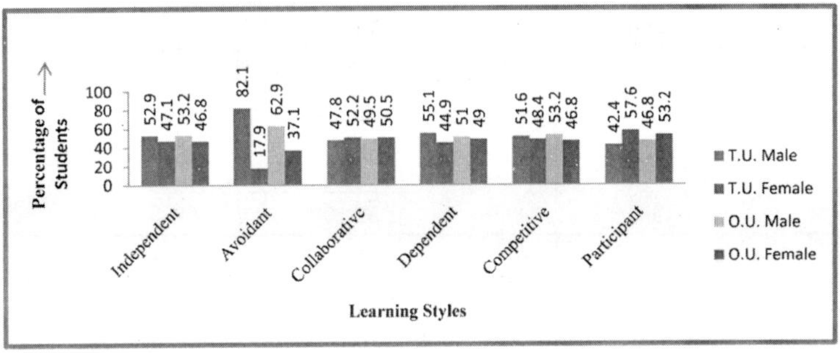

Fig. 24.2: Gender-wise Learning styles of Regular and ODL mode B.Ed. Students

For calculating χ^2-value of independence between gender and university types of B.Ed. Students of different learning styles, only trainees of high level were selected. It can be noticed from Table 24.2 that the calculated χ^2-values of independence between

Table 24.3: χ^2-test of independence between subject area and university types of B.Ed. Students of different learning styles

Learning Styles	University Type	Subject Area				Total		χ^2-value
		Humanities & Social Science		Science & Technology				
Independent Learning Styles	Traditional University	43	(63.2)	25	(36.8)	68	(100)	0.29 N.S.
	Open University	42	(67.7)	20	(32.3)	62	(100)	
	Total	**85**		**45**		**130**		
Avoidant	Traditional University	21	(75.0)	07	(25.0)	28	(100)	0.004 N.S.
	Open University	26	(74.3)	09	(25.7)	35	(100)	
	Total	**47**		**16**		**63**		
Collaborative	Traditional University	51	(55.4)	41	(44.6)	92	(100)	2.45 N.S.
	Open University	62	(66.7)	31	(33.3)	93	(100)	
	Total	**113**		**72**		**185**		
Dependent	Traditional University	33	(67.3)	16	(32.7)	49	(100)	0.02 N.S.
	Open University	35	(68.6)	16	(31.4)	51	(100)	
	Total	**68**		**32**		**100**		
Competitive	Traditional University	50	(54.9)	41	(45.1)	91	(100)	3.38 N.S.
	Open University	64	(68.1)	30	(31.9)	94	(100)	
	Total	**114**		**71**		**185**		
Participant	Traditional University	19	(57.6)	14	(42.4)	33	(100)	0.93 N.S.
	Open University	32	(68.1)	15	(31.9)	47	(100)	
	Total	**51**		**29**		**80**		

N.S. = Not Significant.

Note: Figures in Parentheses indicate percentages.

gender, and university types of B.Ed. students of different learning styles are found 0.001, 2.84, 0.05, 0.17, 0.04 and 0.15 respectively. The obtained values were lesser than the Table value (3.84) at .05 level of significance with df:1. Thus, the observed values were not found significant at .05 level. Hence, the gender and university types of B.Ed. students of different learning styles (Independent, Avoidant, Collaborative, Dependent Competitive and Participant) are not significantly associated with each other.

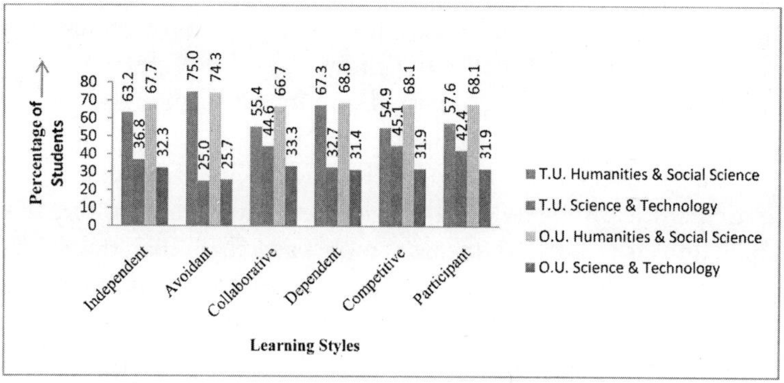

Fig. 24.3: Subject area-wise Learning styles of Regular and ODL mode B.Ed. Students.

It can be noticed from Table 24.3 that the calculated χ^2-values of independence between subject area and university types of B.Ed. Students of different learning styles are found 0.29, 0.004, 2.45, 0.02, 3.38 and 0.93 respectively. The obtained values were lesser than the Table value (3.84) at .05 level of significance with df:1. Thus, the observed values were not found significant at .05 level. Hence, the subject area and university types of B.Ed. students of different learning styles (Independent, Avoidant, Collaborative, Dependent Competitive) are not significantly associated with each other.

Conclusion

Results revealed that there is no significant association between learning styles (Independent, Avoidant, Collaborative, Dependent

Competitive and Participant) and university types of B.Ed. students. There is no association between gender and university types of B.Ed. students of different learning styles (Independent, Avoidant, Collaborative, Dependent, Competitive and Participant). There is no association between subject area and university types of B.Ed. students of different learning styles (Independent, Avoidant, Collaborative, Dependent, Competitive and Participant). The study revealed that both regular mode as well as ODL mode B.Ed. students follow similar type of learning styles. Open University and traditional university B.Ed. teacher trainees have similar type of learning styles irrespective of gender and subject area. Different kinds of learning styles co-existed among ODL mode as well as traditional/regular mode B.Ed. trainees.

Study revealed that the ODL mode B.Ed. trainees follow participant learning style with high level than their counterparts. Open university B.Ed. trainees are more participant than traditional university B.Ed. trainees, so there is need to promote more interactive activities in ODL mode B.Ed. programme. In ODL mode B.Ed. programme, the workshops should provide more chances to participate in different academic activities.

REFERENCES

Aragon, S.R., Johnson, S.D. & Shaik, N. (2002). "The influence of Learning Style Preferences on student success in Online *versus* Face-to-Face Environments". *The American Journal of Distance Education.* 16(4), pp. 227-44.

Hura, G. (2007). "A Comparison of Learning Styles with Student Comfort and Satisfaction in Online and Traditional Learning Environments". *Adult Education Research Conference.* Retrieved from: http://newprairiepress.org/aerc/2007/roundtables/11.

Johnson, G.M. & Johnson, J.A. (2006). "Learning Style and Preference for Online Learning Support: Individual Quizzes versus Study Groups". *ED-MEDIA 2006 Proceeding,* pp. 1861-68. Retrieved from: https://pdfs.semanticscholar.org/b5b3/d91aa00ec569c1114da02b9f7b95bc6261c9.pdf.

Liu, Y. (2007). *A Comparative Study of Learning Styles between Online and Traditional Students.* Retrieved from: http://journals.sagepub.com/doi/abs/10.2190/TJ34-6U66-8L72-2825.

25

Inclusion of Students with Disabilities in Higher Education

Implications for Teachers

Hemendra S. Mistry and *S.C. Panigrahi*

Status of higher education of the students with disabilities and their profiles were studied. The participant consisted of 143 students with disabilities enrolled in the graduate and postgraduate courses of the nine general universities of Gujarat, India. The result of the study indicated very less enrolment of students with disabilities. Participants' profiles in terms of personal, professional, academic, and family background were also studied. This chapter discusses the result obtained, implications for teachers and concludes with the suggestions for improving the status of higher education of students with disabilities.

For a very long time children with disabilities were thought to be incapable of receiving education. This was despite the fact that many distinguished persons with disabilities have made significant contribution to science, arts and literature. To quote a few illustrations, Homer, the immortal Greek poet was blind. Saunderson, who was also a blind person, did most of the mathematical work. Luise Braille who was a blind from his early childhood developed a revolutionary system of reading and writing for the blind. Stephen Hawking who is severely physically handicapped is regarded as one of the most leading physicist of the world. Beethoven a famous musician was blind, deaf and dumb person; Hellen Keller who was blind, deaf and mute from early childhood became a graduate and wrote number of books. So the persons with disabilities are not dis-abled but specially-abled.

Being a second most populous country, India has 26 million disabled, that is 2.21 per cent of its total of a billion and a quarter population (Census, Ministry of Home Affairs, 2011). Among 26 million disabled Indian population, nearly 12 million (45%) are illiterate. Among 14 million (55%) literate disabled population, 13 per cent of them have secondary education and only 5 per cent are graduate and above (Census, Ministry of Home Affairs, 2011). The Government of India has undertaken several initiatives since Independence in 1947 for the education of children with disabilities and efforts have been made towards inclusion of children with disabilities into general education after ratified United Nations Convention on Rights of Persons with Disabilities (UNCRPD) in 2007. India has made considerable progress in terms of putting in place a robust legal framework and a range of programmes and schemes that have improved enrolment rates of children with disabilities in schools (UNESCO, 2019). But when it comes to their higher education, it seems no improvement or almost zero improvement even after decades of implementation of Persons with Disabilities (PwD) Act, 1995 (NCPEDP, 2015 cited in *Hindustan Times*, December 15, 2017). There is only a little over 0.5 per cent students with disabilities are enrolled in the higher education institutions of India (NCPEDP, 2015 cited in *Hindustan Times*, December 15, 2017). Thus, this chapter is an attempt to study the status and profile of students with disabilities in the higher education institutions in Gujarat.

The origin of the inclusive education in India can be traced back to 1966 when first time the Education Commission suggested integration of children with disability into mainstream education. As an experiment of integrated education, the Central Government implemented the scheme of Integrated Education of Disabled Children (IEDC) in selected blocks of the country in 1974. The National Policy for Children (1974) was designed to provide guidelines to the Ministries of the Central Government, State Governments and other agencies for an integrated approach to child development. The success of IEDC scheme led priority consideration of integrated education in Sixth Five Year Plan (1980-1985).

In 1986, the National Policy on Education (NPE) has laid special emphasis on the removal of disparities and to equalize educational opportunities at all levels by attending to the disability specific learning needs of children with disabilities who have been denied equality so far (Ministry of Human Resource Development, 1986). The main objective of NPE was to integrate the physically and mentally handicapped with the general community as equal partners, and to prepare for normal growth and to enable them to face life with courage and confidence. The adoption of Programme of Action (PoA) in 1992 paved a solid ground for this initiative. The successful implementation of Project Integrated Education for Disabled (PIED) resulted in both regular school teachers and students becoming more receptive towards students with disabilities (Azad, 1996).

The implementation of District Primary Education Programme (DPEP) in 1994-95 laid special emphasis on the integration of children with mild and moderate disabilities in the line with world trends. It was one of the largest programmes in terms of funding with the budget of 740 million INR in 149 districts across 14 states (NCERT, 2011). The Persons with Disabilities (Equal Opportunities, Protection of Rights and Full Participation) Act, 1995 required that all States and Union Territories must ensure that children with disabilities have access to the same educational opportunities and basic human rights as their peers without disabilities. The Act further emphasized that, whenever possible, students with disabilities should be educated in regular school settings. The Government of India set up the Ramamurthy Committee (1992) to comment upon NPE/PoA stipulations and made recommendations for early identification of children with disabilities, formulation of stimulation programmes, integrated education of the children with disabilities and bringing about mutual reinforcement of the pedagogies of special and general education.

Since the passage of PWD Act, 1995, a number of other significant initiatives have taken place as well. Those include Sarva Siksha Abhiyan (Education for All) movement launched in 2001 that included a policy of 'zero reject'. It suggested that no child that has special needs could be neglected or denied enrolment on the basis of a disability. These legal mandates have helped to shape the comprehensive National Action Plan for Inclusion in Education of the Children and Persons with Disabilities (IECPD) [Ministry of Human Resource Development (MHRD), 2005]. The main objectives of this plan were to ensure that: (a) no child is denied admission in mainstream education, (b) no child would be turned back on the grounds of disability, and (c) mainstream and specialist training institutions serving persons with disabilities, in the government or in the non-government sector, facilitate the growth of a cadre of teachers trained to work within the principles of inclusion. The National Policy for Persons with Disabilities (2006) recognized that persons with disabilities are valuable human resource for the country and seeks to create an environment that provide them equal opportunities, protection of their rights and full participation in the society.

The landmark passing of Right to Education (RTE) Act, 2009 marks a historic moment for the children of India as it gives guarantee to their right to quality elementary education by the state. RTE provides a right platform to reach the unreached, with specific provisions for disadvantaged groups including children with disability.

University Grants Commission (UGC), a statutory body of Government of India, is supporting universities and colleges in the country to involve in special education activities to empower persons with disabilities. The UGC had started the scheme of assistance to universities/colleges for Higher Education for Persons with Special Needs (HEPSN) since the Ninth Five Year Plan which is basically meant for creating an environment at the higher education institutions to enrich higher education learning experiences of persons with disabilities. Creating awareness about the capabilities of persons with disabilities, construction aimed at improving accessibility, purchase of equipment to enrich learning etc., are the broad categories of assistance under this scheme. The working group report of the development of the Eleventh Five Year Plan (2007-12) recommended inclusion of children with disabilities, disabled friendly schools, policy of inclusive system of education, training to teachers in managing the children with disabilities and formation of disability cell in all higher education institutions (Planning Commission, 2011).

Higher education has its own importance in terms of employability, political power and national development. Diversity in terms of caste, creed and physical is seen in the campus of higher education institutions they need to be ready to cater the needs of such diverse students. Being an important contributory factor for ensuring social justice there is need to provide vertical mobility to deprived sections of society by making higher education accessible to them which in turn will improve the quality of their life (Azad, 2008: 19). Warnock Committee Report (1978) emphasizes the importance of reassessing needs of students with disabilities well before they enter into the world of higher education.

People with disability have a right to get higher education and not making adequate provisions to facilitate their proper education would amount to "discrimination" (The Supreme Court of India as cited in *Hindustan Times*, December 15, 2017). It is not only essential to give necessary education to the persons suffering from the disability but also imperative to see that such education is imparted to them in a fruitful manner so that they would be able to lead an independent, economically self-sufficient and fully participatory life. Lack of inclusive measures in the higher education level limits opportunity of professional growth and suitable employment for these persons with disabilities (TISS, 2018). It directed the government institutions of higher education and other such institutions, which were receiving aid from the government, to comply with the provisions of the Rights of Persons with Disabilities (RPwD) Act, 2016 (*Hindustan Times*, December 15, 2017). The RPwD Act, 2016 (formerly PwD Act, 1995) indicates that persons with disabilities should have access to education at all levels and efforts have been made to improve the status of higher education of disabled. At present, Government of India has undertaken several initiatives for the higher education of persons with disabilities. Some of such initiatives are establishment of equal opportunity cell, coaching schemes for National Eligible Test (NET)/State Eligible Test (SET), Higher Education of Persons with Special Needs (HEPSN), Teacher Preparation for Special Education (TEPSE), financial assistance to visually impaired teachers, National Fellowship for students with disabilities, National Mission on Education through Information and Communication Technology (ICT), Central Polytechnic Scheme for Persons with Disabilities, National Handicapped Finance and Development Corporation (NHFDC) scholarship etc. Despite of these efforts, the enrolment of the students with disabilities in Higher Education Institutions is still very low.

Recognizing RPWD Act, 2016 and its provisions for inclusive education, the National Policy on Education, 2020 asserts that children with disabilities will have opportunities for equal participation across the educational system. The NPE 2020 incorporates several recommendations including non-discrimination, accessible infrastructure, reasonable accommodations, individualized supports, use of braille and sign language in teaching and monitoring among others (MHRD, 2020).

The World Bank Report (2009) suggests that primary enrolment of children with disabilities has considerably improved during 2000s. The enrolment of children with disabilities in regular schools increased sharply from 5,66,921 in 2002-03 to 2.35 million in 2012-13 (NUEPA, 2014). Presently, there are 21,08,918 children with disabilities receiving school education (from classes I to XII) under Samagra Siksha in India (MHRD, 2019). However, it is also evident that their learning outcome remained substantially worse than the rest (Soni, 2013). Thus, despite the Indian Government's efforts to increase the enrolment of children with disabilities, progress has been very slow (Singal, 2016). Even the number of enrolled children with disabilities drops significantly with each successive level of schooling in India (UNESCO, 2019). This could be gauzed from the fact that only 85,877 students with disabilities enrolled in Higher Education Institutions in India against estimated total enrolment of 37.4 million (AISHE, 2019). This is only 0.23 per cent of the total enrolment 3,73,99,388 students in Higher Education Institutions of India. This reveals that the actual figure 85,877 is nowhere close to the expected figure 18,69,969 based on the 5 per cent reservation availed to them. This brings stark reality that despite the twenty years of PwD Act (1995), only 0.23 per cent implementation against the mandated 3 per cent (now 5% under RPWD Act, 2016) raises a question that why the Indian higher education system is not accessible to students with disabilities? To find the answer of this question, the authors have made an attempt to study the enrolment and profile of the students with disabilities in the universities of Gujarat.

Design

The current study involves two-part survey design and reports data obtained from a cross-sectional survey. This study investigates enrolment of students with disabilities in the universities of Gujarat and the demographic profile of students with disabilities enrolled in various courses in the universities. Recruitment for the current study was in nine general universities of Gujarat offering all types of courses in a single campus. The universities are not identified so as to maintain the anonymity of the respondents.

Participants

All the 188 students with disabilities enrolled in all courses and at all levels (Diploma, Graduate, and Post-graduate) of higher education in the nine general universities of Gujarat were included in the study. All the 188 students with disabilities were approached but 45 students with disabilities were denied to participate in survey so that the final sample size was restricted to 143 students with disabilities. The response rate was 76 per cent. Data were collected from 143 students with disabilities across nine general universities *via* survey questionnaire, primarily in paper and pencil format. Informed written consent was obtained from the university authorities and students with disabilities to gather the data from the universities as well as enrolled students with disabilities.

Data Collection Instrumentation

A two-part survey instrument was employed. Part one gathered information about the enrolment of students with disabilities in the universities. Part two employed self-made questionnaire.

Part One: Enrolment Information

Part 1 of the instrument was designed to obtain the information relating to course-wise enrolment of students with disabilities based on the 3 per cent reservation quota availed for them. The data related to the type and category of disability, course and level of education in which the students with disabilities enrolled also collected.

Part Two: Profile of Students with Disabilities

Self-made questionnaire was used to obtain the profile of students with disabilities in terms to their personal information, nature of disability, academic profile and family background. The students with disabilities were asked to provide information about gender, age, habitat, married status, type of disability, category of disability, onset of disability, engagement with disability organization, awareness of PwD Act, 1995, achievement in last year examination, scholarship received, staying place during study, vocational training received, their wish for further continuation of study, parents' education, family economic status, number of siblings and other persons with disability in the family.

Data Analysis

Descriptive statistics, frequency and percentage (%) were used to summarize the profile of students with disabilities.

Result and Discussion

Enrolment of Students with Disabilities

A total of 188 students were found with disabilities, that is only 0.4 per cent of the total enrolment of 48,521 students in the nine general universities. Counting seats based on 3 per cent reservation quota availed to students with disabilities; the expected figure measures 1,455 students with disabilitiesis nowhere close to the actual enrolment 188. The difference between actual and expected enrolment of students with disabilities was found to be 99.06 per cent. Of the total dataset, the male to female ratio was 71:29 (male=134, female=54), with the majority (*N*=167, 89%) students with orthopaedic impairments. Very less number of students were

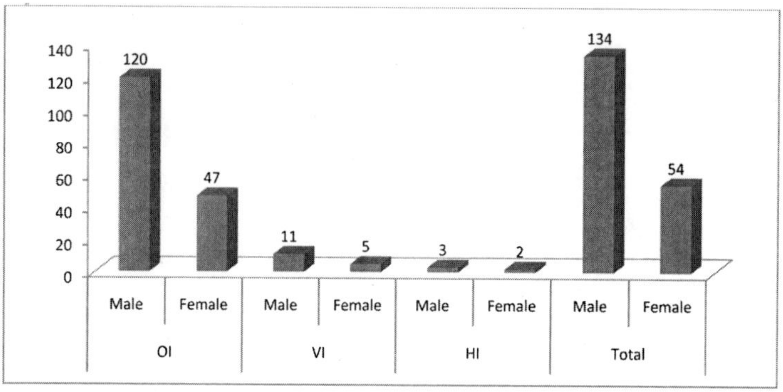

Fig. 25.1. Enrolment of students with disabilities in universities of Gujarat

found with visual impairment (*N*=16, 9%) and hearing impairment (*N*=5, 2%). No student reported with intellectual disability.

Personal Profile

The students with disabilities involved in this survey represented nine general universities of Gujarat, India. As shown in Table 25.1, the majority of the students with disabilities were male (*N*=102, 71%) and in the 21 to 25 year age bracket (*N*=98, 68%). Almost two-thirds of them were from urban areas (*N*=94, 66%) and most of them were unmarried (*N*=137, 94%).

Table 25.1. Personal profile of students with disabilities

Variables	N	%
Gender		
Male	102	71
Female	41	29
Age group		
Less than 20 years	23	16
20 to 25 years	98	68
25 to 29 years	18	12
30 years and above	6	4
Habitat		
Urban	94	66
Rural	49	34
Marital status		
Married	6	4
Unmarried	137	94

Disability Profile

As shown in Table 25.2, the participating students with disabilities varied in type of disabilities, with most of them having orthoapedic impairment (*N*=126, 88%), and a majority falls in mild category of disability (*N*=95, 66%). In terms of onset of disability, the students with disabilities were fairly distributed by birth (*N*=54, 38%) and infancy (*N*=62, 43%). Only 15 per cent of them were engaged with disability organizations working for the welfare for disabled and 31 per cent of them were not aware about the PwD Act,1995 considered as landmark legislative Act for equal opportunities, full participation and protection of rights of persons with disabilities.

Table 25.2: Disability profile of students with disabilities

Variables	**N**	**%**
Type of disability		
Orthopaedic	126	88
Visual	12	8
Hearing	5	4
Category of disability		
Mild (40-60%)	95	66
Moderate (60-80%)	34	24
Severe (more than 80%)	14	10
Onset of disability		
By birth	54	38
By infancy	62	43
By childhood	27	19
Engagement with disability organization		
Yes	22	15
No	121	85
Aware about Persons with Disabilities Act, 1995		
Yes	99	69
No	44	31

Academic Profile

About their academic profile, a majority of students with disabilities were studying in post-graduate degree courses (*N*=91, 64%) from Arts discipline (*N*=52, 37%) and other disciplines such as Engineering, Pharmacy, Fine Arts, Performing Arts (*N*=66, 48%).

A significant numbers of them had either second class (*N*=62, 43%) or first class (*N*=63, 44%) in the last attempted examination. More than 40 per cent of them were receiving some kind of scholarship for their higher education (*N*=60, 42%). Almost half of them were staying either in university hostel (*N*=45, 31%) or paying guest/private hostel (*N*=24, 17%). Less than 20 per cent of the students with disabilities had received some kind of vocational training (*N*=22, 15%) and almost 60 per cent of them wished to continue further their study (*N*=84, 59%).

Table 25.3: Academic profile of students with disabilities

Variable	N	%
Level of education		
Diploma	21	15
Graduation	22	15
Post-graduation	91	64
M.Phil./Ph.D.	9	6
Discipline of study		
Arts	52	37
Commerce	13	9
Science	12	8
Others	66	46
Achievement in last year examination		
Pass class (less than 45% of marks)	18	13
Second class (45 to 60% of marks)	62	43
First class and above (more than 60% of marks)	63	44
Scholarship		
Yes	60	42
No	83	58
Staying place during study		
Own home	74	52
University hostel	45	31
Paying guest/private hostel	24	17

(*Contd.*)

Vocational training		
Yes	22	15
No	121	85
Wish for further study		
Yes	84	59
No	59	41

From the data presented in Table 22.4, related to their parents' education, it was observed that more number of the fathers (*N*=46, 32%) of students with disabilities were illiterate than their mothers (*N*=14, 10%). Even the level of education was found more among their mothers with education more than high schooling (*N*=47, 33%) in comparison to their fathers (*N*=30, 21%). About the family economic condition, majority of them (*N*=102, 71%) were from middle class with more than 2 siblings in family (*N*=98, 68%). A very small percentage of respondent students with disabilities (3%) indicated having other person with disability in their family.

Table 25.4: Family background of students with disabilities

Variables	N	%
Father's education		
Illiterate	46	32
Up to primary schooling	36	25
Up to secondary schooling	31	22
More than high schooling	30	21
Mother's education		
Illiterate	14	10
Up to primary schooling	42	30
Up to secondary schooling	39	27
More than high schooling	47	33
Family economic status		
Rich	4	3
Variables	**N**	**%**
Middle class	102	71

(*Contd.*)

Poor	37	26
Number of siblings		
0	7	5
1	38	27
2 and more than that	98	68
Other persons with disability in family		
Yes	5	3
No	138	97

The low enrolment of students with disabilities made it clear that the universities were not following the PwD Act (1995) strictly. This bring stark reality that despite of the twenty years of Persons with Disabilities Act (1995), only 0.4 per cent implementation against the mandated 3 per cent (now 5% under RTPwD Act, 2016) raises question relating to inaccessible higher education system for students with disabilities. The NCPEDP (2015) survey also supports this finding by revealing only 0.56 per cent seats go to disabled candidates though there is reservation to the extent of 3 per cent in public institutions. This affects to the higher education of students with disabilities despite of the Government's effort for strict implementation of PwD Act (1995) and recommendation of National Policy of Persons with Disabilities (2006) that persons with disabilities will be provided access to the universities to pursue higher and professional courses. Lack of monitoring about the provisions granted under the Act in Higher Education Institutions may also hamper actual implementation. Certain steps need to be taken for improving the scenario students with disabilities in higher education. Now, Government has made strict implementation of RPwD Act (2016) in all the higher education institution but maintaining data about how many of students with disabilities applying, getting admitted and passing out need of an hour. Collaboration between higher education institutions and special as well as inclusive schools can be of great benefit in successful transition of school pass out students with disabilities into higher education.

Results also suggesting that more than 30 per cent of the students with disabilities were unaware about the PwD Act, 1995 and this could have resulted into less numbers of applicants than expected as the students with disabilities who are unaware about the policies and provisions availed for them might not be applying in higher education. The findings of the research studies on school education of children with disabilities also support this finding by revealing that majority of the teachers were unable to support inclusion, not received any training nor had any experience teaching students with disabilities (Shah, Das, Desai & Tiwari, 2013 and Das, Gichuru & Singh, 2013). Awareness drives from Government Education Departments and Higher Education Institutions about the policies and provisions, course-wise number of seats available for the students with disabilities can be of great help in making them aware about their opportunities for higher education. Developing transition goals from school to college/university and a course of study prior to entering into higher education will provide opportunities for persons with disabilities to take the necessary course work as per their interest, aspiration, capabilities and abilities. For instance, students with deafness can be diverted to Commerce, Fine Arts and Performing Arts fields right from the high schooling so that they can build their career in respective fields.

Looking to their career prospect, they are less likely to find job even after successful completion of higher education (AAPD, 2013). Looking at big companies like CII, NASSCOM, FICCI and its strength of member companies, NASSCOM alone must have more than 10,000 companies as its members but not inclusive, not even 1 per cent of the corporate India is inclusive (Abidi, 2018). Lack of employment opportunities might result into disinterest in higher education.

One of the significant findings emerged that out of the three major categories of disability, most of the enrolled students with disabilities were found with orthopaedic impairment (89%) while the representation from the visual (9%) and hearing disability (2%) were very low and not even a single student found with intellectual disability. Generally, the students with orthopaedic impairment do not have much academic related problems except architectural related problems. This brings stark reality that the Indian higher education system is still not inclusive in its true sense for the persons with disabilities other than those with orthopaedic impairment.

The Government of India's efforts for increasing girl child education did not seem any impact on girls with disabilities as only 28 per cent girls with disabilities were found in all the nine universities of Gujarat. Due to mobility problems, students with orthopaedic impairment have to stay either in hostel or as paying guest that will increase the burden of lodging and boarding costs along with their study cost for their higher education. Nearly half of the students with disabilities were residing either in university hostel, private hostel or as paying guest but the hostel facility was not free of cost while Mutiah (1989) reports that the facilities of free boarding and lodging is enjoyed mostly by orthopaedic handicapped students and parents of students with disabilities reported that that learning can be increased and their wards with disabilities will get more exposure by placing them in the hostel. Cost free accommodation in hostels throughout their study could be helpful in improving their academic as well as social skills and can be helpful in minimizing their mobility related problems (Sharma, 2004). Also, the objective to provide some kind of vocational training to the persons with disabilities could not be achieved as only 15 per cent of them had some kind of vocational training. To train them in some kind of vocations can benefit in earning while learning which in turn will help them in minimizing their financial related problems as the study reports half of them had not received any kind of scholarship for their study. Most of the students with disabilities were worried about their future and wanted job security after completion of the study. The vocational training should be imparted in accordance with their interests and aspirations. Majority of them had received less than Rs. 3,000 scholarship amount per year. The Government of India through Department of Disability Affairs is providing scholarship to the students with disabilities of Rs. 700-750 per month for day scholar and Rs. 1,100-1,600 per month to hoteliers for graduation courses (Department of Disability Affairs, 2018). This is a good effort, but the big question emerges here that how one can maintain the entire study cost at higher education level only from such a low amount of scholarship? Less amount of scholarship can lead either to drop-out or low achievement as one cannot maintain the entire study cost in such a low amount of scholarship. Government should provide scholarships with proper amount to all the needy students with disabilities who are pursuing higher education in terms to bring more number of students with disabilities into higher education. The scholarships will also be of great help to them in completing their education without any financial difficulties and their drop-outs can also be minimized as the study reports that nearly 60 per cent of them wanted to continue their higher education up to the post-graduate and doctoral level while one of the major reasons for discontinue of higher education was poor economic condition of their family. Also, strict implementation of the 3 per cent (now 4%) reservation in employment sector will secure their employment. Since the implementation of PwD Act in 1995, it is still question of investigation that how many of the students with disabilities have received jobs in the organizations of government and private sectors on the reservation quota availed for their employment. The secure employment on their reservation quota in turn will lead to growth in their higher education. Awareness regarding the disability policies and Acts should be spread among the higher education institutions, parents and students with disabilities through print or electronic media as nearly 40 per cent of them were not aware even about 3 per cent reservation rule availed to them. Formation of Disability Unit in every university will be of great help in dealing the matters related to disabilities. Though the disability related provisions and policies remaining in the documents but nothing are done in real for the welfare of students with disabilities and thus the cell remains as equality minus disability cell. The research on the activities and help provided by the equality cells to the students with disabilities in the higher education institutions can reveal a true picture regarding the equal opportunities to the students with disabilities in Higher Education Institutions. Formation of Disability Unit in every higher education institution can be of great help to the students with disabilities for their higher education, awareness regarding provisions and schemes, and for guidance and counselling.

The reasons for their less enrolment in universities could also be low family income, illiteracy and less education of their parents as Miceli (2008) also found that disability category, family income and parental level of education significantly impacted on the enrolment of the students with disabilities in colleges.

Implications for Higher Education Teachers

- The teacher at the outset should accept students with disabilities just like other students and should not be hesitate to include them in their classroom.
- The teacher should promote inclusion of students with disabilities and aware about the reservations, policies, provision, legislations and schemes availed for the students with disabilities in terms to make the inclusion of students with disabilities successful in higher education.
- The teacher should encourage and motivate to students with disabilities to pursue higher studies.
- It is the responsibility of a teacher to provide education to all students irrespective of their diversity and thus he/she should be ready to teaching students with disabilities assuming that resources and supporting services may not be available all the time.
- The teacher should aware and collaborate with voluntary organizations (both government and non-government) working for the welfare and rehabilitation of persons with disabilities in terms to receive supporting services for needy students with disabilities.
- The teacher should have a collaborative skill and ready to work in coordination with resource/special teachers

rather than an isolated professional. Moreover, the teacher should coordinate with the parents, head of the institutions, community and peers for improving the learning achievement of students with disabilities.

- The classroom teacher should be able to adjust and adapt curriculum suited to the learning needs of students with disabilities in their class.
- He/she should develop positive attitudes, values and dispositions that creates conducive environment to improve the quality of teaching and learning.
- The teacher should take interest in continuous professional development by attending the training programmes on inclusive education for making the inclusive programme successful.

Conclusion

Looking to the profiles of students with disabilities in higher education and their less enrolment reveals that most of the policies, recommendations regarding the education of students with disabilities have not properly implemented and lots have to be done to improve the status of higher education of students with disabilities. Though the Government of India made attempt to improve the status of higher education of students with disabilities by implementing compulsory the Right to Persons with Disabilities Act (2016) in all the higher education institutions of India but there needs continuous monitoring of extent of implementation of this Act. If they will be encouraged to take higher education and prepare them for a career then in turn they will become productive and successful citizens with leading independent, economically self-sufficient and fully participatory life.

REFERENCES

AAPD (2013, October 3). *AAPD Press Releases.* Retrieved July 8, 2015, from http://www.aapd.com/resources/press-room/press-releases/redefine-disability.htm

Azad, Y.A. (1996). *Integration of Disabled in Common Schools: A Survey-study of IEDC in the Country*. New Delhi: NCERT.

Department of Disability Affairs (2018). *Scholarships for Students with Disabilities*. New Delhi: Ministry of Social Justice and Empowerment. Retrieved on September 20, 2018 from www.disabilityaffairs.gov.in/upload/uploadfiles/files/scholarships2.pdf

Planning Commission (2011). *Draft Report of Working Group on Higher Education: 11th Five Year Plan (2007-2012).* New Delhi: Government of India. Retrieved on May 12, 2012 from http://planningcommission.nic.in/plans/planrel/11thf.htm

Hindustan Times (December 15, 2017). *Disabled people have right to get higher education: Supreme Court.* Available at https://www.hindustantimes.com/india-news/disabled-people-have-right-to-get-higher-education-supreme-court/story-x6kJcs87Zxx2cR6T0rSwBN.html

Miceli, M.A. (2008). "The Associations among Youth Characteristics, Secondary School Experiences, and Enrollment in Two-and Four-year Colleges among Youth with Disabilities" (Doctoral dissertation, University of Maryland, 2008). *Dissertation Abstracts International, 70* (1), 141A.

Ministry of Home Affairs (2011). *Census (2011).* Retrieved from office of the Registrar General & Census Commissioner, Government of India website:http://censusindia.gov.in/

Ministry of Human Resource & Development (2009). *Right to Education Act.* Retrieved from Department of School Education & Literacy, Government of India website: http://mhrd.gov.in/rte

Ministry of Human Resource Development (2005). *Action Plan for Inclusive Education of Children and Youth with Disabilities.* Retrieved from Department of School Education & Literacy, Government of India, website: http://www. education .nic.in/INCLUSIVE.asp

Ministry of Human Resource Development (1966). *Report of Education Commission (1964-66).* New Delhi: GoI.

Ministry of Human Resource Development (1986). *National Policy on Education.* New Delhi: GoI.

Ministry of Human Resource Development (1992). *Programme of Action.* New Delhi: GoI.

Ministry of Human Resource Development (1992). *Report of CABE Committee on Review of National Policy on Education.* New Delhi: GoI.

Ministry of Human Resource Development (1992). *Report of the Ramamurthy Committee (1992).* New Delhi: GoI.

Ministry of Law and Justice (2016). *Right to Persons with Disabilities Act.* Retrieved from Department of Disability Affairs, Government of India website: http://www.disabilityaffairs.gov.in/upload/uploadfiles/files/RPWD%20ACT%202016.pdf

Ministry of Social Justice and Empowerment (1995). *Persons with Disabilities (Equal Opportunities, Protection of Rights & Full Participation) Avt (1995).* Retrieved from Government of India website: http://socialjustice.nic.in/pwdact1995.php

Ministry of Social Justice and Empowerment (2006). *National Policy for Persons with Disabilities.* New Delhi: Government of India. Retrieved on September 19, 2018 from http://www.disabilityaffairs.gov.in/upload/uploadfiles/files/NationalPolicyForPersonswithDisabilities(1).pdf

Ministry of Statistics and Programme Implementation (2016). *Disabled Persons in India: A Statistical Profile.* New Delhi: Government of India. Retrieved on September 19, 2018 from www.mospi.nic.in

Mutiah, P.N. (1989). "Vocational Education for the Disabled Students in Tamil Nadu: A Survey. An Independent Study, Madurai Kamraj University". In A.K. Sharma (Ed. 1997) *Fifth Survey of Research in Education (1988-92).* New Delhi: NCERT.

NUIPA (National Institute of Educational Planning and Administration formerly NUEPA) (2014). *Elementary education in India. Where do we stand? State Report Cards 2012-2013.* New Delhi: NIEPA.

Shah, R., Das, A., Desai, I. & Tiwari, A. (2013). "Teachers' concerns about inclusive education in Ahmedabad, India". *Journal of Research in Special Educational Needs, 16*(1), 34-45.

Sharma, M. (2004). *Development and Try out of an Intervention Programme for Parents of Children with Mental Retardation.* Ph.D. (Education). Vadodara: CASE, The M.S. University of Baroda.

Singal, N. (2016). "Education of children with disabilities in India and Pakistan: Critical analysis of developments in the last 15 years". *Prospects 46*, 171-83 (2016). https://doi.org/10.1007/s11125-016-9383-4

Soni, R.B.L. (2013). *Status of Implementation of RTE Act-2009 in Context of Disadvantaged Children at Elementary Stage.* New Delhi: NCERT.

TISS (2015). *A report on inclusion and accessibility of students with disabilities in higher education.* Mumbai: TISS.

U-DISE Flash Statistics (2016-17). *School Education in India.* New Delhi: NIEPA.

UNESCO (2019). *State of the education report for India 2019: Children with Disabilities.* UNESCO: New Delhi. Available at https://unesdoc.unesco.org/ark:/48223/pf0000368780

UNICEF (2013). *The state of the world's children 2013: Children with disabilities*. New York: UNICEF.

Warnock, M. (1978). *Special Educational Needs: Report of the Committee of Enquiry into the Education of Handicapped Children and Young People*, London: HMSO.

WHO & the World Bank (2011). *World report on disability*. Geneva: WHO.

World Bank (2009). People with disabilities in India: From commitments to outcomes. New Delhi: Human Development Unit, South Asia Region. http://www-wds.worldbank.org/external/default/WDSContentServer/WDSP/IB/2009/09/02/000334955_20090902041543/Rendered/PDF/502090WP0Peopl1Box0342042B01PUBLIC1.pdf

SECTION-V
PROFESSIONAL DEVELOPMENT OF TEACHERS

26

Teacher Education on Professional Ethics of Teachers

P.K. Sahoo

The modern society has focused on the job of teaching to be carried out professionally by a person, called teacher. Two concepts are identified with the concept of teaching. One is a 'person' who does teaching. The other one is the 'teaching job' to be done professionally. Invariably educated parents teach their children in the context of life skills. They also assist their wards in during curricular tasks assigned by the school. A community member may also teach the interested youth on craftsmanship, visual arts, performing art etc. Such persons involved in teaching are not called teachers, even though, they play a major role in education of their wards or community youth on development of desirable knowledge, skills and morals. Second, these persons may do such job because of their passion. Some of the persons engaged in such tasks may charge some benefit in exchange of their teaching. Thirdly, no body may verify the formal qualification of such persons engaged in teaching the community youth. In other words, these persons may not possess prescribed degree on required knowledge and skills to perform such job. The teaching may not take place in any formal institution following the prescribed norms and standards as set by the public governance system. Such people may do teaching job, of course, not qualify to be called as teachers in professional sense. As we understand teachers engaged in formal schools to carry out their jobs as per curricular standards and expectations are different from those who may do the job informally because of their passion or because of the cultural traditions. The industrial society which created the movement of centralised framework of operation of structured school system insisted on the formal educational requirement for teachers' remunerative job replaced by a full time salaried job, the service rules and a set of code of conducts as public employee. The individualised perspective of teacher has been submerged in the ocean of universal code of conduct of teaching job as per expectation of the school system. The requirement of teachers with structured knowledge and formal educational qualifications, of course, with possession of teaching aptitude have been insisted for recruitment purpose. No more teaching is considered as a voluntary participation of a person or as a matter of earning on the basis of socio-cultural traditions. The school system insists on governance of teachers with public interest. Besides possession of structured knowledge in the disciplines concerned with school curriculum, it requires appropriate skills on the part of persons to be qualified for teaching jobs. Moreover, the teaching job is to be carried out as per code of conduct specified for teachers as employee of the organised service sector.

There have been debates over the role of the personality of teachers, besides their formal knowledge and skills to perform varieties of tasks in a school system. The teachers' role in shaping the personality of students appears to be subjective and idealistic in a tradition bound education system. The modern system highlighted the normative values or code of ethics of teachers as universal principles or common guiding factors. The universal norm expected a teacher follow common guidelines irrespective of heterogeneity in teachers' personal faiths, beliefs and values. Teachers' own personal values, beliefs, self-dominating attitudes etc. are of least concern in the formal school system. Instead of such personalised matters, the concept of specification in knowledge system, mastery of professional competencies and working with a common framework of operation of school system have been valued as professional requirement of Teaching Job. Of course, the debates, on teaching to be purely considered as a profession keep on drawing attention of the educationists and thinkers of the modern society. Many question are also raised about the equivalence of teaching professionalism in other jobs like engineering, physicians or legal practices?

Since, a profession is associated with a significant public service, it insists on expertise in the field of knowledge and skills concerning the job, a structured guideline or code of practice, well organised staff management and high degree of individual autonomy and judgement for effective practice (David). The extent to which "teaching meets such parameters will quality be identified as a profession."

Teacher Preparation with Ethical Background

The history of teacher education goes back to the eighteenth century when David Stow of Glasgow established the first normal school for teacher training in UK, i.e. in 1836. Normal school had its meaning in the context of moral education, i.e. setting moral standard or pattern among senior pupils to be trained for teaching job. During this century, similar pattern of teacher training with its roots in religious belief and rote learning spread over Europe and USA. The institutionalised teacher training was patronised by the normal colleges, of course, to a limited number of pupil teachers. During the nineteenth century, the European teacher training institutions produced "disciplined, utilitarian, reliable and of course, religiously based instructors adept in implementing the government imposed revised code of 1862 for the mass of the population with modest state support (Furlong, 2013). Since, teacher education had its root in the denominational 'normal' colleges, the background religious principles, the morals of teachers were governed by religious beliefs which might have promoted indoctrination process in moral development of teachers. The normal college tradition of teacher training was based on the idea of a moral community which was very much different from the ideologies of liberal education. Teachers' personality was, of course, very much valued in the framework of general education oriented teacher education along with the priorities on special training of teaching techniques and skills.

The university based teacher education was encouraged with three years personal education followed by one year professional preparation. The conflicts existed in teacher preparation offered by different management patterns over moral education priorities and priorities of adopting professional techniques and skills in teaching at school level in UK. However, professionalism was kept in the forefront of teacher preparation. Teachers' personality, teaching skills and teachers' commitment to delivery of teaching for betterment of learners were considered valuable during the twentieth century. There remained emphasis on personalised professional-learning. It gave emphasis on more direct control of teachers in classroom practice. The ethics in teaching was interpreted in the perspective of individual teacher proficiency in promoting learners' achievement in the curricular programmes.

Scope of Teacher Ethics

The impact of the post-industrial society noticed in the field of teaching professional and teacher education. Teachers' accountability towards students learning have been emphasised as the sole focus of teaching profession. This has also been expanded to other concerned areas of education system. Teachers' accountability have been spread over to schools, higher education institutions, parents, communities, employers, the government and the nation, the ecological environment and the global society. The broader role of teachers in these contexts have been linked with professional ethics.

As stated above, traditionally, the teachers' role has been confined to the curricular decisions and pedagogical functions. Individual expertise and skills have been linked with ethics concerning benefits of students and quality teaching-learning practices, of course, with least concern with the outer environment. Such notion of isolated autonomy based teacher functions have been changed in the age of global economy. The emphasis on individual role and responsibility in teaching has been expanded to collective roles and responsibility of teachers promoting participatory approach to decision making and interventions in teaching-learning system and institutional management. Teachers' collective responsibility in development of professional knowledge and skills in real school situation has been noticed in the professional development programmes as it is a case of other professions. Teachers' upgrading of knowledge and skills on their individual as well as collective responsibility have covered wide range of activities in dealings with students, own colleagues, administrative functionaries, parents, community members, employers, national and international level welfare agencies. The quality dimensions cover a broad range of ethics in teaching profession which are very much of different nature from traditional vision of professionalism in teaching that focused on teachers' individualized knowledge, autonomy and individual moral responsibility. Currently, the professional groups intervention are being valued with new responsibilities in the era of globalisation. More collectivised and accountable vision of teachers are being projected in professional expertise of teachers. Such visions are accompanied with ethical implications of new role and responsibilities of teachers. In other words, ethics in teaching profession has undergone transformation through collective interventions of experts, members of teaching community and educationists.

In the initial phase of debates over professionalism in teacher education, i.e. during the 1990s, the ethical issues were highlighted in prescriptive and centralised form. The common standards and procedures dominated the teacher education curriculum.

Accordingly, the centralised principles of guiding teacher functions were decided by the statutory bodies. The competency based teacher education curriculum also focused on implementation of prescribed norms and codes of ethics for teachers.

Due to advancement of global economy in education system, the scope of teacher education focus on all the members of teacher communities at different stages of education. Their professional development is brought into the fold of comprehensive and continuous teacher education programmes through alternative means. In continuation to preparatory teacher education programmes for elementary and secondary school education, professional development of all the groups of teachers have been highlighted in the mission of quality teacher education. The issue of professional ethics of teachers in changing perspective of school education (including higher education) have been discussed at length in the policy documents of education (Govt. of India, 2019). The welfare of target group students have been projected for ethical consideration of educational system. Participation of institutions' community members and local authorities have been encouraged to formulate standards of taking care of needs of various groups of students in local context. Hence, what is good and desirable for students are worked out through encouragement of participation of local functionaries of education? The responsibility and accountability matters are also linked with decentralised decision making. The school based decentralised teacher education has been initiated for welfare of in-service teachers as well as for would be teachers in integrated form. Accountability of teacher educators, mentor teachers and teachers have been focused in the context of professional development of teachers. Of course, linking them with international quality initiatives in school education has been on the priority of teacher policy at national level. The process based guidelines have been evolved through integration of experiences in teaching with research outputs in the field of education. Moreover, it is considered ethical to encourage teachers' participation in research with a view to generate practical knowledge base for making teaching-learning process need based, quality oriented and relevant to the ecology of school system.

The contemporary efforts to strengthen professionalism among teachers focuses on improvement of teacher quality. Teacher vision and commitment has been valued in collective form to carry out quality initiatives in school system. The decentralised leadership has been linked with participatory approach of decision making among teachers. In this context, the role of teachers' forums have been considered significant institutional level and national level. Provision of alternative opportunities for enhancement of educational qualifications for teachers on contemporary developments is considered essential criteria of quality initiative in teaching. The high quality engagement in teaching require ethical consideration in context specific grassroots situations. Teachers' professional knowledge and skills integrated with research and missionary spirit for sustainable development have been given high priority in the education policy. This is a challenge for teacher education to gear professional community of teachers towards new responsibilities in teaching, institution development practices, sustainable development in education and society. Major challenge in professional ethics of teachers is visualised in dealing with social inclusion in schooling and development of children of varied groups. Decentralisation with participatory involvement of teachers in decision making insists on fair access of continuing education of teachers. Accountability needs to be viewed in the form of democratic local participation encouraging continuous dialogues among practitioner teachers.

Nature of Ethics in Education and Teaching

Ethics has been defined as "a matter of principled sensitivity to the rights of others and that while truth is good, respect for human dignity is better" (Cavan,1977). Ethics means moral principles that govern a person's behaviour. Ethical behaviour of teachers focuses on their sensitivity towards betterment of students with due carrying out teaching-learning activities. The ethical standards of teaching profession are mostly of applied nature focusing on highlighted dimensions in teaching-learning and evaluation practices. Of course, there are conflicting positions in dealing with ethics as per absolutists and relativists. The absolute ethics insist on universal set principles should guide teachers in their work. Such principles guide teachers what ought and what ought not to be done during teaching. For instance, teachers' sacrifice of personal interest for benefit of students is a kind of absolute ethics of position in teaching profession.

The deontological approach highlights 'duty ethics of principles' in teaching profession like justice, honesty and respect to be adhered by the teachers (Cohen *et al.*, 2010). On the other hand, the relativists' stand on ethics is situation specific in nature. Teachers' ethical behaviour is determined by teaching-learning situation through judicious approach. There may not be absolute guidelines to dictate each and every behavioural component of teaching. Of course, the dichotomous stand may not hold good, since the professional organisations may arrive at consensus on certain broad framework of guidelines, within which there must be ample scope for situation specific appropriate behaviour for achieving the goals of teaching. In this sense, professional ethics in teaching covers a broad scope for evolving ethical discussions keeping in view the complex nature of teaching and endeavour for learners' development. A good code of ethics must be inclusive in nature and foster active participation of the stakeholders, viz. students, teachers, administrators, parents and employers of teachers in evolving ethics in education.

Common Framework of Professional Ethics among Teachers

As stated above, the professional concern has been projected in the form of code of ethics. The professional and associations have major onus on themselves in this regard. Their consensus of values among teachers and teacher educators play significant role in this direction. There have been efforts on the part of National Education Association, Singapore highlighted ethical standards for teachers in the context of responsibilities towards students, parents, community members, employment system and professional organisation. Major highlights of such codes are stated in the following.

I. *Teachers' Responsibilities Towards Students*

- Responsibilities towards students cover fairness in dealing with students irrespective of their social, cultural, psychological, racial and religious background.
- Treat students with care for individual needs.
- Encouraging students to pursue learning for all round development.
- Assist students to work democratically.
- Respect for individual rights (including rights to education of child of 6 to 14 years age group) and maintaining confidentially in information about individual students.
- No extra remuneration for teaching job except in accordance with government norms.

II. *Teachers' Responsibilities Towards Parents*

- Honouring the prime responsibility of parents towards education of their wards.
- Encouragement of students engagement in learning at home and sustain their confidence level.
- Informing parents about progress of their wards and gathering necessary information from their parents.

III. *Teachers' Interaction with Community*

- Teachers' interaction with community members to generate learning resources for school.
- Teachers' contribution to strengthen community health, environmental preservation, eco-friendly activities in the school and community.

IV. *Teachers' Ethics in the Context of Employment*

- Adhere to the norms and standards as prescribed by the

statutory bodies for employment and promotion purposes with fairness.

- Fulfil the requirement of competencies for specific positions without adopting unfair means for holding a position.
- Follow the service rules.
- Provide detailed information about professional activities with fairness.
- Being fair in required recommendation concerning the works of other teachers.
- Co-operating with the school in quality management.

V. *Teachers' Responsibilities Towards Professional Organisation*

- Taking membership of teachers' professional organisations and active participation in professional activities.
- Contribute significantly to activities of professional bodies in policy formulation, quality enhancement measures and transformation in educational policies and practices.
- Strengthen leadership in professional organisations' functions.
- Adopt flexibility in the process of quality improvement of education.
- Such responsibilities are of universal nature and are applicable to every teacher. However, they cannot be prescriptive while transforming them into action of teachers in conceptuality. This requires participatory approach in dealing with ethical issues concerning improvement in the teachers themselves, learners' development, development of institution, community progress and welfare of the profession as a whole.

Issues Concerning Development of Professional Ethics among Teachers

Two major areas of discussion have emerged concerning evolving professional ethics in teaching profession and educating teachers about ethical issues while dealing with teachers' multiple responsibilities. The first kind of debates have been left to philosophical approaches concerning applied ethics and professional ethics of teachers. Different approaches to teachers' professional ethics has been reviewed with elaboration by Pawel, K. on following points.

A. *Deontological Approaches: Ethics of Duty for Teachers*

This approach is linked with the code of ethics or code of conduct as evolved at control level. Written codes of conduct for teachers are stated for obligations of teachers universally. The criticism of such approach is focused on general spheres of teaching profession. The codes do not cover detailed moral sphere. What is good for students in specific context and what kind of action is appropriate in what context cannot be covered in detail by written codes of conduct, Moreover, the written codes may be communicated promoting authoritarianism in teaching profession. Hence, just restricting to norms, principles and contracts, ethical issues can be interpreted as formal and mechanical in nature. Deep involvement of a teacher in exploring ethics and its meaningfulness to teaching profession has restricted scope in the form of written guidelines to teachers. Teachers' own vision in dealing with ethical issues in education cannot be reflected appropriately in such normative approach.

B. *Consequentialist Approach: Output based Ethics*

The morality is considered in the context of outcome of expected behaviour among students. Teacher ethics is geared towards maximisation of benefits to the students. Teachers' actions leading to optimum learning outcome of larger percentage of students is considered valuable. Teacher effectiveness and school quality are judged by the criteria of learning outcome of students. Such approach pragmatism has been valued in the globalised society. The result oriented practices adopted by teachers are rewarded by the accreditation bodies. This approach has limitations with regard to lack of wholeness in measurement theories and its application in teaching-learning system. Moreover, the issue of inclusiveness in learners' development is not reflected in measurement of students' performances in different areas of proficiency.

The attitude of maximising results neglect other areas of students' development mostly of personal nature. Moreover in the age of market economy, competitiveness is valued among institutions to project externally assessed quality of institutions and attracting the clienteles to the institutions in terms of production of better results. In this approach, the focus of teachers, students and parents remain mainly on outcome of learners in examinations. Teachers' moral is boosted in the context of students' performances in board or university examinations and their placement in jobs. Such ethics is highly utilitarian in nature.

C. *Aetiological Approach: Ethics of Virtue*

This approach is highly personalised in nature. The *Guru* or teacher is considered as embodiment of all virtues. He can influence his disciplines through his personality to adopt virtuous conducts. The teacher can inspire, guide and emulate students to follow the paths of virtue. Consciously and unconsciously the students follow virtuous actions of the teachers. Mysticism is linked with such approach. Teachers' virtues in day to day professional life is observed by the students. The virtues like honesty, generosity, compassion austerity, love, righteousness, peace, patience, benevolence and sacrifice are reflected in everyday teaching practices. Such approach is very much personal and subjective in nature, not giving much scope for dialogues on the nature of virtues in teaching. Distinctions between virtue and vice are mostly dictated as per missionary guidelines

D. *Axiological Approach: Ethics of Value*

Value based life and value based profession are guiding principles for teaching activities as per such approach. Subjective analysis of values and its implications for objectively noticed behaviour of teachers are reflected in such approach. The eternal values of love for truth (*satyam*), love for right conduct (*shivam*) and love for beauty (*sundaram*) are considered cardinal principles of teachers' performance inside classroom and outside the classroom. Teachers motivate students to analyse values and engage them in different kinds of individualised and group based activities to unfold the eternal values existing inside themselves. Of course, different types of contextual values are developed among students through teachers' initiatives and encouragement. The social and constitutional values are also prioritised in teachers' ethics.

E. *Personalistic Approach: Ethics of the Person*

This approach is called personality approach. This approach is of inclusive nature, where code of ethics, virtues, values and learners' benefits are submerged in teacher behaviour. Various responsibilities to be carried out by teachers must be delivered through commitment of teachers. Treating human development oriented actions are not considered as the means, rather teachers' action to treat humanity must be considered as an end. It insists on development of personality giving major emphasis on humane action. Good means leads good results. Such approach insists on rigorous teacher practices based on in-depth analysis based on observation, and reflection with commitment to bring improvement in teachers' ownself. It takes care of different ethical considerations like character formation, value orientation, dedication to work for betterment of life, love for learning, love for efficient and effective action, and skilful application of technology to solve critical problems. Teachers' caring behaviour for personal growth of students, guiding students to adopt suitable means for learning experiences and promoting their autonomy and active involvement in learning are the examples of such ethics. It signifies their facilitators' role in teaching with full trust on students in this respect. Humanitarian approach in teacher behaviour is promoted through such personal ethics.

Teacher Education on Professional Ethics

In view of professional education of teachers' the questions are raised whether ethics can be taught to in-service teachers? Which content can be taught? How it can be taught? What are the approach methods and techniques to develop teacher ethics? etc. The teacher education curriculum covers specific credit based courses on personality development. However, mostly such issues are dealt in by hidden curriculum of teacher education.This is a general notion that the knowledgeable and skillful teachers may not be committed to teaching profession. Their decision making in curriculum design and unit plans may not incorporate ethical issues like: What is good for students? What is desirable? What is essential for students' personality development? What is eco-friendly knowledge? How students enjoy autonomy in learning process? How students' decision making is accommodated in curriculum design and unit plans? How students' learn comfortably without stress and burden? How students' alienation from classroom environment can be minimised or how students home environment can accommodate different kinds of expected curricular experiences? etc. There are also other questions related to ethics like: How students can be dealt with love and affection? How students' self-can be respected by teachers and *vice-versa*? How to develop humane environment in teaching and learning? How verbal and non-verbal languages and communication can generate confidence in learning, free expression of views with modesty, how to tolerate differences? How to solve problems through collective endeavour? How to enjoy learning? How to recognise the essence of collective living in human life? etc. There have been different programmes for value education and personality development of teachers as a component of pre-service and in-service education curriculum with limited formal approach. Strengthening professional ethics among teachers focus on special pedagogical concerns, as stated in the following.

Authoritarian Approach on Ethics

Teacher educators presenting their experiences on ethics and communicating to student teachers to follow code of ethics are centralised and authoritarian in nature. The missionary institutions very often interlink virtues and religious values with teachers' ethics. Teacher educators persuade and convince pupil teachers to accept code of ethics. It includes cognitive involvement of pupil teachers for getting clarifications and strong beliefs to honour the mission chiefs. In such approach open inquiry is least recognised in learning ethics. In general, the public funded formal education institutions do not have such model of teaching ethics. Of course, they adopt communication model based orientation to make pupil teachers aware of the code of ethics applicable to every teacher.

Dialogue Approach on Ethics

Ethics is not indoctrination among professionals. If indoctrinated, teachers to adhere to ethical principles in practices which does not take its root in real situations. Ethical values spreaded among teachers may not be practicable. Centralised ethics are not built on the basis of practitioner teachers' experiences in dealing with complex nature of teachers job. Hence, the practical ethics among professionals must address to the ethical standards of teachers community centralised manner. The methodology of evolving ethical debates must be of participatory nature. The moral guidelines may not be considered absolute in nature. The ethical standards must take into consideration prolonged dialogue among participant teachers.

It will be worthwhile to state that the professional obligations should not be restricted to the prescribed duties. A profession covers responsibilities which are to be carried out by the professionals judiciously. The concept of "beyond of duties" in teaching profession covers the ethical issues beyond individuality to sociality and then to transcendently (Guha, 2014). The judicious operation of genuine responsibilities must be fair in nature. Such fairness is nurtured through dialogues among teaching community members.

The dialogue among professionals is not restricted to the concept of exchange of opinions and analysing the ethical matters. Dialogue involves to individual opinion of others, listening to everybody's opinions and see what all that means (Bohn, 2004).

It means everybody to see the meaning together and arrive at the conclusion by overruling all the assumptions. Sharing of common meaning indicate participatory approach or togetherness in evolving ethical principles. Two concepts have been discussed by Bohn in the process of dialogue is "to partake of" and "to take part in". It involves every member of teaching community must be a part of the group to decide on ethics and every teacher must take part in such debate. The individual views would be absorbed into the group views. It will lead to emergence of a common mind. Unlike authoritarian approach, there is no place for convincing the followers or persuade them about a set of code of conducts decided in a centralised platform. Dialogue promotes the spirit of collectivism. The whole group of professionals constantly move towards coherence. The individual views are submerged into the collective. Collective views emerge through the process of dialogue. In the process of collective dialogue we go beyond opinions and arrive at new meaning of ethical principles. Such ethics are of creative nature.

Students Teachers Collective Inquiry and Self-reflection on Ethics

One such approach is classroom meeting model. The classroom meeting model contrived by Glasser (1956) highlights the mechanism where students and teachers join collectively in an open environment. The non-judgemental discussion takes place on personal problems, behavioural problems and academic issues for developing a caring social group, self-discipline and behavioural commitment. Even though classroom meeting model of teaching for social problems solving its implication for dealing with ethical behaviour of students teachers in school internship programme and teaching practices can be valued through this model in teacher preparation course.

(i) The teacher educators must develop conducive environment for voluntary participation of pupil teachers with warm, purely personal and concerned relationship among participants. They must be encouraged to share experiences without fear and inhibitions.

(ii) Each pupil teacher poses his own problem on ethical behaviour. The group poses several issues and constraints in dealing with critical situations ethically. They discuss probable consequences of continuing with problematic conditions of teaching ethically.

(iii) Each student-teacher makes his value judgement on carrying out their behaviour. They are asked to justify why they prefer certain behaviour.

(iv) The group identifies alternative courses of action. They decide which one should be preferred.

(v) The last phase is related to student teachers commitment to carry out identified ethical behaviour. Their committed involvement in classroom teaching practices and other kinds of internship activities can be observed by the mentors and teacher educators. Further discussions may take place as a follow up measure.

The role of teacher education, in such model, is of facilitation oriented nature. Teacher behaviour is governed by the principles of involvement, non-judgemental attitude and classroom group participation in decision making process. The skills of interpersonal relationship among teacher educators and pupil teachers as well as open group discussions are valued in such model. Such approach involves collective learning experiences of ethics among teachers.

There are other models of value development among pupil teachers like value analysis model, value development model, role playing model and social inquiry model of teaching. Group participation strategies leading to value clarification analysis of value conflicts and value based decision making are adopted to solve teachers' problems in dealing with students, managing school affairs and community welfare practices.

Professional Development of Working Teachers on Ethics

Ethical issues concerning day-to-day teaching-learning practices are resolved through experience and practical knowledge of teachers. The behavioural dimensions of ethics in individual teachers activities can be focused through action research studies. Action research can be classified under two categories, viz. practical action research and participatory action research. The practical action research focuses on studying local practices, involving individual or team based teaching-learning activities, teachers' self-development and implementing ethical behaviour in teaching and other related activities in a school. It can be used as a method for improvement in own ethical behaviour in teaching and other related activities in a school. It can also be used as a method for improvement in own ethical behaviour in the context of day-to-day teaching in real school situation. Teachers' commitment in improving teaching-learning practices by recognising the students' autonomy can be studied through such method. Its application is very much relevant to explore the impact of ethical behaviour of teachers on students' colleagues, parents and community members.

Action research project plays significant role in development of professional ethics on following assumptions:

- Teachers take own initiatives to bring improvement in their ownself;
- Teachers are committed to continue professional development and development of students.
- Teachers keep on reflecting on their own practices continuously.
- Teachers involve students and other teachers to reflect on his teaching practices.

The process is considered as dialectics action research spiral (Mills, 2011) to improve on their own practices by conducting study on themselves on continuous basis. The four components of action research design consists of development of action plan, identifying areas of focus and action of data, analysis and interpretation of data. The components are interrelated with each other. The teacher researcher may involve other colleagues and students to assist him in ethical oriented practices. Quantitative and qualitative data, multi-method approach for data analysis on teachers' activities and classroom dynamics, self-reflection and collective reflection on ethical practices can be encouraged through such projects.

Another kind of action research, viz. Participatory Action Research (PAR) is conducted to empower teachers and students on ethical issues in the context of local level schools. The emphasis is led on empowering cluster school teachers or subject teachers in the area of ethics in teaching and other related responsibilities of teachers. Different ethical issues are discussed and practitioner teachers participate collectively to resolve various issues. The project encourages participatory and collaborative actions on formulating action plans, action, observation and reflection on spirit form collective dialogues. Critical reflections on different components of the project are carried out by the teacher participants to encourage reform in collective activities of teachers ethical considerations like teachers autonomy, collective efforts to solve critical problems, participatory approach in resolving conflicts, fairness in decisions on the interest of learners and their development are encouraged among professional group members. The issues concerning total quality management of institution are dealt very well by the participant teachers through teacher research.

Conclusion

Education for professional ethics cannot be practical through indoctrination and communication model based instruction. Congenital environment must be created in teacher education institutions for development of ethics among teachers. Encouragement must be given to working teachers for continuous professional development activities on ethical issues concerning development of self, appropriate decision making and ethical approaches on students development, institutional practices and eco-friendly approach to teaching. Participatory approach must be promoted in teacher education programmes promoting open dialogue of the student teacher educators' school teachers students, parents and other stakeholders of school system. Constructive approaches in teacher development programmes must be grounded in school based practices. Professional bodies of teacher educators and teachers have to play significant role in this regard.

REFERENCES

Cavan, S. (1977). Review of J.D. Douglas's (1976). "Investigative social research Individual and Team Field Research", *American Journal of Sociology, 83*(3).

Cohen, L. *et al.* (2010). *Research Play Significant Role in this regard.* 9939hj Methods in Education, London: Routledge.

Furlong John (2013). *Education—An Anatomy of Discipline*: New York: Routledge.

Pawel, Kazmierezak, *Teacher's professional Ethics*, PDF, W. Marcin Kazmierczak, Maria Teresa Signes.

Bohn David (2007). *On Dialogue*, London: Routledge.

Guha, D. (2014). "Professional Ethics in a Education" in Sahoo, P.K. *et al.*, eds. *Quality Education in India*, Vol. 2, New Delhi: Concept.

A.C.T.D.E.T. (2006). *Teacher's Code of Professional Practice.* Retrieved from http//www det.act.gov.–data assets pdf-file 0007/17992 or–code profession ate practice pdf.

27

Teachers' Professional Development

Emerging Issues

Gyanendra Kumar Rout

Professional development of teachers refers to the generation of all those updated skills required to execute a task of teachers and academicians in academic teaching-learning situations. It means by which members of academic community at higher education level maintain, improve and broaden their knowledge and skills and, develop the personal qualities required in their professional lives. Professional development may also come in the form of pre-service or in-service professional development programmes. These programmes may be formal, or informal, group or individualized. Individuals may pursue professional development independently, or programmes may be offered by human resource departments. Five streams of reform, both singly and in combination, present complex challenges to teachers as individuals and as members of a wider professional community. Those challenges are: (1) Reforms in subject matter teaching (standards, curriculum, and pedagogy), (2) Reforms centred on problems of equity among a diverse student population, (3) Reforms in the nature, extent, and uses of student assessment,

(4) Reforms in the social organization of schooling, (5) Reforms in the professionalization of teaching Professional development must be constructed in ways that deepen the discussion, open up the debates, and enrich the array of possibilities for action. Ground for optimism resides in those "innovations on the margin" that embody principles consonant with the complexity of the reform task and with the capacities and commitments of a strong teacher workforce.

One of the parameters to judge the progress and status of any nation is to see its educational system. Today's students shall be tomorrow administrators. Therefore, a good educational system produces good students, and good students are produced by good teachers, obviously. Thus, the teachers are one of the prime agents of socio-economic change in a country. The National Policy on Education of India (1986/1992) has given very clear directives on this issue, "The Professional development of teachers reflect the socio-cultural ethos of a society; it is said that no people can rise above the level of its teachers. The Government and the community should endeavour to create conditions which will help motivate and inspire teachers on constructive and creative line."

Quality improvement is closely related to teacher professional development. In a recent UNESCO publication attempt has been made to collate various definitions of TPD which is in fact defined as "professional growth a teacher achieves as a result of gaining increased experience and examining his or her teaching systematically." The concept of professional development is broader than career development which is defined as the growth that occurs as the teacher moves through professional career cycle. Sometimes, staff development is considered synonymous to professional development though staff development is generally used in reference to in-service training.

Professional Development of Teachers

Professional development of teachers refers to the generation of all those updated skills required to execute a task of teachers and academicians in academic teaching-learning situations. It means by which members of academic community at higher education level maintain, improve and broaden their knowledge and skills and, develop the personal qualities required in their professional lives (Behera, 2009). Professional development may also come in the form of pre-service or in-service professional development programmes. These programmes may be formal, or informal, group or individualized. Individuals may pursue professional development independently, or programmes may be offered by human resource departments. Professional development opportunities can range from a single workshop to a semester-long academic course, to services offered by a medley of different professional development providers and varying widely with respect to the philosophy, content, and format of the learning experiences. But, at the heart of professional development is the individual's interest in lifelong learning and increasing their own skills and knowledge.

Professional Development and the Reform Agenda

Five streams of reform, both singly and in combination, present complex challenges to teachers as individuals and as members of a wider professional community. Those challenges are illustrated, though not exhausted, in the descriptions that follow. The test of teachers' professional development opportunities resides in their capacity to engage teachers in this kind of study, investigation, and experimentation required to understand and undertake the multiple challenges described here, and to grasp the relationships among them.

Reforms in Subject Matter of Teaching (Standards, Curriculum, and Pedagogy)

Reforms in subject matter standards, curriculum content, and pedagogy increasingly aspire towards more ambitious student outcomes. Among them one would count the shift to a whole language and literature-based approach to language arts, the new mathematics standards, proposals for integrated science curricula and the like. Among them, too, one would place conceptions of "authentic achievement" that requires a fundamental change in the nature of students' intellectual tasks and teacher-student relations (Baker, 2005; Newmann, 1990). These reforms constitute a departure from canonical views of curriculum and from textbook-centred or recitation-style teaching. They demand a greater facility among teachers for integrating subject content, and for organizing students' opportunities to learn. They represent, on the whole, a substantial departure from teachers' prior experience, established beliefs, and present practice. Indeed, they hold out an image of conditions of learning for children that their teachers have themselves rarely experienced (Barko, 2004).

In addition, individual teachers may be pressed to move on many fronts at once (Hargreaves, 1990; Little, 1990; Buczynski, S., and Hansen, C.B. (2010). Elementary teachers must absorb the changes in content and method associated with an entire spectrum of the elementary curriculum. Secondary teachers are asked to consider possibilities for interdisciplinary curricula at precisely the time they are asked to reconsider their approaches to subject matter teaching the latter reinforced by new state curriculum frameworks, standardized test protocols, subject-specific university admission requirements, textbook design, and the like. Meanwhile, reforms aimed at "critical thinking" sit in tension with the basic skills reforms that began in the 1960s and are still a prominent part of the urban school improvement landscape (Desimone, 2009).

Reforms Centred on Problems of Equity among a Diverse Student Population

Equity reforms respond to the persistent achievement disparities among students from differing family backgrounds, and are aimed at altering both the demonstrated achievement and school completion rates of the lowest achieving groups. Over the past decades, such reforms have centred largely on remedying individual student deficiencies. Although more recent analyses have pointed with increasing specificity and persuasiveness towards institutional structures and norms that define and contribute to student failure

(Fine, 1991), programmatic remedies continue to focus on students' individual skills (and deficits). (We could ask the question, for example, why does tracking in the high school persist despite so much discrediting evidence?) There are a few exceptions in which reforms in school organization target specifically the structures of students' opportunity to learn.

Advances in professional development, too, have centred on problems of diversity and equity in individual classrooms assisting teachers to identify and alter classroom practices that contribute to student failure and that undermine "equal opportunity to learn". The most promising of these efforts engage teachers collectively in studying classroom practices in ways that sometimes lead to more systemic changes at the school level (Cochran-Smith and Lytle, 1992). They do so by building a norm conducive to the close scrutiny of well-established practices and by building a capacity for organizational change (Doherty, 2010a).

Reforms in the Nature, Extent, and Uses of Student Assessment

Reform proposals argue for more widespread and rigorous use of authentic assessment. Yet the technical advances in assessment have typically lagged behind the formulation of standards and the advances in curriculum design. State and local policy-makers continue to judge the success of reform efforts on the basis of standardized test scores. Components of statewide tests that strike teachers as most "authentic" (for example, writing samples or open-ended math reasoning items) are also those most difficult and expensive to develop and to score. In areas other than language arts and math, they may also be relatively underdeveloped especially where they call for synthesis across subject areas, as in the "exhibitions" favoured by the Coalition of Essential Schools. At the local level, teachers' expressed interest in and commitment to alternative forms of assessment far exceeds their professed skill and confidence in constructing, evaluating, or incorporating such alternatives and also exceeds the resources presently available from the research and test development communities. Yet local discussions do not and cannot wait upon the psychometricians advances. In schools embarked upon reinventing, redesigning, and restructuring themselves, teachers wrestle with the criteria for good work, and the forms in which it might be expressed (Doherty, 2010b).

Reforms in the Social Organization of Schooling

The recurrent strains of criticism throughout the ealier days culminate in the widespread agreement that business as usual will not suffice. The convergence of interest (and funds) around the broad image of "school restructuring" has been quite astounding. The call to more systemic reform permeates initiatives in "school restructuring" supported by states, private foundations, and, to a lesser extent, projects sponsored by teachers' associations in concert with local schools and districts.

The most ambitious of these initiatives have in common that they are oriented towards principles, not programmes or specific practices. The Coalition of Essential Schools, for example, is united by a commitment to nine principles for the "redesign" of secondary schools. Predictably, teachers' commitments to these principles are provisional and uneven in that regard, we have what might appear to be a conventional "implementation of innovation" situation. But the dilemma for school leadership and for professional development goes far deeper in this instance: there is no well-developed picture of what these principles look like in practice. In the scramble to define a model, isolated cases of success become the focus of lore. Central Park East springs to mind, but few others (Meier, 1992; Baker, 2005). And no matter how persuasive the precedent set by any success story, broad principles require close attention to each local context. To fit opportunities for professional development to a campaign for the principled redesign of schooling is arguably a different matter indeed from organizing the training and support to implement a programme or a set of readily-transferable practices. Yet we lack descriptions of restructuring initiatives that supply a detailed portrait of the learning demands on teachers and the corresponding professional development responses.

Reforms in the Professionalization of Teaching

The "professionalization" reforms at the national and state levels centre on teachers' demonstrated knowledge base (as reflected in standards for preparation programme accreditation and candidate assessment), on conditions surrounding teacher certification and licensure, and on the structure of career opportunities in teaching. At the local level, professionalization tends to take the form of extended assistance to new teachers, expanded career opportunities for experienced teachers, and experiments in site-based decision making. For purposes of this chapter, these reforms are interesting principally for the way in which they bear upon the four reform movements discussed above that is, for the way in which they equip teachers both individually and collectively to play an informed and active role in defining the enterprise of education and the work of teaching (Czerniawski, Guberman & MacPhail, 2016).

This is not the place to repeat all the major arguments surrounding the professional standing of the teaching occupation, although the reforms have spawned a large and growing literature. Two comments seem germane. First, state and local policy-makers seem most readily disposed to support appeals to "professionalization" where they see it as (1) sustaining a reasonably well-prepared and stable teacher workforce; and (2) coupled with assurances of local accountability for student outcomes. Second, initiatives that promise "professionalization" of teaching increasingly expand opportunity and reward in exchange for increased obligation. Teachers are expected to contribute to the support of beginning teachers and to participate in other ways in the improvement of schooling and teaching.

These five streams of reform cannot be done well piecemeal, nor are they reforms that succeed if attempted only in isolated classrooms. As Fine (1992) puts it, the present ventures pursue the "big systemic, educational question..." of transforming whole systems into "educationally and emotionally rich communities of learners". This suggests quite a different organization of learning opportunity (and obligation) than one that supplies teachers with measured increments in knowledge, skill, and judgement from a known pool of "effective" classroom practices.

Emerging Issues

In the present reform context, three issues dominate policy considerations in the design of professional development:

(1) The sheer complexity of the reform tasks being proposed, together with the relative absence of tested principles, policies, and practices; the contradictions across policies; and the propensity to seize upon early-stage experiments as "models".

(2) The problem of "fit" between the task of reform and the prevailing models of professional development in particular, the dominance of a training paradigm built on "knowledge consumption", and the lesser support for an inquiry and problem-solving paradigm built around "knowledge production".

(3) The relative inattention to teachers' "opportunity to learn" within the salaried work day and work year an issue in the social organization of teachers work in schools and their participation in a wider professional community.

The Complexity and Uneven Pace of Systemic Reform

Complexity and ambiguity are inherent features of the more ambitious reforms, making progress uneven and difficult to detect. The picture is complicated further by the internal contradictions of the reform movement itself, e.g. in the competing views of schooling and teaching inherent in the basic skills reforms that still dominate urban reform *versus* the more "ambitious" outcomes embodied in the original standards and in other reform initiatives that emphasize higher order thinking. Confronted with complexities, ambiguities, and contradictions, individuals and institutions move forward in fits and starts. The professional development problem mirrors the larger problem of reform in several ways.

Limited grasp of possibilities: Asked to participate in the redesign of their work and workplace, participants at first invent a narrow range of responses or solutions. Conventional forms of professional development and support grounded in "training" are poorly conceived to help people expand the possibilities for learning, teaching, and schooling. Rarely do they contend with fundamental debates and disagreements about the purposes of schooling, the relationships between teachers and students, and the obligations of teachers to a wider larger community. It seems unlikely that teachers' sense of possibility will be enlarged in the absence of expanded information, deeper discussion and debate, and a tolerance for public dispute over fundamental matters.

Policy collisions and the legacy of past reforms: Most plans for systemic reform or restructuring underestimate the sustained impact of long-standing policy and practice. Teachers and administrators witness "policy collisions" between present reforms and their predecessors, many still reflected in statute, regulation, policy, and local habit. Darling & Hammond (1990) goes on to argue: "In several respects, policy accretion is a more difficult problem than the older problem bemoaned by reformers (which has not left us) of ingrained tradition. ...This can create an Alice in Wonderland world in which people ultimately begin to nod blithely at the inevitability of incompatible events"(Harris, Jones, and Huffman, 2017).

Pressures for fast-paced implementation: Systemic change is also undermined when local and state leaders attempt to reduce conceptual and practical complexities in the interest of a fast-paced implementation. The California curriculum frameworks serve as one example of a complex policy instrument that is experienced in distilled form by classroom teachers. It is observed that, at least from the vantage point of the teachers interviewed, the mathematics curriculum framework consisted of a 'statement'... and its transmission to them occurred when they were handed new textbooks, selected by the local administration after being approved by the state as compatible with the framework" (Higher Education Academy, 2005).

The magnitude of the task: Observers remind us of the sheer difficulty of the reform task, and the toll that it takes on people. The work of systemic reform is enormously difficult, frustrating, slow and rewarding. Fine (1992) says once-discouraged teachers are "back" in droves but they must contend with powerful dilemmas.

Political will: The success of the trail-blazing individuals and institutions will rest ultimately on a crucial fund of political will. Whatever the shortcomings of the knowledge base on which reform stands, we can nonetheless assert that we have sufficient knowledge to move forward; we have "the knowledge, methods, assessment strategies to transform our classrooms into engaging, critical and creative sites of intellectual growth and personal development" (Fine, 1992). What remains uncertain is whether we have the political will to employ our knowledge in the service of public (and particularly urban) education. Professional development, in this view, will prove fruitless if it fails to cultivate and sustain political will.

The available (though rare) accounts of large-scale restructuring efforts thus underscore the *systemic* character of reform and, correspondingly, the *collective* capacity needed to achieve and sustain it. But professional development practice remains, on the whole, highly individualistic. "Rates of participation vary enormously, generating radically different profiles of professional development for teachers with comparable experience and teaching assignments" (Lanier and Little, 1989; and Arends, 1983). These differences appear to persist even in schools formally "committed" to reform initiatives.

A shift to "school-based" initiatives does not necessarily alter the variable pattern of individual practice. Schools associated with the Illinois Writing Project showed promising changes in language arts scores, but in the urban schools "typically less than half of the teachers in each building attended the voluntarily, after-school workshops." What we do not learn is why. Were teachers opposed to the assumptions and practices of the Writing Project? Unimpressed with the quality of the workshops, or already expert in the practices? Pressed by the demands of too many projects, or too burdensome a teaching load? Committed to other activities that required time, thought, and energy? Not persuaded that participation would make a difference to the students they taught? Discouraged by failures of administrative leadership? Truly discouraged about teaching?

Here we have a tension between institutional imperatives and individual prerogatives, between the conditions necessary to attempt systemic change and the conditions that engage individual teachers in their work. At best, these are in harmony; at the least, we must learn the sources of conflict between them. We will be better served by knowing the grounds on which teachers choose to participate or not. As a context for professional development, reform movements place a premium on institutional perspectives. They may absorb all of the resources available for teachers' professional development, leaving little in the way of subsidy for individually-inspired intellectual pursuits that may also, in quite different ways, make a difference to the character of schooling. (Megginson and Whitaker, 2007).

In any event, the complexities and tensions illustrated here are not resolved by any simplistic distinction between "voluntary" and "mandatory" occasions of professional development. More productive will be careful consideration of teachers' professional obligations and opportunities, of the balance and tension between individual latitude and collective endeavour, and of the resources and rewards devoted to each.

Problems of "fit": Professional Development Models and the Task of Reform

Without becoming preoccupied by barriers to reform, we might highlight five issues that states and localities confront in matching professional development to the challenges surrounding systemic reform.

Innovation on the margins. The training paradigm dominates the world of teachers' professional development. Short-term skill training workshops for outnumber teachers' study groups and well-conceived teacher research. But the training paradigm has also come under assault: Critics charge that most training places teachers in passive roles as consumers of knowledge produced elsewhere; that the "workshop menu" is fragmented in content, form, and continuity at precisely the time when teachers are confronted with the challenge of redesigning the way we do schooling (Moore and Hyde, 1981; Little, 1989).

Alternative approaches of the sort described above have gained the admiration of teachers, administrators, school boards, and state policy-makers. Some, to be sure, have grown in stature and reach over the past decade. The history of the Bay Area Writing Project is a case in point; the BAWP model now guides a large number of local and regional projects in many states, and serves as the basis for comparable projects in mathematics and science. It has attracted state and local district funding.

On the whole, however, innovative approaches to teachers' professional development those that correspond most closely to the principles outlined above remain small in scale and number. Most have been supported with private moneys (foundation and corporate funding) and have made relatively little impact on the configuration of publicly-supported professional development. Such partnerships have formed between individual activists in universities and schools or districts, or between individual consultants and schools, or between departments of education and local schools. In large institutions, multiple "partnerships" may operate in ignorance of one another's efforts, or in pursuit of quite different or even conflicting goals.

Lord (1991) maintains that the subject matter collaboratives have "magnified the impact of local resources both human and financial", but provides no detail. Meanwhile, the risks associated with moving from the margins to the centre are well-known: teacher-centred programmes.

The limitations of packaged knowledge and standardized programmes: Given the option, district and school administrators say they will opt for a "well-packaged programme" of staff development (Little *et al.*, 1987). Packaged programmes have an understandable appeal. They are readily defended, managed, and evaluated. Most district-sponsored staff development is oriented towards the acquisition of specific knowledge and skill; assessing "impact," though it is rarely done, is relatively straightforward (especially if centred on changes in observable teacher behaviour).

Alternative approaches, by comparison, are conceptually and pragmatically messier. The main benefits that participants derive from teacher networks, study groups, curriculum experiments, and the like may be more broadly intellectual, motivational, and attitudinal. By acknowledging the importance of teachers' intellectual curiosities and capacities, and by crediting teachers' contributions to knowledge and practice, such approaches may strengthen the enthusiasm teachers bring to their work and the intellectual bent they display in the classroom. Over the long run, teachers who participate in experiences of this sort might be expected to show higher rates of classroom innovation and to inspire greater enthusiasm for learning on the part of their students. Nevertheless, appropriate comparisons with conventional staff development are likely to prove very difficult. This is due in part to differences in programme aims, content, and format, and due in part to the difficulty of tracing the crucial longer-term consequences for individual teachers.

The proliferation of classroom- and school-based studies over the past two decades has fed the organized professional development marketplace. "Research says" is a common preface to many workshop presentations and exercises, serving as a warrant for recommended practice. But "research says" has increasingly become a means for exercising institutional authority rather than for informing teachers' judgments or framing their own inquiries. Teachers are typically less well positioned than district specialists or outside consultants to invoke research (or challenge it) as a warrant for action they have less routine access to sources of research, less time to read and evaluate it, and less familiarity with its arcane language.

What is inevitably hidden in the effort to "translate" research are all the ways in which the research findings conflict, or are limited by design flaws, or reflect particular conceptions of the phenomena under study. What also is missing is an invitation to teachers to act not only as consumers of research but also as critics of research and producers of research to be participants in a more visible and consequential manner. An alternative to the formulation "research says", reads something like: "The way this question has been framed in most research is...." Or: "There are three main approaches to this problem in research so far. Here's what each has produced...." These formulations leave open the possibility that the available research knowledge is incomplete and that there is room for discovery. They neither romanticize teachers' knowledge nor unduly privilege researchers' claims.

The status of the "knowledge base" in support of systemic reform is uncertain. Some argue that the base is strong, others that it is more hortatory and ideological than it is theoretically coherent or empirically defensible. Advocates of reform argue that we know enough to make considerable difference in the ways that students experience school and the benefits they derive from schooling. Whatever the strength of that claim, it also seems certain none of the knowledge we assert will be adequate to account for the complexities of any specific context, and that there is no substitute for local invention and inquiry. These circumstances prompt various responses to the burgeoning "teacher research" movement (not the first such movement in this century). In recent symposia on the subject, debate revealed widely diverse and competing views teachers' preparation to engage in "research", the nature of research topics and methods, conventions associated with legitimation of research, and issues surrounding the political control of research agendas and products (Hefnawi, 2017).

The dominance of "training" over problem solving: States and local school districts have learned in part, anyway the lesson of the "implementation problem" and the importance of adequate local support. In the late 1970s, one could reasonably charge that "many... education reform efforts fell short primarily because planners seriously underestimated teacher training needs" (McLaughlin, 1990). An adequate supply of well-conceived training opportunities seemed a major contributor to implementation success. More than a decade later, we boast a more sophisticated understanding of the implementation problem, casting it as a complex interaction between external policy variables (clear statutes, effective authority, and the like) and the micro-contexts shaped by individuals' and groups' commitments, histories, and politics. Our conception of implementation has evolved "from early notions of implementation as transmission or as a problem of incentives or authority to conceptions of implementation as bargaining and transformation" (McLaughlin, 1990) expresses certain skepticism about the power of policy mandates, especially those that take the form of special projects aimed at "discrete elements of the education policy system" instead of embracing the systemic nature of problems and the systemic character of local practice.

But districts' strategies for reform, at least with regard to teachers' professional development, do not appear to capitalize fully on what we have learned about the importance and variability of local contexts and about the transformational nature of reform. "In-service" activities tend to be linked to special projects or to discrete components of "reform", and to embody a relatively traditional conception of classroom experience. The most sophisticated of these make some provision for follow-up in the form of classroom consultation and coaching.

The training-and-coaching strategy that dominates local professional development has much to recommend it when considered as a balanced part of a larger configuration, and when linked to those aspects of teaching that are properly rendered as transferable skills. But the training model is problematic. The content of much training communicates a view of teaching and learning that is at odds with present reform initiatives. It is not at all clear, for example, that any form of training is adequate to develop the "substantive conversation" that Newmann (1990) envisions, nor is the content of training set against the content of local belief, practice, and policy in any meaningful and detailed way. In addition, principles of "good training" are frequently compromised in practice. In particular, schools and districts demonstrate far less capacity for classroom consultation and support than is required by the training and coaching model. Those persons typically designated as "coaches" or "mentors" are far outnumbered by their clientele of regular classroom teachers. They are further constrained by school workplace cultures that perpetuate a norm of privacy and constrain advice-giving (Little, 1989). Finally, to attain results from the training/coaching model requires a consistency of purpose and a coordination of effort that is not the norm in many districts. Rather, districts parade a litany of short-term goals in their response to various state mandates and incentives, local constituencies, or the individual enthusiasms of superintendents, school board members, or others.

Having launched such criticisms, it is to reiterate that the skill training and coaching model to which so many districts seem wedded has demonstrated consistent results in those cases where training content can be represented as a repertoire of discrete practices, and where classroom performance is oriented towards specified student outcomes. At their best, local activities incorporate the wealth of research on effective training and support that we can trace to the various "implementation of innovation" studies and to studies of specific professional development ventures (Buczynski & Hansen, 2010). Nor are these remarks in any way meant to impugn the knowledge, skill, thoughtfulness, or good intentions of those persons designated by local districts as staff development specialists, coaches, mentors, and the like. Rather, the aim is to record the dominance of the training model, the possibilities it offers, and the constraints on its effectiveness.

The Workplace and Teachers' Opportunity to Learn

Concentration on formal programmes of professional development tends to obscure issues of obligation, incentive, and opportunity in the salaried work day and work year. Investigation of teachers instructional assignments, ratio of in-class to out-of-class time, and school-level affiliations (departments, grade levels, friendship nets) provides us both with a perspective on *motivation* or *pressure to learn* and with a description of those *opportunities to learn* that are embedded in the social organization of schools (Little, 1990; Hargreaves, 1990).

Teachers' central reasons and opportunities for professional development begin with the teaching assignments they acquire, the allocation of discretionary time, and other work conditions encountered day by day. They begin, that is, with a teacher's experience of what it is to teach and to be a teacher in general, and in particular circumstances. To some large degree, it is only in relation to the daily experience of teaching that one can anticipate the contributions of more structured opportunities that range from independent reading to formal coursework, conference attendance, skill training workshops, leaves or sabbaticals, participation in committees or special projects, and scheduled consultation with colleagues (Goswami, 2010).

Reform movements tend to orient us towards an institutional (and largely functionalist) perspective. By this perspective, the schools' capacity for supporting the professional development of teachers is expressed in a system of obligations, opportunities, and rewards. Teacher's obligations for professional preparation and development reside formally in certification and recertification requirements, teacher evaluation standards, and other personnel policies and practices. They are communicated informally by institutional norms regarding teachers' performance (Gosha, Billionniere, Gilbert & Ramsey, 2010).

In privileging the institutional and collective view, however, the language of reform underestimates the intricate ways in which individual and institutional lives are interwoven. It under-examines the points at which certain organizational interests of *schools* and occupational interests of *teachers* may collide. Critics of reform movements stress the tendency to "de-skill" teaching and a corresponding tendency to legitimate institutional surveillance and coercion under the rubric of "vision" and "instructional leadership" (Carlson, 1992; Hargreaves, 1990). Carlson (1992) describes the principled opposition mounted by a teachers' association to the "spectre of standardization" they detected in basic skills reforms built around programmed materials, pre-arranged objectives, and batteries of standardized tests. Smylie and Smart (1990), examining sources of support for and opposition to merit pay and career ladders, note that "the primary beliefs and assumptions that guide the development of relationships among teachers include norms of independence and professional equality" and it is naive to suppose that such programmes will generate widespread support unless they resolve "social and normative incongruities". Each of these cases is consistent with the observation that members of an occupational community may find that "what is deviant organizationally may be occupationally correct" (Van Maanen and Barley, 1984; Mouza, 2009).

As the arena in which teaching traditions and reform imperatives confront one another most directly and concretely, the school workplace is both the most crucial and the most complex of domains in which we play out the possibilities for teachers' professional development (Ostashewski, 2010). Teachers' motivations, incentives, and frustrations come foremost from the immediacy and complexity of the classroom teachers' responses to the students they teach and the circumstances in which they teach them. Idiosyncratic classroom realities may take precedence over broader institutional interests, leading teachers to protect a "strategic" or "elective individualism" (Hargreaves, 1990; Flinders, 1988). The impetus to protect one's autonomy may be intensified by various circumstances surrounding collegial and institutional life the norms underlying peer acceptance and admiration, and the fabric of relations between teachers and administrators. Taking the workplace seriously requires more than shifting staff development resources and activities to the school site (Harris, Jones, and Huffman, 2017).

Conclusion

Five streams of reform present a challenge of considerable complexity, scope, and ambiguity. Yet the present pattern of professional development activity reflects an uneven fit with the aspirations and challenges of present reform initiatives in subject matter teaching, equity, assessment, school organization, and the professionalization of teaching. Much "staff development" or "in-service" communicates a relatively impoverished view of teachers, teaching, and teacher development. Compared to the complexity, subtlety, and uncertainties of the classroom, professional development is often a remarkably low-intensity enterprise. It requires little in the way of intellectual struggle or emotional engagement, and takes only superficial account of teachers' histories or circumstances. Compared to the complexity and ambiguity of the most ambitious reforms, professional development is too often substantively weak and politically marginal.

Professional development must be constructed in ways that deepen the discussion, open up the debates, and enrich the array of possibilities for action. Ground for optimism resides in those "innovations on the margin" that embody principles consonant with the complexity of the reform task and with the capacities and commitments of a strong teacher workforce.

REFERENCES

Arends, R. (1983). *Teachers as Learners: A Descriptive Study of Professional Development Activities*. Paper presented at the annual meeting of the American Educational Research Association, Montreal.

Baker, P.H. (2005). "Managing Student's Behaviour: How Ready are Teachers to Meet the Challenge". *American Secondary Education, 333*(3), 51-64.

Barko, H. (2004). "Professional Development and Teacher Learning: Mapping the Terrain". *Educational Researcher, 33*(8), 3-15.

Behera, S. (2009). "Academic Staff College: Ideas & Issues". *University News, 47*(4), 10-15.

Buczynski, S. & Hansen, C.B. (2010). "Impact of Professional Development on Teacher Practice: Uncovering Connection". *Teacher and Teacher Education, 26*(3), 599-607. doi: 110.1016/j.tate.2009.09.006.

Carlson, D. (1992). *Teachers and Crisis: Urban School Reform and Teachers' Work Culture.* New York: Routledge.

Cochran-Smith, M. & Lytle, S.L. (1992). *Interrogating cultural diversity: Inquiry and action.* A paper presented at the annual meeting of the American Educational Research Association, San Francisco.

Czerniawski, G., Guberman, A. & Mac Phail, A. (2016). "The Professional Developmental Needs of Higher Education-based Teacher Educators: An International Comparative Needs Analysis". *European Journal of Teacher Education.*

Darling-Hammond, L. (1990). "Instructional Policy into Practice: The Power of the Bottom Over the Top." *Educational Evaluation and Policy Analysis, 12*(3), 339-347.

Desimone, L.M. (2009). "Improving Impact Studies of Teachers' Professional Development: Towards Better Conceptualizations and Measures". *Educational Researcher, 38*(3), 181-199.

Doherty, I. (2010a). *Aiming for Systemic Change Through an Embedded Continuing Professional Development Initiative.* Paper presented at the Curriculum, Technology and Transformation for an Unknown Future: Ascilite 2010. Sydney, Australia.

Doherty, I. (2010b). "Staff Development Workshops for Teaching with Web 2.0 Tools". In C.D. Maddux, D. Gibson & B. Dodge (Eds.), *Research Highlights in Information Technology and Teacher Education 2010:* Chesapeake, V.A: SITE.

Fine, M. (1991). *Framing Dropouts: Notes on the Politics of an Urban Public High School.* Albany: State University of New York Press.

Fine, M. (1992). *Chartering Urban School Reform: Philadelphia style.* Philadelphia: CUNY Graduate Centre/Philadelphia Schools Collaborative.

Flinders, D.J. (1988). "Teacher Isolation and the New Reform". *Journal of Curriculum and Supervision, 4*(1), 17-29.

Gosha, K., Billionniere, E., Gilbert, J. & Ramsey, M. (2010). *Developing a Framework for Teacher Professional Development Using Online Social Networks.* Paper presented at the Society for Information Technology & Teacher Education International Conference (SITE) 2010. C.A.: San Diego.

Goswami, D. (2010). "Teacher training programme of Academic Staff College, Gauhati University: An Appraisal". *University News 48*(10), 22-28, March 8.

Hargreaves, A. (1990). "Teachers' Work and the Politics of Time and Space". *Qualitative Studies in Education, 3*(4), 303-20.

Harris, A., Jones, M. and Huffman, J. (2017). *Teachers Leading Educational Reform: The Power of Professional Learning Communities.* London: Routledge Press.

Hefnawi, A. (2017). "Towards an Effective Teachers Professional Learning". *Journal of Social Science, 3*(1), 453-66.

Higher Education Academy (2005).*Consultation on a framework for professional standards.* http://www.heacademy.ac.uk/news/20_3370.htm (accessed 6 October, 2015)

Little, J.W. (1990). "Conditions of Professional Development in Secondary Schools". In M.W. McLaughlin, J. Talbert & N. Bascia (Eds.), *The Context of Teaching in Secondary Schools: Teachers Realities,* (pp. 187-223). New York: Teachers College Press.

Little, J.W. (1989). "District Policy Choices and Teachers Professional Development Opportunities". *Educational Evaluation and Policy Analysis, 11*(2), 165-79.

Lord, B. (1991). *Subject-area Collaboratives, Teacher Professionalism, and Staff Development.* Paper presented at the annual meeting of the American Educational Research Association, Chicago.

McLaughlin, M.W. (1990). "The Rand Change Agent Study: Macro Perspectives and Micro Realities". *Educational Researcher* (December), 11-16.

Megginson, D. and Whitaker, V. (2007).*Continuing Professional Development* (2nd ed.) London: Chartered Institute of Personnel and Development.

Meier, D. (1992). "Reinventing Teaching". *Teachers College Record, 93*(4), 594-609.

MHRD (1986) *National Policy on Education,* New Delhi. Government of India.

MHRD (1992) *National Policy on Education, Programme of Action,* New Delhi. Government of India.

Moore, D. & Hyde, A. (1981). *Making Sense of Staff Development: An Analysis of Staff Development Programmes and their Costs in Three Urban School Districts.* Chicago: Designs for Change.

Mouza, C. (2009). "Does Research-Based Professional Development Make a Difference? A Longitudinal Investigation of Teacher Learning in Technology Integration". *Teachers College Record, 3(*5), 1195-1241.

Newmann, F.M. (1990). “Linking Restructuring to Authentic Student Achievement”. *Paper presented at the Indiana University Conference.* Madison, W.I.: University of Wisconsin, National Centre on Effective Schools and National Centre for Educational Research. University of Wisconsin.

Ostashewski, N. (2010). *Online Technology Teacher Professional Development Courselets: Design and Development.* Paper presented at the Society for Information Technology & Teacher Education International Conference (SITE) 2010. C.A.: San Diego.

Smylie, M.A. & Smart, J.C. (1990). “Teacher support for career enhancement initiatives: Programme Characteristics and Effects on Work.” *Educational Evaluation and Policy Analysis, 12*(2), 139-55.

Sparks, D. & Loucks-Horsley, S. (1990). “Models of Staff Development.” In W.R. Houston, M. Haberman & J. Sikula (Eds.)., *Handbook of research on teacher education*, (pp. 234-50). New York: Macmillan.

UNESCO (2003). *Teacher Professional Development: An International Review of Literature*, Paris.

Van Maanen, J. & Barley, S.R. (1984). “Occupational Communities: Culture and Control in Organizations”. *Research in Organizational Behaviour*, 6, 87-365.

28

Content Competencies for Professional Development of Teachers

Rama Gupta

Right to Education Act has been implemented in India with the aim of providing quality compulsory primary education to all children of 6-14 years age group. As the teachers and students are the main part of education system, students' achievement in various subjects is a major issue for ensuring quality primary education and as a key input the teachers' role, their subject knowledge, motivation and competency affects students directly. This chapter aims at content competencies of primary school teachers and students' academic achievement to find out what specific interventions in training can help teachers to improve their content competencies and teaching competencies.

Quality is essential for education at every stage. While universalization of elementary education is governments' commitment, improving and sustaining the quality of basic education is equally important. Good quality teaching and learning in the classroom are vital to ensure effective learning outcomes that provide children with literacy, numeracy and other skills, enhance their creative and emotional development, and equip them with values and attitudes that enable them to be active and engaged citizens leading meaningful and valued lives. Good quality teaching and learning environment assures effective learning outcomes. (UNESCO, 2000a).

The rising concerns with quality of education were strongly reflected in the protocols of World Conference on Education for All (1990) in Thailand and also in the World Education Forum in Dakar, Senegal (2000). In India, the policies on education repeatedly emphasize on ensuring and imparting quality education at primary stage. India faces many hurdles in educational development due to multiple of poverty, caste system and social ethos (EFA Report, 2008). It is the duty of teachers to impart education to students that helps them in proper personality development.

Quality Education demands quality teachers. The Education Commission (1964-66) says, "Of all different factors which influence the quality of education and its contribution to national development, the quality, competence and character of teachers are undoubtedly more significant. Nothing is more important than securing a sufficient supply of high quality of recruits to the teaching profession providing them with the best possible professional preparation and creating satisfactory conditions of work in which they can be fully effective."

The students belong to different background, abilities, habits and thoughts. Teacher is the key input in the school system, they enable learners to acquire basic skills such as literacy and numeracy in the early years of schooling.The learning achievement and quality of our schools has to be improved. The policies adopted by government under SSA, have brought major progress in access to schooling and now close to 97 per cent children of age 6-14 are enrolled in primary schools.

However, this single minded goal of providing access to schooling has not resulted in learning. School system has not always been able to retain the large flow of new entrants and ensuring successful completion of elementary schooling. The retention of children in school is deeply related with quality of education. If the quality of education and student's academic achievement in schools is not satisfactory, the number of dropouts will increase.

'Achievement' is a term used to indicate learning outcomes. The learning outcomes of instructional processes are called as learning achievement. Instruction on subject study provides a scholarship to learners. Thus, accomplishment or proficiency in a given skill is termed as achievement. It is one of the most important outcomes of any educational setup. "Academic achievement refers to the degree to which the pupil has moved towards the objectives of the school. These objectives are goals in the direction of which the curriculum seeks to change the pupils" (Remmers and Gage,1956).

According to Annual Survey of Education Report (ASER) 2018, only 50.3 per cent of class 5 students could read a simple class 2 level text and only 27.8 per cent could do basic division in rural areas. ASER (2019) reports for early years schooling shows that half of all children in Standard III are at least two years behind in language outcomes where the curriculum expects them to be.

The achievement level of children at primary stage, especially at the terminal class V is important, because at this level, the children complete the level of primary education and enter to the next level, i.e. the upper primary and then secondary education. Language is the basic necessary prerequisite for all types of learning and is useful in our day-to-day activities so learning achievement of class V students in language has been taken for the present study.

In any education system, the level of students learning depends substantially on teachers' competencies and teaching-learning conditions. The competencies has been defined as—"Competencies are the requirements of a competency based teacher education, which includes the knowledge, skills, and values the student, must demonstrate for successful completion of the programme" Houstan (1987). Teacher competence refers to the right way of conveying units of knowledge, application and skills to students." The right way here, includes knowledge of content, processes, methods and means of conveying content in an interesting way, involving the activities of students. DPEP, Tamil Nadu (1996).

The term 'competence' refers to 'a desired quality of job performance'. A competent teacher can carry out all tasks effectively. (Lakshmi, 2000). Thus, competencies aim at transforming inborn qualities and abilities of individuals into visual utilities. These are essential to be nurtured among the teachers for making them efficient and effective. These competencies are designed on theoretical and conceptual understanding to empower teachers to perform their responsibilities with professional insights and confidence.

DPEP, Tamil Nadu (1966), DPEP, Tamil Nadu (1996), NCTE (1998), Bhat (1998) made efforts towards identification and categorization of teacher competency and found that there are several ways in which competencies can be classified. The teachers' content competencies are an important part of every category of competencies, because content upgradation is one of the major areas of human resource development.

Teachers' subject specific teaching competencies have been selected for the present study in which content competencies and teaching competencies are included. Knowledge of content is the necessary condition for good teaching. Content competencies are related to specific stage of education and it assures to what extent a teacher has achieved mastery over the content areas.

The content or subject matter in a subject is very crucial as the instructional interactions are carried out using it. The teacher with lesser command over the subject may have difficulty in visualizing learning experiences in creative ways. He will surely select those that are teacher predominant. It is significant that content in a particular subject is rendered into meaningful themes such that the learners can understand. Every teacher thus needs not only to know how content can be 'treated' but also to develop competence to actually do it.

The success of standards based reform depends on teachers' ability to foster both basic knowledge and advanced thinking and problem solving among their students (Loucks-Horsley, Hewson, Love, & Stiles, 1998; National Commission on Teaching

& America's Future, 1996), and such effective practices require teachers to have a deep understanding of the content they teach (Ma, 1999). Professional development is considered an essential mechanism for deepening teachers' content knowledge and developing their teaching practices. As a result, professional development could be a cornerstone of systemic reform efforts designed to increase teachers' capacity to teach to high standards (Smith & O'Day, 1991).

In any education system, the level of students learning depends substantially on teachers' competencies and teaching-learning conditions. For any curricular reform teacher change is required. It leads to a persistent questioning of teachers' content knowledge and expertise. Professional development includes pre-service and formal in-service training to upgrade the content knowledge and pedagogical skills of teachers and is widely viewed as an important means of improving teaching and learning.

In UP most of the teachers appointed in Parishadiya Primary Schools have studied all the subjects up to 10th standard and then they choose Art, Science or Commerce stream but they teach all the subjects. In this situation, the question arises that how much content knowledge is acquired by the teachers who are teaching students up to 5th grade. It is really of great importance to find out whether students' learning achievement is being affected by teachers' content knowledge.

Teachers' knowledge of content should be assisted by proper transaction of syllabus to the students for effective teaching and meaningful learning outcomes. Thus, it is also important to know whether the teachers are having knowledge of proper teaching methods or not and how much help students are getting by the use of these teaching methods. Are teachers' content knowledge and teaching competencies associated with students' achievement at primary stage? The present study aims to study the association of teacher competencies and students' achievement and find out that what specific interventions in training will help teachers to improve their content competencies and teaching competencies.

Objectives and Methodology of the Study

(1) To study the association between teachers' content competency and students' achievement level in Hindi at primary school stage in the context of gender and teaching experience of teachers.

(2) To study the association between teachers' general teaching competency and students' achievement in Hindi at primary school stage in the context of gender and teaching experience of teachers.

Hypotheses

(1) Content competency of teachers in Hindi is associated with students' achievement in Hindi at primary school stage in the context of gender and teaching experience of teachers.

(2) General teaching competency of teachers is associated with students' achievement in Hindi at primary school stage in the context of gender and teaching experience of teachers.

Research Method: Survey method has been adopted in the present study. Both qualitative and quantitative methods have been used.

Population: All the teachers working at Parishadiya Primary Schools of Eastern UP and their students of class V constitute the population of the study.

Sample: 100 teachers teaching Hindi at Parishadiya Primary Schools of Eastern UP and all their students of class V constitute the sample. Multistage random sampling and cluster sampling method has been applied for selecting sample. Out of total 75 districts of UP, 25 districts are included in Eastern UP, 20 per cent of the population, i.e. 5 districts—Allahabad, Jaunpur, Mirzapur, Pratapgarh and Varanasi—were selected randomly for the data collection. From each district, one block has been selected randomly and 20 schools were selected randomly from every Block.

From each school of sample, 1 teacher and all the students of class V were selected. Thus, from one district, 20 teachers and all their students studying in class V were selected as sample.Thus, sample of 100 teachers teaching Hindi in class V and 1592 students of Class-V have been selected. Out of 100 teachers teaching Hindi, 51 gent teachers and 49 lady teachers were selected. Out of 100 teachers teaching Hindi, 51 teachers having less than 10 years of teaching experience (Less Experienced Teachers) and 49 teachers having more than 10 years of teaching experience (More Experienced Teachers) were selected.

Tools: The tools used for research work are:

1. Hindi Achievement Test-class V.
2. Hindi Achievement Test for Primary Teachers.
3. Teaching Competence Observation Schedule.

All the 3 tools were developed by the researcher and the reliability and validity of tools were established.

Data Collection

For collection of data, 'Hindi Achievement Test for Primary School Teachers' has been administered on sample teachers and three classes of every teacher were observed with the help of 'Teaching Competency Observation Schedule'. For assessing achievement levels of class V students of sample teachers, 'Hindi Achievement Test Class V' has been administered.

Analysis Procedures: The chi-square test of independence has been applied for analyzing the data.

Analysis and Interpretation

Association between Teachers' Content Competency and Students' Achievement in Hindi

To study the association between teachers' content competency and students' achievement level in Hindi, the teachers were categorized in low, medium and high groups on the basis of scores of 'Hindi Achievement Test for Primary School Teachers' and classification was based on sum of scores of teachers on test after calculating its mean value and standard deviation.

Low Group = < (Mean-SD)
Average Group = (Mean-SD to Mean+SD)
High Group = > (Mean+SD)

The students taught by high, average and low group teachers in Hindi were also categorized into the group of high achiever students, average achiever students and low achiever students on the basis of marks obtained in 'Hindi Achievement Test Class V' and by calculating the Mean value and standard deviation. Then chi-square test of independence was applied to study the association between content competency of teachers in Hindi and students' achievement in Hindi.

Association between Teachers' Content Competency and Students' Achievement in Hindi

Table 28.1: χ^2 Value of Test of Independence between teachers' content competency and student's achievement in Hindi

Students' Achievement	Teachers' Content Competency				
	High	**Average**	**Low**	**Total**	**Value**
High	53 (56)	154 (161)	82 (71)	289	11.25 Significant at .05 level
Average	192 (204)	591 (583)	262 (258)	1045	
Low	66 (50)	143 (144)	49 (64)	258	
Total	**311**	**888**	**393**	**1592**	

Note: Figures in Parentheses indicate expected frequencies.

It can be observed from Table 28.1 that the calculated χ^2 value of independence test is 11.25 which is greater than Table value (9.48) at .05 level of significance with df: 4. The observed value is significant hence the null hypothesis that students' achievement in Hindi is independent of teachers' content competency is rejected at .05 level.

It can be said that students' achievement level in Hindi is associated with teachers' content competency in Hindi.

Association between Gents Teachers' Content Competency and Students' Achievement in Hindi

Table 28.2: χ^2 Value of Test of Independence between gents teachers' content competency and students' achievement in Hindi

Students' Achievement	Gents Teachers' Content Competency				
	High	**Average**	**Low**	**Total**	**χ^2 Value**
High	50 (36)	95 (101)	33 (41)	178	13.35 Significant at .05 level
Average	84 (103)	302 (290)	124 (117)	510	
Low	32 (27)	69 (75)	31 (30)	132	
Total	**166**	**466**	**188**	**820**	

Note: Figures in Parentheses indicate expected frequencies.

It can be observed from Table 28.2 that the calculated χ^2 value of independence test is 13.35 which is greater than Table value (9.48) at .05 level of significance with df: 4. The observed value is significant hence the null hypothesis that students' achievement in Hindi is independent of gents teachers' content competency is rejected at .05 level.

It can be said that students' achievement level in Hindi is associated with gents teachers' content competency in Hindi.

Association between Lady Teachers' Content Competency and Students' Achievement in Hindi

It can be observed from Table 28.3 that the calculated χ^2 value of independence test is 15.14 which is greater than Table value (9.48) at .05 level of significance with df: 4. The observed value is significant hence the null hypothesis that students' achievement in Hindi is independent of lady teachers' content competency is rejected at .05 level.

Table 28.3: χ^2 Value of Test of Independence between lady teachers' content competency and student's achievement in Hindi

Students' Achievement	**Lady Teachers' Content Competency**				
	High	**Average**	**Low**	**Total**	**χ^2 Value**
High	35 (27)	72 (94)	67 (53)	174	15.14 Significant at .05 level
Average	64 (72)	269 (248)	126 (139)	459	
Low	22 (22)	76 (75)	41 (42)	139	
Total	**121**	**417**	**234**	**772**	

Note: Figures in Parentheses indicate expected frequencies.

It can be said that students' achievement level in Hindi is associated with lady teachers' content competency in Hindi.

Association between Less Experienced Teachers' Content Competency and Students' Achievement in Hindi

Table 28.4: χ^2 Value of Test of Independence between Less Experienced Teachers' content competency and students' achievement in Hindi

Students' Achievement	**Less Experienced Teachers' Content Competency**				
	High	**Average**	**Low**	**Total**	**χ^2 Value**
High	30 (31)	79 (75)	11 (14)	120	1.20 Not significant at .05 level
Average	116 (116)	279 (280)	52 (51)	447	
Low	24 (23)	54 (56)	12 (10)	90	
Total	**170**	**412**	**75**	**657**	

Note: Figures in Parentheses indicate expected frequencies.

It can be observed from Table 28.4 that the calculated χ^2 value of independence test is 1.20 which is less than Table value (9.48) at .05 level of significance with df: 4. The observed value is non-significant hence the null hypothesis that students' achievement in Hindi is independent of less experienced teachers' content competency is not rejected at .05 level.

It can be said that students' achievement level in Hindi is independent of less experienced teachers' content competency in Hindi.

Association between More Experienced Teachers' Content Competency and Students' Achievement Level in Hindi

Table 28.5: χ^2 Value of Test of Independence between more experienced teachers' content competency and students' achievement in Hindi

Students' Achievement	More Experienced Teachers' Content Competency				
	High	**Average**	**Low**	**Total**	**χ^2 Value**
High	41 (37)	73 (79)	57 (55)	171	2.61 Not significant at .05 level
Average	123 (130)	292 (281)	192 (195)	607	
Low	37 (34)	68 (73)	52 (51)	157	
Total	**201**	**433**	**301**	**935**	

Note: Figures in Parentheses indicate expected frequencies.

It can be observed from Table 28.5 that the calculated χ^2 value of independence test is 2.61 which is less than Table value (9.48) at .05 level of significance with df: 4. The observed value is non-significant hence the null hypothesis that students' achievement in Hindi is independent of more experienced teachers' content competency is not rejected at .05 level.

It can be said that students' achievement level in Hindi is independent of content competency of more experienced teachers.

Association between Teachers' General Teaching Competency and Students' Achievement Level in Hindi

To study the association between teachers' general teaching competency and students' achievement level in Hindi, the teachers were categorized in low, medium and high groups on the basis of sum of scores of general 'Teaching Competence Observation Schedule' for primary school teachers teaching Hindi. The classification was based on scores of observation schedule after calculating its mean value and standard deviation.

Low Group = < (Mean-SD)
Average Group = (Mean-SD to Mean+SD)
High Group = > (Mean+SD)

The students taught by high, average and low competent group teachers in Hindi were also categorized into the group of high achiever students, average achiever students and low achiever students on the basis of marks obtained in 'Hindi Achievement Test Class V' by calculating the Mean value and Standard deviation. Then chi-square test of independence was applied to study the association between general teaching competency of teachers in Hindi and students' achievement in Hindi.

Association between Teachers' General Teaching Competency and Students' Achievement Level in Hindi

It can be observed from Table 28.6 that the calculated χ^2 value of independence test is 14.31 which is greater than Table value (9.48) at .05 level of significance with df: 4. The observed value is significant hence the null hypothesis that students' achievement in Hindi is independent of teachers' general teaching competency is rejected at .05 level.

Table 28.6: χ^2 Value of Test of Independence between teachers' general teaching competency and student's achievement in Hindi

Students' Achievement	Teachers General Teaching				
	High	**Average**	**Low**	**Total**	**χ^2 Value**
High	75 (60)	200 (226)	80 (68)	355	14.31 Not significant at .05 level
Average	157 (168)	658 (628)	170 (189)	985	
Low	39 (43)	157 (161)	56 (48)	252	
Total	**271**	**1015**	**306**	**1592**	

Note: Figures in Parentheses indicate expected frequencies.

It can be said that student's achievement level in Hindi is significantly associated with teachers' general teaching competency in Hindi.

Association between Gents Teachers' General Teaching Competency and Students' Achievement Level in Hindi

Table 28.7: χ^2 Value of Test of Independence between gents teachers' general teaching competency and students' achievement in Hindi

Students' Achievement	Gents Teachers' Competency				
	High	**Average**	**Low**	**Total**	**χ^2 Value**
High	51 (37)	89 (101)	34 (37)	174	14.54 Not significant at .05 level
Average	91 (112)	325 (310)	119 (112)	535	
Low	39 (32)	86 (89)	28 (32)	153	
Total	**181**	**500**	**181**	**862**	

Note: Figures in Parentheses indicate expected frequencies.

It can be observed from Table 28.7 that the calculated χ^2 value of independence test is 14.54 which is greater than Table value (9.48) at .05 level of significance with df: 4. The observed value is significant hence the null hypothesis that students' achievement in Hindi is independent from gents teachers' general teaching competency is rejected at .05 level.

It can be said that students' achievement level in Hindi is associated with gents teachers' general teaching competency in Hindi.

Association between Lady Teachers' General Teaching Competency and Students' Achievement Level in Hindi

Table 28.8: χ^2 Value of Test of Independence between lady teachers' general teaching competency and students' achievement in Hindi

Students' Achievement	**Lady Teachers' General Teaching Competency**				
	High	**Average**	**Low**	**Total**	**χ^2 Value**
High	25 (17)	91 (100)	35 (35)	151	7.54 Not significant at .05 level
Average	50 (53)	321 (316)	108 (110)	479	
Low	10 (16)	97 (94)	35 (33)	142	
Total	**85**	**509**	**178**	**772**	

Note: Figures in Parentheses indicate expected frequencies.

It can be observed from Table 28.8 that the calculated χ^2 value of independence test is 7.54 which is less than Table value (9.48) at .05 level of significance with df: 4. The observed value is non-significant hence the null hypothesis that students' achievement in Hindi is independent of lady teachers' general teaching competency is not rejected at .05 level.

It can be said that students' achievement level in Hindi is independent of lady teachers' general teaching competency in Hindi.

Association between Less Experienced Teachers' General Teaching Competency and Students' Achievement Level in Hindi

Table 28.9: χ^2 Value of Test of Independence between general teaching competency of less experienced teachers' and students' achievement in Hindi

Students' Achievement	Less Experienced Teachers' General Teaching Competency				
	High	**Average**	**Low**	**Total**	**χ^2 Value**
High	22 (25)	73 (69)	30 (30)	125	4.21 Not significant at .05 level
Average	90 (85)	234 (232)	95 (102)	419	
Low	22 (23)	56 (62)	35 (28)	113	
Total	**134**	**363**	**160**	**657**	

Note: Figures in Parentheses indicate expected frequencies.

It can be observed from Table 28.9 that the calculated χ^2 value of independence test is 4.21 which is less than Table value (9.48) at .05 level of significance with df: 4. The observed value is non-significant hence the null hypothesis that students' achievement in Hindi is independent of general teaching competency of less experienced teachers is not rejected at .05 level.

It can be said that students' achievement level in Hindi is independent of general teaching competency of less experienced teachers.

Association between More Experienced Teachers' General Teaching Competency and Students' Achievement Level in Hindi

It can be observed from Table 28.10 that the calculated χ^2 value of independence test is 11.27 which is greater than Table value

(9.48) at .05 level of significance with df: 4. The observed value is significant hence the null hypothesis that students' achievement in Hindi is independent of general teaching competency of more experienced teachers is rejected at 0.05 level.

It can be said that students' achievement level in Hindi is associated with general teaching competency of more experienced teachers.

Table 28.10: χ^2 Value of Test of Independence between general teaching competency of more experienced teachers' and students' achievement in Hindi

Students' Achievement	More Experienced Teachers' General Teaching Competency				
	High	**Average**	**Low**	**Total**	**χ^2 Value**
High	17 (28)	111 (107)	40 (33)	168	11.27 Not significant at .05 level
Average	118 (101)	369 (381)	112 (117)	599	
Low	23 (28)	114 (107)	31 (33)	168	
Total	**158**	**594**	**183**	**935**	

Note: Figures in Parentheses indicate expected frequencies.

Main Findings

- The students' achievement level in Hindi is associated with teachers' content competency in Hindi.
- The students' achievement level in Hindi is associated with gents teachers' content competency in Hindi.
- The students' achievement level in Hindi is associated with lady teachers' content competency in Hindi.
- The students' achievement level in Hindi is independent of less experienced teachers' content competency in Hindi.
- The students' achievement level in Hindi is independent of content competency of more experienced Teachers.

- The student's achievement level in Hindi is associated with teachers' general teaching competency in Hindi.
- The students' achievement level in Hindi is associated with gents teachers' general teaching competency in Hindi.
- The students' achievement level in Hindi is independent of lady teachers' general teaching competency in Hindi.
- The students' achievement level in Hindi is independent of general teaching competency of less experienced teachers.
- Students' achievement level in Hindi is associated with general teaching competency of more experienced teachers.

Discussion

The findings indicate that students' achievement level in Hindi is significantly associated with teachers' content competency in Hindi subject. It leads to conclusion that students' achievement in Hindi subject is influenced by the content competency of their teachers at primary stage. For better achievement and performance in Hindi subject students depend on their teachers. In most of our primary schools teaching is still teacher centred shifting the focus towards student centred approach requires upgradation of content knowledge of in-service teachers.

The students of government schools do not get much academic help at home. Content knowledge of teachers needs to be updated by means of regular in-service training for expected learning outcome of school children. Teacher development programmes must ensure that every teacher gets motivation and receives proper orientation in content areas of school subjects for better learning. In the context of present study, subject knowledge must be upgraded among primary teachers along with their skills of reading, writing, speaking, listening, thinking, working and understanding.

The course content has been changed in the new books according to New Curriculum Framework-2005. Hence, the teachers need upgradation of content knowledge according to modified curriculum that gives importance to critical thinking and new ideas of students. Teachers can find scope for extra activities related to subject when they are having a sound knowledge of content. During in-service training programmes, care should be taken for making child centred lesson plans and its practice by teachers on difficult content areas and emerging pedagogies at the primary level for their professional development.

Association between Students' Achievement in Hindi and Teachers' General Teaching Competency in Hindi

The students' achievement level in Hindi is significantly associated with teachers' general teaching competency in Hindi. It leads to conclusion that students' performance in Hindi subject might be influenced by the general teaching competency of Hindi teachers.

The classroom observation reveals that still the traditional methods like textbook method and rote memory have dominated the classroom practices. The teachers choose the methods of teaching by which they can complete the course. Innovative methods of teaching-learning are not used by the teachers. This may be due to lack of motivation of teachers to adopt innovative teaching-learning practices.

The inadequate duration of training of teacher education courses, lack of competent faculty in education colleges, large scale deficiencies of resources and infrastructures of different kinds, advancement and change in curriculum for which teachers have not received training but is essential for performing their tasks are the major reasons which calls for proper training of teachers. The teachers' guide should be used by teachers to reinforce their knowledge.

This is hightime that in-service teachers should be motivated to initiate innovative practices in the class focusing child centred approach and joyful activities. During in-service programmes emphasis should be given on practical activities like group work, demonstration lessons, observation lessons and field studies. The instructional practices at primary stage require an urgent shift from teacher oriented activities towards student centred activities as per National Curriculum Framework.

On the basis of above discussion, it may be concluded that the most important aspect needed to be addressed in professional development of teachers is tanning up content competencies through training and improved teaching/learning materials. A good teacher is well informed not ignorant. Teachers should have a rich, extensive and available field of perceptions about the subject matter for which they are responsible. In this context, ample scope should be provided for in-service education of every teacher for their professional development. Appropriate training provisions should be available for training of teachers at Block Resource Centres (BRCs), Cluster Resource Centres (CRCs) and at school level.

Suggestions

- The in-service training programmes for teachers should take care of content to be taught by the teachers in the class. Mostly training programmes focus on how to teach but very few of them tell what to teach.
- The in-service education programmes should deal adequately with the deficiencies in the academic and professional background of teachers. The nature of knowledge in each subject is quite distinct and this demands for subject specific training of teachers in each subject. Teachers teaching Hindi also need special assistance for understanding the basics of Hindi teaching, in order to improve students' performance.
- The content or subject matter in a subject is very crucial as the instructional interactions are carried out using it. Hindi is perceived as a very easy subject by most teachers in UP, so they think that anyone can teach it. Teachers need training for systematic teaching of Hindi as language.
- Content or subject matter is knowledge in a subject or discipline and so, it is abstract. Teachers should be told about proper and sequential organization of syllabus and they should practice it in training programmes.

- The role of various components of Hindi subject—stories, poems, biographies, comprehension and grammar should be made clear to teachers for better subject teaching according to students' need.
- The factual information in Hindi discipline needs to be organized for students in such a way that they show some relevance to daily life or create enthusiasm and curiosity, challenge the intellect and compel learners to seek to understand them completely. Teachers need proper orientation for this competence.
- Teacher's deficiency in the mastery of different school subjects can be identified through using Achievement Tests. After identifying teachers' deficiencies in content areas suitable training inputs can be designed to enrich and update their content knowledge.
- New textbooks should be written for teachers with an approach to provide content knowledge for primary level.
- The focus of textbooks should be based on providing content knowledge that enables student teachers to proceed to follow constructivist approach.
- In pre-service training, the lesson plans should be based on the constructivist approach so that pupil teachers may practice it during their internship.
- Required resources and infrastructure should be made available for proper training.
- Proper monitoring should be done for ensuring that there is no misalignment between teachers, students, school administration and parents.

REFERENCES

Annual Status of Education Report (2018). website:www.asercentre.org/keywords/p/346.html

Annual Status of Education Report (2019). website:www.asercentre.org//p/359.html

Bhat, V.D. (1998). *Identification of Essential Competencies for Primary Teachers.* RIE, Mysore.

Das, R.C. (1999). *Quality Concerns in Elementary Teacher Education*, New Delhi: NCTE.

Griffin, P. (2008). "Linking Pupil and Teacher Competence in Reading and Mathematics in Vietnam". *Educational Research for Policy and Practice*, 7(1), Heidelberg, Germany Springer.

Gupta, K.M. (1996). "Teachers' Performance in Mathematics and Reading Test". *Indian Educational Review. 31*(1) 92-104.

Gupta, R. (2013). A Study of Students Learning Achievement at Primary School Stage in the Context of Subject Specific Teaching Competency and Work Motivation of Teachers. Unpublished Ph.D. thesis, University of Allahabad, Allahabad.

Houstan, W.R. (1987). "Competency based Teacher Education" in M.J. Dunkin (Ed.). *The International Encyclopedia of Teaching and Teachers Education*; Oxford: Pergamon Press Ltd.

Kundu, Ahmad and Das (1999). Impact of Innovative Teachers' Training, Teacher Competencies and Motivation on Attendance and Community–School Relationship. SIEMAT, Allahabad.

Loucks-Horsley, S., Hewson, P.W., Love, N. & Stiles, K.E. (1998). *Designing Professional Development for Teachers of Science and Mathematics.* Thousand Oaks, CA: Corwin.

Ma, L. (1999). *Knowing and Teaching Elementary Mathematics: Teachers' Understanding of Fundamental Mathematics in China and the United States.* Mahwah, NJ: Lawrence Erlbaum.

Madhusudan, J.V. and Yeli R.S. (2004). "Effect of Teacher Competency on Students Achievement at Minimum Levels of Learning". *Journal of All India Association for Educational Research, 16*(1&2).

NCERT (2005). *National Curriculum Framework.* New Delhi: NCERT.

NCTE (1998). *Competency Based and Commitment Oriented Teacher Education for Quality School Education*, Initiation Document, NCTE, New Delhi.

Padhi, J.S., Jadho, V.G. and Rath, K.B. (1998). "Enhancing Pupil Achievement", *The Primary Teacher, 23*(1):25-29.

Raj Rani and Pandey, S. (2000). "Hard Spots in Mathematics Teaching at Primary Level: Implications for Need based In-service Training". *Teacher Education, 34*(2), 1-15.

Rao, M.P. (2002). "Teacher Competencies and Learners' Achievement in Tribal Areas of Karnataka". *Indian Educational Review. 38*(2).

Remmers, H.H. & Gage, N.L. (1956). *Educational Measurement and Evaluation.* New York: Harper and Brothers Publishers.

Sahoo, P.K. and Das, B.C. (2010). "Priorities of Research in Teacher Management at Primary Stage". *Researches and Studies,* Vol. 61, University of Allahabad, Allahabad.

Sahoo, S.N. (2002). *Forecasting Need for in-Service Education of Primary School Teachers in the Tribal Districts of Orissa*: Ph.D. Unpublished Thesis, Kota Open University, Kota.

Sharma, N. (1997). *Evaluating Children in Primary Education.* New Delhi: Discovery Publishing House.

Srivatava, P. (2002). "A Study of Achievement in Mathematics and Teaching Learning Process of Class V Students". *The Primary Teacher, 27*(4), 64-70.

Smith, M.S. & O'Day, J. (1991). "Systemic School Reform". In S.H. Fuhrman & B. Malen (Eds.), *The Politics of Curriculum and Testing: The 1990 Yearbook of the Politics of Education Association* (pp. 233-267). Bristol, PA: Falmer Press.

UNESCO (2000a). The Dakar Framework for Action: Education for All- Meeting Our Collective Commitments. World Education Forum, Dakar.

UNESCO (2007) Global Monitoring Report 2008, Education for All by 2015: Will we make it? Paris: UNESCO/Oxford University Press.

Yadav, M.S. and Nikalje, V.M. (2006). "Knowledge Dimensions in Teacher Education". *Journal of Indian Education, 32*(2).

29

Accountability of Pre-Service Teacher Education Programme

Usha Mishra and *Prerna Mandhyan*

Pre-service teacher education programmes are considered as a part of the process of making a quality teacher. From here, the accountability of this programme starts that output of this process should be qualitative. Mostly quality of teachers is evaluated by outcomes of the students that are quantitative in nature based on standardized scores. The study is focused on the accountability of pre-service teacher education programme. Defining briefly accountability in terms of specifically teacher education programme. This chapter will lead to the perception of teachers' quality. Evaluation of teachers will be discussed further.

This study examines the ways in which teacher qualifications and other school inputs are related to student achievement. The present chapter highlights the limitations of using performance indicators based on test or examination scores as accountability measures at the school- and system-level, or indeed, as measures of student learning outcomes.

Teachers make a difference. Indeed, of all the factors that education leaders can control, the quality of teaching has perhaps the greatest potential effect. Policy has begun to reflect this perspective, most prominently in the provision of the Right to Education Act of 2009 (RTE) that requires that all public school teachers in core academic areas be highly qualified by 2012. Teacher qualifications and preparation are likely to remain in focus even as the policy environment for education reform shifts.

Few topics in education have captured as much attention from policymakers and practitioners as the connection between teaching quality and student achievement. The research has clearly shown that quality teaching matters to student learning. Teacher quality has been consistently identified as the most important school-based factor in student achievement, and teacher effects on student learning have been found to be cumulative and long-lasting.

One important purpose of research on teacher education programme is to provide an empirical basis for changes to policy and practice regarding the structure, content, and timing of teacher preparation, and many research methods can contribute to causal understanding. Causal understanding is built upon a body of research that usually begins with descriptive analysis and empirical efforts to identify correlations, and the development of competing theories of behaviour.

For many years, educators and researchers have debated which school variables influence student achievement. As policymakers become more involved in school reform, this question takes on new importance since their many initiatives rely on presumed relationships between various education-related factors and learning outcomes. Some research has suggested that "schools bring little influence to bear upon a child's achievement, that is independent of his background and general social context". Other evidence suggests that factors like class size, teacher qualification, school size, and other school variables may play an important role in what students learn.

While some evidences suggest that better qualified teachers may make a difference for student learning at the classroom, school, and district levels, there has been little inquiry into the effects on achievement that may be associated with large-scale policies and institutional practices that affect the overall level of teachers' knowledge and skills in a state or region.

Accountability: An Overview

Accountability—the mechanism by which institutions meet their obligation to report to others about how their resources have been used and to what effect—is a central concept in democratic societies (Trow, 1996). It can function through a variety of structures, including government regulation, private markets, and self-regulation (Trow, 1996).

The success of any plan for improving educational outcomes depends on the teachers who carry it out and thus on the abilities of those attracted to the field and their preparation. Accountability mechanisms are important tools for improving teacher education and could be an excellent ongoing source of the kind of information. Two types of accountability bear directly on teacher education, one related to programmes and one related to teachers:

1. The direct monitoring of teacher preparation programmes, by means of programme approval and accreditation, and
2. The monitoring of individual teachers, through certification and licensure.

States and professional accrediting bodies exert direct influence over the operations and content of teacher education programmes. Certification and licensure policies affect teachers directly, but they also affect preparation programmes, which have the goal of certifying their graduates in particular areas and preparing them for the tests that states requirement of prospective teachers.

Teachers' Quality

There is no firm consensus within the field as to exactly what constitutes high-quality teaching or a quality teacher. However, it will be useful to establish a working definition of teacher quality for the purposes of this chapter. The clearest and potentially most useful example identified in our review of the literature comes from the Centre for High Impact Philanthropy (Donarldson & Peske 2010: 7).

A quality teacher is one who has a positive effect on student learning and development through a combination of content mastery, command of a broad set of pedagogic skills, and communications/interpersonal skills. Quality teachers are life-long learners in their subject areas, teach with commitment, and are reflective upon their teaching practice. They transfer knowledge of their subject matter and the learning process through good communication, diagnostic skills, understanding of different learning styles and cultural influences, knowledge about child development, and the ability to marshal a broad array of techniques to meet student needs. They set high expectations and support students in achieving them. They establish an environment conducive to learning, and leverage available resources outside as well as inside the classroom.

Specifically, the early-childhood literature emphasizes: the importance of knowing how to best promote children's social and emotional needs, organize the learning environment for young children, help children make connections, and encourage language skills and higher order thinking. The assumption is that quality early-childhood teachers possess these abilities, which will translate into academic and developmental success in future schooling and life.

These definitions suggest that teaching quality in practice constitutes a set of actions and activities that improve student outcomes. In investigating the meaning of quality, the research literature has examined a wide range of student outcomes. Much of the recent work in the field has focused particularly on quantifiable indicators of educational performance such as student test scores. "Hard" performance measures of these kinds have the appeal of quantifying a key outcome of student learning in a relatively objective and standardized manner for large numbers of students and teachers. In fact, test scores and other quantitative measures are an essential foundation of the research programmes that have generated key insights regarding the importance of quality teaching and supported consensus that teaching has the largest in-school impact on student learning and school leadership exerts the next-largest influence. Ravitch and others believe that some findings from test-based research studies may be flawed and deserve further scrutiny. Researchers have also examined a variety of "softer" (i.e. less readily quantifiable) measures that capture the behavioural, social, and developmental impacts of teaching.

Despite those different approaches to the issue of teaching quality and a healthy level of debate within the field, an examination of the literature identifies three main approaches to defining teaching quality and the interplay between effective teaching and increased student learning:

- Research that focuses on teacher qualifications,
- Research on ways to influence the human capital pool, and
- Contextual factors that act as mediating influences.

Research on teacher qualifications includes attention to academic degrees, certification, coursework, teacher preparation programmes, and teacher test scores. A common thread in the following review is a focus on teacher qualifications as they relate to student achievement. The researcher draws heavily on several major syntheses to characterize major findings on the relationship between teacher qualifications and student performance, with an emphasis on standardized test scores.

Perhaps the most prominent conceptual framing that has been brought to bear on the issue of teaching quality in the past few years is that of human capital management. This term encompasses the larger set of human-resource management processes and professional-development practices that operate to recruit, develop, deploy, retain, and evaluate quality teachers. A human-capital perspective is primarily concerned with getting well-qualified teachers into the profession and enhancing their effectiveness (and that of the larger system) once they are in the classroom.

A wide array of cross-disciplinary research has explored the ways in which context, broadly understood, influences the effectiveness of teaching and learning, including connections between context and the impacts of reform and policy initiatives. This work has encompassed topics as varied as "sense making" or how teachers and students interpret and perceive reforms, family and societal influences, and working conditions.

Teacher Evaluation for the Purpose of Accountability

Teacher evaluation is often used both for the improvement of teaching and learning and for accountability purposes (Baratz-Snowden, 2009). Research suggests that the best school systems do not allow ineffective teachers to remain in the classroom for long (Gordon, Kane, and Staiger, 2006; Kane, Rockoff and Staiger, 2006). Hanushek (2009) estimates that eliminating the least effective 6 to 10 per cent of teachers would bring student achievement up significantly.

Traditional Teacher Evaluation

In most public schools, evaluation of provisional, non-tenured teachers occurs at least once a year, with tenured teachers generally evaluated less often.The most widely used form of teacher evaluation has traditionally been classroom observations that measure evident classroom processes, including specific teacher practices, interactions between teachers and students, or other holistic aspects of instruction (Goe, Bell, & Little, 2008). Sometimes, teachers and administrators conduct pre- and post-observation conferences, and teachers are often required to "sign off" on their evaluations (Donaldson, 2009; Donaldson & Peske, 2010). The majority of summative ratings on teacher evaluations are "satisfactory" or above (Donaldson & Peske, 2010) and teachers often find little value in the evaluation process (Baratz-Snowden, 2009; Duffett, Farkas, Rotherham, & Silva, 2008).

Some of the problems associated with these traditional evaluations include: poor evaluation instruments, little school district guidance on the substance of teacher evaluations, the lack of time for evaluators to conduct evaluations, the absence of high-quality feedback to teachers in the evaluation process, and few consequences (either positive or negative) attached to the evaluations (Donaldson, 2009; Donaldson & Peske, 2010). Further, because few teachers are identified as unsatisfactory or ineffective, it has been suggested that such evaluations are perfunctory in nature (Baratz-Snowden, 2009). Some researchers say that teacher evaluations often result in little instructional improvement and the continued employment of weak teachers (Donaldson & Peske, 2010).

Bonding Teacher Evaluation to Student Achievement

Partially, in response to the identified weaknesses of traditional measures of teacher evaluation, there has been growing interest in linking evaluations of teacher effectiveness directly to student learning, with "value-added" models among the most prominent examples of this trend. While the current discussion focuses on the use of value-added models for teacher evaluation, that type of analysis can also be applied to investigate any number of issues, including the effectiveness of particular interventions or programmes, trajectories of individual student learning, and patterns of school improvement.

Value-added approaches seek to quantify the contribution of specific teachers, schools, or programmes to student test performance while taking into account the differences in prior achievement and perhaps other measured characteristics that students bring with them to school. The promise of value-added models rests in their ability to directly link individual teachers to the performance of their own students. Compared with other methods, value-added analysis may come considerably closer to isolating the amount of growth in student learning attributable to a particular teacher. Accordingly, proponents of value-added approaches argue that because such methods are more objective and able to account for such non-school factors as poverty or family background, they represent a more appropriate basis for evaluating teacher performance.

However, significant questions remain as to how or whether value-added measures should be used for formal teacher evaluation. While recognizing potential value in using such methods for low-stakes purposes, researchers are typically more cautious about their application for high-stakes decisions, such as teacher dismissal. The practical challenges include the danger of using test scores as the sole measure of student performance, the lack of data for all teachers in all subjects, the need to consider the possible unintended consequences that might result from widespread use of value-added measures, the question of how to attribute improved student performance when multiple teachers are involved, and data quality issues. Critics also point out that value-added measures fail to identify specific teacher practices that lead to improved student achievement. Additionally, researchers have raised methodological questions about the instability of value-added measures over time whereby teacher effects fluctuate substantially from one year to the next, as well as potential biases that may be inherent to the models themselves (Ladd, 2008).

Multiple and Alternative Teacher Evaluation Criteria

A variety of efforts are underway to broaden the scope of teacher evaluation to include multiple measures of performance, so that determinations of teacher effectiveness are not based narrowly on a single test score (Goe *et al.*, 2008). In addition to tested achievement, teacher evaluation criteria might include classroom artefacts' such as lesson plans or student work, documents on a range of teacher behaviours, or somewhat less tangible factors like teacher beliefs and expectations. These criteria can be measured using such tools as standardized classroom observation tools, protocols for the analysis of classroom artefacts, student ratings of teachers, self-reports from teachers, peer reviews, or teacher portfolios. Among these techniques, researchers are paying increasing attention to standardized classroom observation tools.

Through the Classroom Assessment Scoring System (CLASS), the early-childhood community is able to employ several measures to assess teacher quality. CLASS examines three domains in which teachers interact with children: emotional supports, classroom organization, and instructional supports. Evaluating teachers on all aspects of their interactions gives a stronger picture of the contributions teachers make to the child's educational experiences.

To sum up, the researcher can say the teacher education programme poses particular conceptual and empirical challenges:

- There are no well-formed theories that link teacher preparation to student outcomes.
- The complex nature of schooling children makes it difficult to identify empirically the role of teacher preparation among the many intertwined influences on student outcomes.
- The use of strict experimental design principles can be problematic in some educational settings. Teacher candidates are sorted into teacher preparation programmes in non-random ways, just as beginning teachers are no randomly sorted into schools and groups of students: consequently, it is difficult to control for all the important factors that are likely to influence student outcomes.

Improving learning outcomes for children is a complex process. Both common sense and sophisticated research (e.g. Sanders and Rivers, 1996; Aaronson, Barrow, and Sander, 2003; Rockoff, 2004; Rivkin, Hanushek, and Kain, 2005; Kane, Rockoff, and Staiger, 2006) indicate that teachers have enormously important effects on children's learning and that the quality of teaching explains a meaningful proportion of the variation in achievement among children. However, understanding that teachers are important to student outcomes and understanding how and why teachers influence outcomes are very different; our charge required us to think carefully about the evidence of the effects of teacher preparation. Student learning is affected by numerous factors besides teaching, many of which are beyond the control of the educational system. Even the factors that are affected by education policy involve intricate interactions among teachers, administrators, students, and their peers.

Teacher candidates bring certain abilities, knowledge, and experiences with them as they enter teacher education programmes. The candidates then experience a variety of learning opportunities as part of their teacher education. After completing their training, candidates who pursue teaching likely enter classrooms that vary greatly within and across schools on a variety of dimensions, including the characteristics of students, the curriculum, the school climate, and the neighbourhood climate. Each source of variation affects individual student achievement: taken together, they complicate the search for the empirical relationship between teacher education and student outcomes.

Recommendations Based on Empirical Evidence

It is clear from our review of accountability in teacher education programme that the existing evidence does not support a strong conclusion about the effectiveness of the current accountability process in teacher education. Thus, there would be significant value in investment in research and development to improve the research base and technical infrastructure for teacher education accountability. In addition, although empirical links between teacher preparation and student learning have not been established, current accountability mechanisms could likely use information that is available. Specifically, accountability systems could better integrate in their evaluations indirect evidence, such as consensus about the intellectual foundations and priorities in academic fields and findings about promising instructional approaches.

As part of the broader research agenda on teacher education, the researcher recommend research on developing valid means of establishing links between teachers' preparation and outcomes for students that could be used in accountability policies for teacher education programmes.

The evaluation should focus specifically on evidence of learning and effects on outcomes. On the first point, the recommended evaluation should focus on the nature and rigour of the evidence base used to inform approval and accreditation standards and processes. The evaluation should also include an assessment of the near- and long-term effects of these mechanisms on key processes and, especially, K-12 student outcome measures. On the second point, the evaluation should assess the extent to which the information gathered in accreditation reviews serves as a force for ongoing improvement at the programme level and whether and how it could contribute to a broader knowledge base about teacher education programme.

Both further research and an evaluation of existing accountability mechanisms are critical. All teacher education programmes should be able to demonstrate that their graduates can teach in ways that have been shown empirically to lead to gains in K-12 student learning. As research strengthens the knowledge base that can be used for accountability purposes, it will be possible to better examine many questions. In particular, as stronger indicators are developed, states and independent associations that are involved in teacher education programme approval and accreditation will be able to use them as a basis for their accreditation standards and reviews.

Finally, we suggest that accountability ought to focus on assessments that show programme graduates can practice effectively. Workforce trends across sectors reflect heightened demand for workers at all levels who can demonstrate their knowledge and skill; high-stakes teacher certification tests are an example of this phenomenon in the teacher labour market. But passing a paper-and-pencil test is different from demonstrating effective teaching practices, and a few states are developing performance assessments that are or will be part of their teacher certification requirements.

Most relevant for our purposes, however, is the observation that, despite changes in the rhetoric, teacher education programme accountability is still overly dependent on input and process requirements. Many states continue to require programmes to offer particular courses, set minimum admissions standards, ensure minimum contact hours with faculty and student teacher supervisors, and the like. The national accrediting bodies have made progress towards implementing outcome-oriented standards, but much remains to be done. The researcher envisions an accountability system that is based primarily on the evaluation of programme graduates' ability to use instructional practices that facilitate K-12 student learning in core subjects. Although such an approach is likely to be more difficult and expensive than the current one, it is a fundamental need if teacher education is to reflect the ultimate outcome, student learning.

More systematic information about the development and content of tests used for teacher accreditation or certification is needed. Accountability is a complex component of the education system and one that provokes strong opinions. Questions about the quality of the nation's teachers go to the heart of many contentious issues in education policy. For example, discussion of licensure, certification, and accreditation naturally suggests comparisons with other fields in which these issues arise, such as medicine, law, accounting, and various technical occupations. This comparison in turn raises questions about the status of teaching as a field. Whatever the answer to that question, it seems reasonable to ask that teacher candidates and teacher preparation programmes be held to high standards and that the accountability system used be both professionally responsible and publicly credible.

The existing research base on the link between teacher education programme characteristics and student outcomes suggests several steps that Government can take to ensure high quality teacher education programme that translates into effective teaching and, in turn, more positive gains in student achievement. Here, the researcher draws on this evidentiary base to outline a few recommendations:

1. All teacher preparation programme components should be grounded in teaching practice. The evidentiary base

strongly supports the idea that pre-service teachers gain substantially from more frequent and higher quality opportunities to gain hands on experience, explore teaching methods, practice with curricula, and encounter situations and challenges they are likely to confront after the preparation programme has ended. Preparation programme coursework requirements likely can be streamlined in some areas (e.g. foundations courses) to make room for more practical courses and experiences.

2. Students need high quality field experiences. This point is related to the first. Most programmes feature field experience requirements; what separates them is how those field experiences are structured to maximize what pre-service teachers can learn from them. The field experience should have explicit goals that are linked closely to teacher practice. Cooperating teachers should be selected carefully. The preparation programme should monitor the experience closely, with frequent contact with the student and cooperating teacher.
3. Teacher content knowledge should be emphasized in mathematics and science but perhaps not in other subjects. There is good evidence that teachers of mathematics and science perform better with more extensive grounding in those subjects. However, it may be preferable to substitute mathematics and science courses with mathematics and science education courses that both teach content and emphasize the link to teaching strategies. Moreover, there is no good evidence of a content knowledge effect in less technical subjects (e.g. social studies). It is likely that course work devoted to teaching practice or pedagogy would be a more productive use of student time, if the goal is improving student achievement.
4. Pedagogy matters, but how students learn it is as important as what is taught. Pedagogy should be tied to the content area the teacher will be teaching in the future, and should

be grounded in actual classroom skills. Students should acquire hands-on experience with pedagogical techniques, through field experiences, a capstone, or practice in the classroom. Again close and explicit ties to the actual practice of teaching appear to make pedagogical course work substantially more effective.

5. Teacher education programmes should be judged by their outputs rather than their inputs. In the era of accountability, education has begun to move beyond being satisfied with the counting of inputs: dollars, certified teachers, curricular programmes, and the like. A premium now is placed on outputs, primarily student learning. A similar principle can guide standards for teacher preparation. Studies suggest that there is great variation in programme structures and programme offerings, even within the same state. We know too little about how preparation programmes should be structured to impose standards for inputs or offerings beyond some minimum. Instead, we likely can benefit from encouraging experimentation and innovation in preparation programme structure and curriculum in both traditional and alternative routes but holding programmes accountable for the quality of the teachers they produce.
6. Alternative certification programmes should also focus on employing strategies identified here as linked to student achievement. Most of the recommendations made here can be and are incorporated by alternative route programmes. In fact, several studies reviewed here incorporate alternatively certified teachers explicitly into their research on preparation programme effectiveness (Boyd *et al.*, 2009). Several of the features of strong programmes, such as the focus on hands on experience, are already at the centre of many alternative certification programmes. As alternatively prepared teachers grow in number, it will become even more important for them to focus on preparation strategies linked specifically to student achievement.

The quality of the nation's teachers has been the subject of sharp critiques, and so have many teacher education programmes. Yet, teacher education programme is often treated as an afterthought in discussions of improving the public education system. Federal and state policy-makers need reliable, outcomes-based information to make sound decisions, and teacher educators need to know how best to contribute to the development of effective teachers. Clearer understanding of the content and character of effective teacher preparation is critical to improving it and to ensuring that the same critiques and questions are not being repeated 10 years from now.

REFERENCES

Aaronson, D., Barrow, L. and Sander, W.L. (2003). *Teachers and Student Achievement in the Chicago Public High Schools*. (WP 2002-28). Research Department, Federal Reserve Bank of Chicago.

Accountability Initiative (2012). *PAISA Report*. New Delhi: Centre for Policy Research.

Boyd, D., Grossman, P., Lankford, H., Loeb, S. and Wyckoff, J. (2005). "How Changes in Entry Requirements Alter the Teacher Workforce and Affect Student Achievement". *Education Finance and Policy, 2*: 176-216.

Boyd, D., Grossman, P., Lankford, H., Loeb, S. and Wyckoff, J. (2009). *Teacher Preparation and Student Achievement*. http://www.teacherpolicyresearch.org/portals/1/pdfs/EEPA TeacherPrepVA.pdf

Cochran-Smith, M. and Fries, K. (2005). "Researching Teacher Education in Changing Times: Paradigms and Politics". In M. Cochran-Smith and K. Zeichner (Eds.), *Studying Teacher Education: The Report of the AERA Panel on Research and Teacher Education*. Mahwah, NJ: Lawrence Erlbaum Associates.

Darling-Hammond, L. and Bransford, J. (2005). *Preparing Teachers for a Changing World: What Teachers should Learn and be Able to do*. San Francisco, CA: Jossey-Bass.

Donaldson, L. Morgaen. (2009). "Principals' Approaches to Cultivating Teacher Effectiveness: Constraints and Opportunities in Hiring, Assigning, Evaluationg, and Developing of Teachers". *Educational Administration Quarterly*. Vol. 49, Issue 5. pp. 838-82.

Donaldson, L. Morgaen and Peske, G. Heather (2010). *Supporting Effective Teaching Through Teacher Evaluation*. Centre for American Progress.

Douglas O. Staiger, Robert Gordon and Thomas J. Kane. (2006). *Identifying Effective Teachers Using Performance on the Job*. The Hamilton Project, The Brookings Institution.

Duraisamy, P. (2002). "Changes in Return to Education in India, 1983-94: By Gender, Age-cohort and Location." *Economics of Education Review*, No. *21*: 609-22.

Duffet, A., Farkas, S., Rotherthan, J. Andrew and Silva, E. (2008). *Waiting to be Won Over: Teachers Speak on the Profession, Unions, and Reform.*

Goe *et al.* (2008). *Teacher Quality and Student Achievement: Making the most of Recent Research*. TQ Research & Policy. National Comprehensive Centre for Teacher Quality.

Geo, Laura; Bell, Courtney; Little, Olivia (2008). *Approaches to Evaluating Teacher Effectiveness: A Research Synthesis*. ERIC. https://eric.ed.gov

Hanushek, E.A., & Rivkin, S. (2007). "Pay, Working Conditions and Teaching Quality". *The Future of Children, 17* (1), 69-86. http://www.futureofchildren.org/usr_doc/7_04.pdf

Hanushek, Eric and Steve Rivkin (2006). "Teacher Quality", In *Handbook of the Economics of Education*, edited by Eric Hanushek and Finis Welch. North. Holland.

Harris, D.N. & Sass, T.R. (2007). Teacher Training, Teacher Quality, and Student Achievement (Working Paper No. 3). Washington, DC: National Centre for Analysis of Longitudinal Data in Education Research. http://www.caldercenter.org/PDF/1001059_Teacher_Training.pdf

Ladd, F. Helen. (2008). Returns to Teacher Experience: Student Achievement and Motivation in Middle School. CALDER Working Paper No. 112.

Muralidharan, Karthik, and Venkatesh Sundararaman (2011). "Teacher Performance Pay: Experimental Evidence from India." *Journal of Political Economy*, No. *119* (1): 39-77.

Podgursky, M., Monroe, R. & Watson, D. (2004). "The academic quality of public school teachers: An analysis of entry and exit behaviour." *Economics of Education Review*, *23*, 507-18.

Pratham (2012). *Annual Status of Education Report.*

Preparing Teachers Building Evidence for Sound Policy. http://www.nap.edu/catalog.php?record_id=12882

Rivkin, Steven G., Erics A. Hanushek and John F. Kain. 2005. "Teachers, Schools, and Academic Achievement." *Econometrica*, No. *73* (2): 417-58.

Rockoff, Jonah E. 2004. "The Impact of Individual Teachers on Student Achievement: Evidence from Panel Data." *American Economic Review*, No. *94*(2): 247-52.

Sanders, W.L. & Rivers, J.C. (1996). *Cumulative and Residual Effects of Teachers on Future Students Academic Achievement*. Knoxville, YN: University of Tenessee Value-Added Research and Assessment Centre.

Snowden-Baratz, J., (2009). "Fixing Tenure—A Proposal for Assuring Teacher Effectiveness and Due Process". *Education,* K-12. www.americanprogress.org

Thomas, J.Kane, Jonah E. Rockoff and Douglas O. Staiger (December 2008). *Economics of Education Review*, Volume 27, Issue 6, pp. 615-631.

Trow, M. (1996). "Trust, markets and accountability in higher education: A comparative perspective". *Higher Education Policy, 4*: 309-24.

Urbanski, A. (1988). "Teacher Professionalism and Teacher Accountability Towards a More Genuine Teaching Profession." *Educational Policy, 12*(4), 449-57.

Wright, S. P., Horn, S.P. & Sanders, W.L. (1997). "Teachers and Classroom Context Effects on Student Achievement: Implications for Teacher Evaluation". *Journal of Personnel Evaluation in Education, 11*, 57-67.

30

Needs Analysis for Professional Development of Teacher Educators

P.K. Sahoo and *Brijesh Kumar*

Teacher educators' role is very much significant in development of professional competencies among teachers through pre-service and in-service teacher education programmes. Teacher educators are engaged in professional activities to enable student teachers and working teachers to learn professional knowledge, skills and attitude. In other words, the efficient teacher educators facilitate teacher learning effectively. Teacher educators are often held accountable for teacher quality. There is an urgency to pay attention to "the education of teacher educators or to local and larger policies that would support the development of teacher educators who are prepared to meet the complex demands of teaching teachers for the twenty-first century" (Smith Marily Cochran, 2020). Grundy and Stanley (1995) highlighting the professional support continuing experience education among teacher educators stated that teacher educators working in innovative education projects can develop "new ways of working, forge links with the teaching profession which will provide powerful opportunities for the development of teachers as learners and schools as learning communities." Adamson (2012) viewed the new role of teacher educators in development of (a) having knowledge of student teachers understanding specific concepts; (b) using such knowledge to design appropriate teaching materials; (c) making student teachers aware of their own views and uncertainties; (d) engaging student teachers to be confronted with different concepts, and (e) providing experiences to help student teachers to construct new meaning of experiences and arriving at conceptualisation.

Professional Development of Teacher Educators

Professional development of personnel in education system, especially teachers and teacher educators is a complex process. It is inclusive in nature. It involves collaboration among different continuous meaningful interaction among teachers and other community members. Professional development of teacher educators influences professional teachers. There may not be one structured model of professional development of teacher educators. There are conceptuality in the form of stages of teacher education, areas of specialisation, subject teaching competency orientation, institutional mission, socio-cultural conditions of the stakeholders, nature of school system etc. This has been stressed by that "schools and educators must evaluate their needs and cultural beliefs and practices to decide which professional development model may be most successful in that particular context." This was also highlighted that professional development has to be considered within a framework of social, economic, and political trends and events.

The teacher educators must focus on the needs of teacher and the priorities of school curriculum for which teacher education programmes take initiative in meeting such needs. Professional development of teacher educators and teachers need a broad and inclusive perspective keeping in view the focus of teacher development.

Areas teacher educators must update their knowledge and skills on following aspects:

- General Pedagogical knowledge covering understanding of learners, learning environment etc.
- Subject matter knowledge covering subject content and concerned discipline.
- Pedagogical content knowledge including knowledge of curriculum and curricular materials.
- Knowledge of students, context socio-cultural environment of school.
- Knowledge of mechanism to bridge theory and practice.
- Evaluation of learning outcome and clinical learning.
- Knowledge of strategies to create and sustain conducive learning environment.
- Multicultural perspectives of teacher preparation to deal with varied groups of school children, ethnic and language background.
- Knowledge and attitude to develop constitutional values among teachers on liberty, equality, fraternity and justice.
- Knowledge and skills on how to use technology covering various strategies and tools for professional development practices.

Teacher educators' education is considered education. So far Master of Education programme has been considered as basic requirement for development of professional skills and knowledge among teacher educators. Of late, NCTE (2014) expanded the scope of stage specific. M.Ed. programme for elementary stage teacher education and secondary stage teacher education respectively. However, in view of multiple role of teacher educators in teacher education and school education require continuous upgradation of their knowledge and skills from time to time.

The NCTE Curriculum Framework for teacher education (2009) insisted on "Comprehensive and enduring arrangement for the professional development of teacher educators." In-service education for teachers as well as teacher educators has been focused clearly in the context of shift in teachers role to: learner centric, flexible teaching-learning processes, learner agency, participation in learning, knowledge is constructed evolving, learning as a collaborative, social process, multidisciplinary, educational focus, assessment for learning, self-assessment to enhance motivation, through continuous non-threatening processes, to record progress over time (JV Commission Report, 2012). Various measures were projected for development of knowledge and research base among teacher educators. The NCTE subcommittee on teacher educators' education (2014) highlighted that the teacher educators need space and time to realistically understand the roles and functions expected of them in pre-service and in-service teacher education programmes. They must be exposed to varied experiences in such programmes and reflect on their role to make the programmes more effective and efficient.Their role in understanding policy perspectives, curriculum design, implementation of programmes, research based practices in teacher education and development of professional attitudes and values draw special attention of educationists.

In this regard Justice Verma Commission (2012) recommendation on faculty development for all the teacher educators is very much significant. He stated, "Faculty development programmes for teacher educators should be institutionalised." The draft National Education Policy (2019) highlighted professional development of education faculty of "The Department of Education at the respective universities must also offer continuing education programmes for the professional development (PD) of the faculty, education of teacher educators must focus on teaching methodology, classroom innovations and student motivation of textbooks and innovation of literature in different languages can be a part of (PD). Of late, there have been initiatives in organising PD of teacher educators at elementary stage and secondary stage through different organisations like CTE, IASE, SCERT, RIE and UGC HRDC such programmes can be of two types: Institution programme at the initial stage of job and refresher courses during the teaching career within a span of one to three years. Research experiences on PD of teacher educators has been in negligible state in the country.

One may witness researches on in-service education of teachers in the Indian context. However, one study on induction programme for teacher educators at elementary stage adds a new dimension to studies on technology intervention to teacher educators development by Bhat and Manjul (2009). They argued that limited efforts were made in the direction of improvement of professional capabilities of teacher educators in India. Hence, they conducted a study on development of an ICT platform to help DIET faculty to be effective resource person in teacher education. Professor Bhat developed entire web page. Different instructional inputs were uploaded to the page being linked with necessary reference materials, audio and video materials. The facilitation was made through email and on workplace. The participants' activities were found encouraging. They developed skills for making optimum use of training package for their professional development.

The present study has been conducted to explore the needs PD among elementary and secondary stage teacher educators in objectives. The objectives of the study was to assess the relevance of different areas of PD by the teacher educators and to study the highest need weightage of teacher educators on different areas of PD.

Methods and Procedure

The population of the study covered all the teacher educators of secondary education and elementary education teacher education institutions of Northern Zone of India: 900 teacher educators consisted of the sample (500 secondary and 400 elementary). A questionnaire consisted of 50 questions on six areas of PD, viz.:

1. Knowledge of Education Discipline.
2. Teacher Education Policy and Curriculum.
3. Teacher Learning Practices.
4. ET and ICT.
5. Research and Development.
6. Quality of Teacher Education.

Each area was also divided into sub-areas. In all, there were 17 sub-areas of needs for PD.

The respondents were to give response on relevance of each item for PD and their own need for PD in the concerned subarea. The responses were categorised taking into consideration mean value of responses subarea-wise under different components. Descriptive analysis procedure was adopted in the context of objectives of the study.

Analysis and Interpretation of Data

I. *Professional Development on Knowledge of Education Discipline*

Table 30.1: Priority Areas and most preferred Needs of Professional Development of Teacher Educators of Secondary Knowledge of Education Discipline and Perspectives and Elementary Programmes

Sl. No.	Component	Training Needs weightage in percentage B.Ed. D.El.Ed. TE TE N=500 N=400	Priority area (in %) Most Preferred (MPNW) B.Ed.TED. El.Ed. TE B.Ed. TE D.El.Ed.TE N=500 N=400 N=500 N=400	
1.	Discipline based knowledge on Education	52.00 58.15	97.40	95.25
2.	Theoretical understanding of New Paradigms of Teaching and Teacher Learning, Teacher Development	51.00 52.50	96.00	96.5
3.	Understanding of student teachers' personality, Teaching and professional ethics	53.00 54.50	97.00	95.5
4.	Understanding self- and Personality Development of Teacher Educators	52.00 53.75	96.20	96.25

Table 30.1 reveals that almost all the teacher educators (96 to 97%) respondents of B.Ed. as well as D.EI.Ed. programme considered this area as relevant for teacher educators professional development. Majority of elementary level teacher educators (52 to 55%) gave most preformed responses on their need for PD in this area comparatively similar number of secondary level teacher educators (51 to 53%) gave highest preference to the need for PD on following components:

- Discipline based knowledge on Education.
- Theoretical understanding of new paradigms of teaching, Teacher Learning and Teacher development.
- Understanding of student teachers personality, Teaching aptitude, expectations needs, attitude values and professional needs, attitude ethics.
- Understanding self- and Development of personality of teacher educators, their professional ethics and competencies.
- The data reveal meaningfulness of PD in this area for almost a major section of teacher educators of elementary level as well as secondary level TEP.

II. *Professional Development on Teacher Education Policy and Curriculum*

Table 30.2 indicates the relevance of PD on Teacher education policy and curriculum as perceived by a vast majority of teacher educators (95 to 98%) respondents from B.Ed. and D.EI.Ed. programme. It is worthwhile to note that majority of teacher educators from elementary level TEP (54 to 56%) gave highest preference to the need for PD in this area. Of course, comparatively lower number of teacher educators belonging to secondary level TEP (49 to 50%) gave highest need weightage on PD in different areas, such as:

Table 30.2: Priority Areas and most preferred Needs of PD of TEs of Secondary and Elementary level on Teacher Education Policy and curriculum

Sl. No.	**Component**	**Training Needs weightage in percentage B.Ed. D.EI.Ed.TE. TE N=500 N=400**	**Priority (in %) B.Ed.TED. EI.Ed.TEB.Ed. TE D.EI.Ed.TE N=500 N=400 N=500 N=400**	
1.	National and International efforts for transformation in school system and Teacher Education. Development curriculum of Teacher Educators	49.00 54.00	97.60	95.25
2.	Development of Teacher competencies means methods and approaches	49.00 54.75	98.00	96.50
3.	Understanding school curriculum, subject content pedagogy objectives	50.00 56.25	97.00	95.75

- National and International level for transformation in school system and Teacher Education, Development of Teacher Education curriculum and Role of Teacher Educators.
- Development of Teacher competencies means methods, models and approaches.
- Understanding school curriculum, subject context, objectives and pedagogy.
- This is significant to note that the elementary level teachers expressed comparatively higher need to PD in this area than that of their secondary level counterparts.

III. *Professional Development on Teacher Learning Practices*

This is the core component of Teacher Education Process. Perusal of Table 30.3 reveals that almost all teacher educators (96 to 98 %) with elementary and secondary teacher education background appreciated PD in this area of Teacher Education. This is noticed that a large majority of elementary stage teacher educators (55 to 57 %) gave highest need weightage on this area. Comparatively, a moderate percentage of Teacher educators from secondary stage TEP gave highest need weightage on different aspects of Teacher Learning process. They read as:

Table 30.3: Teacher Learning Practices

Sl. No.	Component	Training Needs weightage in percentage B.Ed. D.El.Ed. TE TE N=500 N=400		Priority in percentage B.Ed. TED.El.Ed.TE N=500 N=400	
1.	Teacher learning practices on competency of innovative teaching-learning	48.80	55.00	98.40	97.25
2.	School Internship: Management TEI school coordination Planning, Supervision of Interns learning practices	52.00	56.75	96.00	98.00
3.	Conducting field studies projects, Field Experiment and TEI School interaction	50.00	56.50	98.00	96.75
4.	Assessment and Evaluation of student teachers performance	52.20	57.00	97.00	98.00

- Competency of Innovative Teaching and Teacher Learning process.
- School Internship and Management.
- Conducting Field studies, project and field experiment.
- Assessment and evaluation of student teachers theory and practicum.

On this area of PD, the elementary level of teacher educators expressed higher need than that of their secondary level counterparts.

Table 30.4: Priority areas Professional Development on ET and ICT Theory and Practicum on Educational Technology (ET) and Information and Communication Technology (ICT)

Sl. No.	Component	Training Needs weightage in percentage B.Ed. D.El.Ed.TE TE N=500 N=400	Priority (in %) B.Ed.TED.El.Ed. TE N=500 N=400	
1.	Knowledge and skills of ET and ICT	57.50 50.00	96.40	97.25
2.	Design and Development of Teacher Learning Resources application of ICT in Teacher Learning. Application of ICT in Teacher Learning	51.40 56.00	96.00	94.75

It can be noticed from Table 30.4 that almost all teacher educators from elementary and secondary level TEP (95 to 98%) valued the significance of PD in this area. A large chunk of elementary (50 to 56%) level teacher educators as well as secondary level teacher educators (51 to 58%) gave highest preference to their need for PD on the following:

- Knowledge and skills of ET and ICT.
- Design and development of Teacher Learning resources and application of ICT in teacher learning.

Since, this is most relevant area of contemporary practices of teaching-learning, the expressions of teacher educators from elementary and secondary stages appear to be very close to each other.

Table 28.5: Research and Development

Sl. No.	Component	Training Needs weightage in percentage B.Ed. D.El.Ed. TE TE N=500 N=400	Priority in percentage B.Ed.TED. El.Ed.TE N=500 N=400	
1.	Research Methodology in Education Knowledge and skills	50.40 57.50	96.20	95.00
2.	Action Research Design for development of action Research for development of Institutional programmes and innovative Practices Application of ICT in Teacher Learning	49.60 56.00	97.00	95.50

It can be observed from Table 30.5 that a large majority of teacher educators (96 to 97%) irrespective of course background gave high priority to PD in the area of research and development. Of course, there was disciplinary response of teacher educators from B.Ed. and D.El.Ed. programme with regard to their need for PD. It was noticed that a large majority of elementary teacher educators (56 to 58%) gave highest weightage to their need for Research and Development related PD in comparison to their

B.Ed. counterparts. A moderate number of B.Ed. teacher educators (around 50 %) gave highest weightage to PD on:

- Research methodology in education.
- Action for institutional level Teacher educators are more keen to learn R&D in comparison to their B.Ed. counterparts. This may be due to Research degree as are of the desirable criteria for B.Ed. colleges recruitments they may not give more importance for in-service education teacher educators as well as secondary teacher educators are more prone towards professional development. Of course, the elementary teacher educators are more keen to join PD activities with regard to teacher education policy and curriculum, Teacher learning practices Research and Development and Quality of Teacher Education. This may be due to their multifarious role in pre-service as well as in-service teacher education of working teachers at elementary schools. The in-service programmes of teacher education has not been valued so much at secondary stage as it is in the case of elementary school teachers. This may be because of several major schemes adopted for promotion of elementary education as a matter of constitutional obligation. The elementary level teacher educators' keenness for their professional development is well appreciated.

The findings of the study have implications for teacher development programmes at higher education stage through UGC HRDC as well as through the scheme of PMMMNMTT teachers and Teaching. Especially, the missions intention to bridge the gap between teachers and teacher educators can be fulfilled through encouraging workplace based projects on PD of teacher educators working in elementary and secondary level teacher education institutions. Opportunities for blended learning in different areas of PD as highlighted above need to been encouraged through university teaching departments and research centres. Research based teaching-learning projects need to be in comparison to their elementary level counterparts.

Table 30.6: Quality of Teacher Education

Sl. No.	Component	Training Needs weightage in percentage B.Ed. D.EI.Ed.TE TE N=500 N=400	Priority in percentage B.Ed.TED. EI.Ed.TE N=500 N=400	
1.	Total Quality Management of Teacher Education teacher educators	50.40 56.75	96.20	95.00
2.	Futuristic Planning of Teacher Education and sustainable Development in Education Application of ICT in Teacher Learning	49.80 57.00	97.40	97.25
3.	Strategies of implementation of TEP and programme Evaluation	48.00 54.75	97.60	97.25

This can be observed from Table 30.6 that 96 to 98 per cent of teacher educators of elementary and secondary level teacher education agreed on the relevance of PD in Quality of Teacher Education. This is noticed that a larger number of teacher educators of D.EI.Ed. programme (55 to 57%) gave highest weightage of need to PD in this area. Comparatively lower percentage of B.Ed. programme teacher educators (48 to 50%) gave highest weightage to need to PD in the items:

- TQM in Teacher Education.
- Futuristic Planning in Teacher education.
- Strategies of implementation of TEP and programme evaluation.

This result also indicates elementary natures more favour to take part in PD in Quality issues of Teacher education than that of their secondary level counterparts.

Discussion

The findings of the study reveals that the teacher educators at elementary stage as well as at secondary stage recognised of the significance of PD in the context of their knowledge and attitude towards current developments in teacher education and necessary skills required for performing their role in teacher education institutions. Of course, a moderate (around 50-55%) size of teacher educators expressed highest need for PD in above stated areas. Teacher educators' role in enabling student teachers of pre-service programme for development of professional competencies is very much significant. In this regard, their knowledge and skills concerning different components of teacher development are to be updated from time to time. The need analysis on all the six areas of PD reveal that the elementary promoted through PD of teacher educators Research skills must be nurtured through its application in innovative teacher learning programmes undertaken at teacher education institutional level. Suitable integration of ICT based knowledge and skills with pedagogic knowledge and skills can lead to development of professional competencies of teachers through PD schemes. There have been continuous efforts to conduct in-service education programmes for DIET personnel in different aspects of PD through state level agencies. National level projects like IGNOU DPEP had sound effect on different states teachers and teacher educators. Such kind of technology integrated projects need to be expanded towards workplace based PD of elementary teacher educators. Similarly, the institutions like NIEPA and SIEMAT must focus on quality management training aspects of in-service teacher educators. The SCERTs at state level, organise capacity building programmes for teacher educators of DIETs. The RIEs involvement in massive orientation of working teachers on specific areas of teacher competencies are commendable. However, empowerment of teacher educators to facilitate in-service education of working teachers must be given top priority. The centralised structured programmes of in-service education should be transformed into workplace based continuous efforts for PD among teacher educators. Conceptuality is to be highlighted in meeting specific needs and problems of teacher educators in institutional environment. Alternative approaches may be adopted to encourage teacher educators' participation in resolving PD related issues through collaborations and sharing of experiences in teacher development practices.

REFERENCES

Bhat, V.D. and Manjula, R. (2009). Web based Induction programme for elementary teacher educators, in IGNOU, DPEP, (2009), New Delhi, Technology-Mediated learning for Professional Development at Elementary Education level.

Bob Adamson (2012). *Review, International Comparative Studies in Teaching and Teacher Education*, 28.

Glundy, S. and Gorden Stanley (1995). "Restructuring teacher education", *Australian Journal of Teacher Education*, Vol. 20, Issue 1.

Government of India, MHRD, New Delhi (2012). *Justice M. Verma Commission Report on Teacher Education.*

Marilyn Cochran-Smith M.C. Lexie Grudnoff, Lily Orland-Barak & Kari Smith (2020). "Educating Teacher Educators: International Perspectives". *The New Educator*, 16:1, 5-24, c DOI: 10.1080/1547688X 2019.1670309.

NCTE Guidelines (2014). In Government of India, New Delhi, *The Gazette of India*, Part II-Sec 4, 1st December 2014.

NCTE, New Delhi (2009). *National Curriculum Framework for Teacher Education.*

Inclusive Education and Professional Ethics of Teachers

Minakshi Biswal

The Upanishad declares, *Ekoham Bahusyam* (I am one, I became many), *Anuraniyom, Mahat mahiyan* (He is present in all, smallest particle to largest matter). From these two declarations, it is obvious that all are different forms of God. There is nothing in this universe except God. Thus, everyone has the right to get everything in general and education in particular. Education is the birthright of every child. No one can deny them from their birthrights. Inclusive education is the manifestation of education for all. Education for all in UNESCO document (2009) declares:

1. Expanding and improving comprehensive early childhood care and education, especially for the most vulnerable and disadvantaged children;
2. Ensuring that by 2015 all children, particularly girls, children in difficult circumstances and those belonging to ethnic minorities, have access to and complete, free and compulsory primary education of good quality;

3. Ensuring that the learning needs of all young people and adults are met through equitable access to appropriate learning and life-skills programmes;
4. Achieving a 50 per cent improvement in levels of adult literacy by 2015, especially for women, and equitable access to basic and continuing education for all adults;
5. Eliminating gender disparities in primary and secondary education by 2005, and achieving gender equality in education by 2015, with a focus on ensuring girls' full and equal access to and achievement in basic education of good quality; and
6. Improving all aspects of the quality of education, and ensuring excellence of all so that recognized and measurable learning outcomes are achieved by all, especially in literacy, numeracy and essential life skills.

The last decade has seen enormous changes in our public schools. One of the greatest changes is in the amount of diversity in the classroom. Teachers are being called upon to teach students with a wide range of abilities and needs. Perhaps the factor that has had the greatest impact on diversity is the movement towards the inclusion of students with disabilities in the general education classroom.

The UNESCO (2008) definition states that inclusive education is: "an ongoing process aimed at offering quality education for all while respecting diversity and the different needs and abilities, characteristics and learning expectations of the students and communities, eliminating all forms of discrimination" (p. 3). It is clear, then, that thinking has moved on beyond the narrow idea of inclusion as a means of understanding and overcoming a deficit and it is now widely accepted that it concerns issues of gender, ethnicity, class, social conditions, health and human rights encompassing universal involvement, access, participation and achievement (Ouane, 2008). Arnesen *et al.* (2009) note that "inclusion may be understood not just as adding on to existing structures, but as a process of transforming societies, communities and institutions such as schools to become diversity-sensitive" (p. 46). Inclusive education is educating All students in age-appropriate general education classes in their neighbourhood schools, with high quality instruction, interventions and supports so all students can be successful in the core curriculum. Inclusive schools have a collaborative and respectful school culture where students with disabilities are presumed to be competent, develop positive social relationships with peers, and are fully participating members of the school community. The UNESCO Policy Guidelines on Inclusion in Education (2009) set out Educational justification, Social justification, and Economic justification.

The results of research conducted by (Das, Kuyini, P. Desai, 2013) showed that nearly seventy per cent of the regular school teachers in Delhi had neither received any training in special education nor had experience teaching students with disabilities. It was even more troubling to see that nearly eighty seven per cent of the teachers did not have access to support services in their classrooms. It is, therefore, not surprising to see teachers rating themselves not competent in each of the ten competency categories. Research indicates that negative attitudes of teachers and their lack of skills impede the successful implementation of inclusive education programmes.

One of the greatest barriers to achieving this goal is the preparation teachers receive at the pre-service level. Several researchers (Pugach and Allen-Meares, 1985; Baker and Zigmond, 1990; Schumm and Vaughn, 1995; Giancreco, Dennis, Cloninger, Edelman, and Schattman, 1993) have noted the lack of professional training in inclusive techniques and practices for general and special education teachers. And Welch (1996) also discussed the differences in philosophies and theories between general and special education at the pre-service level. If teacher education programmes are to prepare educators to be successful in the classrooms of the future they must reconceptualize and redesign their approach to pre-service preparation of teachers.

Innovative Teacher Preparation Model

It is for sure that if quality education in inclusive education is the aim of this century then definitely innovative model for teacher training is essential.

The main aims of teacher training for inclusive education are:

- Improve pre- and in-service training, mentorship and team-building.
- Promote the use of new and alternative methods for teaching.
- Encourage teachers to organise their work in teams and to apply problem oriented teaching methods as well as paying respect to diversity and different learning styles among their pupils.
- Prepare teachers for child friendly school.
- Motivate to change their attitude.
- Train them to be teachable and accountable.
- Prepare multi-talented teacher.
- Inculcate sincerity in teachers.

To achieve these aims, the training model has to have:

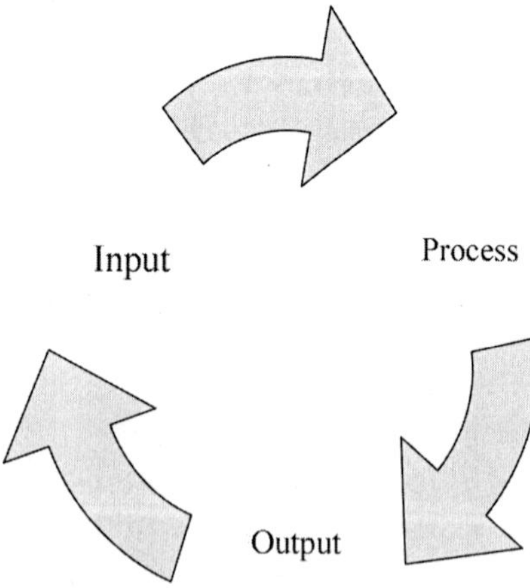

Input of the Model

The Input of this model consists of two elements. These are:

- Collaborative Teaching.
- Change of attitude.

Collaborative Teaching

Collaborative teaching integrates the strengths of multiple experts in a synthetic endeavour. It also provides an expanded number of teaching styles that may connect with more student learning preferences. At its best, collaborative teaching allows students and faculty to benefit from the healthy exchange of ideas in a setting defined by mutual respect and a shared interest in a topic. At its worst, collaborative teaching can create a fragmented or even hostile environment in which instructors undermine each other and compromise the academic ideal of a learning community and civil discourse. It includes:

- Co-teaching.
- Collaborative Planning.
- Cooperative Learning.
- Integrated Curriculum.
- Integrated Activities.
- Collaborative Evaluation.
- Group Process Skills.

These cater to the needs of Learners having different learning styles. Always two is better than one. Students get attached to different personalities. As they see two teachers planning together and working together, they also learn to be together and respect their teachers equally. This celebrates diversity, acknowledges individual differences, actively involves students in learning, and provides more opportunities for personal feedback.

Change of Attitude

This is the most important aspect of the teacher training. Through the entire process of teacher's training if there is no change in their attitude, then all the effort is useless. Thus, to change the attitude of the teachers, the following exercises should be taken into practice. These are:

- Positive mind programming.
- Positive self-talk.
- Reading of literature on human values.
- Taking up social service activities.
- Reflecting on the ultimate goal of life.

These activities definitely develop a positive attitude towards the disabled and disadvantaged group of the society. In turn, the teachers will develop the feeling of sympathy and empathy towards them and ultimately they will take it as a Divine and life changing work.

Process of the Model

The process includes:

- Techniques and Strategies.
- Innovative Teaching-Learning Methods which create multiple learning experiences.

Techniques and Strategies

The process to achieve the aim and attaining concept is known as technique and strategy. This looks into the preparation, transaction and evaluation of curriculum. As in-service teacher training is more tedious and expensive, so, pre-service teacher training should be enriched with:

- Accommodation.
- Curriculum.
- Activities.
- Evaluation.
- Effective Practices.

- Modifying Materials.
- Resources and Supports.
- Instructional Arrangements.

These elements enhance the software and hardware of the teacher-training programme. With this a concrete structure it is easy to train the progressive teachers to accommodate all varieties of students in their classroom. Theoretically they get well equipped.

Innovative Teaching-Learning Methods

The theory gets concretized when practiced. Various methods are:

- Role playing.
- Simulation.
- Field-based Experience.
- Inclusion model.
- Practicum.

These give proper practice for providing Multiple experiences. As students are from various societies and different mental make ups, they need varied range of learning experiences to attain concept.

Output of the Model

GIGO emphasized on the proper input and Systematic process. As the Input, and process, so, the Output. The outputs of this entire process are the teachers who are:

- Strongly committed to the purpose of Inclusive education.
- Sensitive to the needs of the students.
- Able to construct a welcoming and positive school climate.
- Recognize individual differences and implement learning strategies for all.
- Have team spirit, i.e. to promote collaborative learning.
- Have aptitude and attitude for research and action research.
- Multi-talented balancing of educational services, i.e. designing programmes for diverse needs.

- Be a good mentor.
- Having positive attitude towards life.
- Having Holistic Vision.
- Having Humanistic perspectives.

With this model, the teaching in Inclusive education becomes an enjoyment and worship rather than only discharging duty.

REFERENCES

UNESCO (1994). *The Salamanca Statement of Framework for Action on Special Needs Education.*

UNESCO (1999). *Reports on African Regional Experts Forum*, Dakar, Senegal.

Bess, James L. (2000). *Teaching Alone, Teaching Together: Transforming the Structure of Teams for Teaching.* San Francisco: Jossey-Bass.

Davis, James R. (1997). *Interdisciplinary Courses and Team Teaching. Phoenix: American Council on Education/Oryx Press Series on Higher Education.*

Das, Kuyini, Desai (2013). "Inclusive Education in India: Are the Teachers Prepared?", *International Journal of Special Education*, Vol. 28, No. 1.

Jerry, W. Whitworth, D. (Ed.) (1999). "A Model for Inclusive Teacher Preparation Electronic". *Journal for Inclusive Education*, Vol. 1, No. 2, Art. 3.

http://corescholar.libraries.wright.edu/ejie/vol1/iss2/3

SECTION-VI
QUALITY ASSURANCE IN TEACHER EDUCATION

32

Teacher Education Towards Excellence

M.S. Lalitha

Equality, quality, and quantity, the three interrelated terms have characterized a triangle of Indian education which has been an elusive concept. The term equality refers to the constitutional commitment of providing equal educational opportunities for all in access and quality education, irrespective of caste, creed, religion, and gender. The term quality refers to providing at least the minimum knowledge, understandings, and skills required for minimum quality life and to meet the challenges faced by the world. It goes without saying that any quantitative expansion endangers ensuring quality. The present context in school education can be understood in the light of meeting the challenges posed by the efforts made to integrate these three terms. The draft National Policy on Education, 2020 has visualized the above stand in mentioning that the policy statement is based on the foundational pillars—access, affordability, equity, quality, and accountability. In this context of education, the importance of teachers' role in preparing young people for successful, responsible, and productive lives is recognized unquestionably the world-over. There is growing evidence to support that effective teachers make powerful impact on students (Hattie, 2003). Further, there is a broad consensus that teacher quality is the single most in-school factor influencing student achievement (OECD, 2005).

Teacher education is considered as a pivotal sub-system of the education system. Teacher education for any level goes hand in hand with development of school education. In other words, a proper system of teacher education determines the quality of teachers, who, in turn, determine the quality of education at any level from pre-primary to higher education, including education of the special groups. In any country, teacher education programmes are designed to prepare effective teachers. Further, there is always a concomitant relationship between school education and teacher education in any country. In India, the undergraduate programmes in teacher education especially for secondary school teachers were conducted mostly in separate autonomous or affiliated colleges, although the faculty for teacher education have always been supplied by the university departments. This has led teacher education to remain as a separate entity away from university system for a long time until recently. Many universities across the country are involved in secondary teacher training programmes mainly as four-year integrated undergraduate teacher education programmes. However, teacher training institutes/District Institutes of Teacher Education are involved in elementary/pre-primary teacher education 0n the country.

Challenges from Changing Context in School Education

The quality of school education is closely associated with the quality of teacher education provided to teachers who form the backbone of school education. In the twenty first century, the school education in India has been facing many challenges which in turn have posed challenges to teacher education system in the country. They are briefly reviewed below.

Quantitative Expansion in School Education

The nation is committed to bring all school going children to schools or to alternative mode of education under the Right to Children to Free and Compulsory Education Act or Right to Education Act enacted by the Parliament of India on 4th August, 2009, which came into force on 1st April, 2010. The implementation of Right to Education in India has created new demands on the school systems for providing age specific and stage specific education by developing appropriate programmes. The nation is committed to bring all school going children to schools or to alternative mode of education which has led to expansion of schooling facilities. The expansion in school education has posed a demand for production of increased number of teachers who are competent and professionally qualified. To manage the expansion needed in school education as well as in higher education, it has become inevitable for the government to have a partnership with private sector. Thus, many private organisations have opened educational institutions including teacher education institutions, resulting in the increased financial burden for the beneficiaries, namely parents/students, thus creating a threat to the issue of equity in quality education. This issue of affordability of quality education by all may further be threatened by allowing private sector partnership in education which, however, is inevitable. The government is making all out efforts to make quality education affordable by all irrespective of the socio-cultural background of the beneficiaries through many initiatives. For example, the nationwide programmes like, Sarva Shiksha Abhiyan (SSA) and Rashtriya Madhyamik Shiksha Abhiyan (RMSA) are intended to improve standards of school education by strengthening both infrastructural and instructional facilities in schools mainly in terms of improving quality of teachers through a large number of in-service teacher education programmes.

Technological Advancements Affecting Content and Process of School Education

The education system in most of the countries in the world is in a state of flux because of rapid technological changes and open and competitive economies. This has posed new challenges to school education, and hence to teacher education. The technological developments have made a big dent in all walks of life, irrespective of socio-economic background of individuals in the society. These developments have impacted education system at all levels, pre-primary through higher secondary education. They have created new demands on school education calling for changes not only in the curriculum, but also in the teaching-learning processes. There has been a paradigm shift in the understanding of the learner, curriculum and its access, the teaching-learning processes and assessment of learning. This has created a demand on teachers to judiciously integrate technology in curriculum designing, curriculum transaction and evaluation keeping in view the contextual realities and without losing the advantages of what has stood the test of time. Hence, teacher education needs to respond aggressively to the changed demands on the types of teachers to be prepared. This further necessitates the needed changes in the content and processes of teacher education and in the roles of teacher educators themselves. The curriculum and structural revisions in school education and higher education envisaged in the New Policy on Education (NPE), 2020 appear to respond to the challenges posed by technological advancement on school education and hence, teacher education.

Changing Global Perspectives on Education

One of the most significant developments in the new millennium is the publication of the report of the International Education Commission on Education for the Twenty-First Century entitled 'Learning: The Treasure Within', prepared under the chairmanship of Jacques Dellor (UNESCO, 1996). The Commission has identified four pillars of Education and proposed the concept of learning society. They are—Learning to know, implying developing the skill of learning; Learning to do, implying skill of putting what is learnt into practice; Learning to be, meaning to develop one's total personality in all dimensions and be able to act with greater autonomy, judgement and personal responsibility; Learning to live together requiring developing a feeling of oneness and work towards the common goal of development of all. These pillars suggest the direction in which the school education in general and teacher education in particular require reformation in the new millennium. World over there is an emphasis on developing among learners twenty first century skills and competencies. They include proficiency in higher order thinking, critical thinking, creativity and innovation, entrepreneurship skills, problem solving abilities skills, cooperative and collaborative skills and technology skills and media literacy.

The students need to be prepared for a new knowledge society where information is easily accessible for which they need to acquire not only information accessing skills but also appropriate interpretative skills. In the knowledge-based society of the twenty first century, it is being realized that there is no rigid compartmentalization in different subjects of study. The students have more flexibility in the choice of the subjects of study and the learning of any particular subject is not within the boundary of that subject but rather is more interdisciplinary, trans-disciplinary and integrative in nature. The NPE 2020 has addressed to this issue in its policy statement.

This changed scenario in school education calls for new perspectives in content and process of school education. The new methods of teaching and learning need to be more reflective and facilitative in nature. They can include approaches like, self-learning, mutual learning (co-operative) and collaborative learning. The evaluative practices need to be more collaborative (involving student, peers, and teacher as well as community), continuous, comprehensive and self-reflective. The teacher not only facilitates learning of students instead of transmitting knowledge/ information, but also a co-learner with his students and sometimes learns from students.

The developing trends in social and political contexts as well as in technological advancements have led to a value crisis. The school education and in turn the teacher education need to address to this issue and focus on developing appropriate values among students. This has implications for content and processes both in school education as well as teacher education.

Teachers of today need to be equipped not only with the latest subject expertise and effective pedagogic practices but also with the capability to assist students to meet the challenges of the emerging knowledge-based society. Changes in the perspectives on school education pose concomitant demands on the needed changes in our perspectives about and practices in teacher education.

While taking quality of education to world standards, the New Education Policy 2020, proposes to allow selective foreign universities to enter India to start their own campuses. This, however, may pose challenges to teacher education programmes offered in different universities. This is because teacher education can no longer remain as a separate entity, rather it is going to get integrated with other degree programmes offered by the universities. This, however, may further threaten the issue of equity in quality higher education in general, and teacher education in particular.

Present Scenario in Teacher Education

The expansion in school enrolment both at primary and secondary school levels has led to a demand for teachers far exceeding supply there has been. This has led to the mushroom growth of teacher education institutions and unwieldy expansion in teacher education programmes especially with respect to elementary and secondary levels. There has been different types of programmes and alternative modes of training.

Greater participation of private sector and almost negligible involvement of public sector (Government) has led to uncontrolled expansion of the teacher education system. No assurance of providing for required infrastructural and instructional facilities and without the recruitment of qualified faculty in required numbers, can possibly lead to the dilution of quality of teacher education system.

The size of the intake has also got expanded with large number of teacher trainees are getting admitted to teacher education programmes with different types of background abilities, aptitudes, aspirations, and motivations. The demand for trained teachers and the belief that a training certificate ensures prospects of obtaining teacher's jobs has led to teacher education a lucrative business proposition. As a result, large number of teacher education institutions of poor quality has come up. This, in turn, appears to have posed a great challenge to institutions which monitor the quality of teacher education institutions. The increased demand for teachers and shortage in their supply has led to the concept of Para-teachers in many states. These are the unqualified teachers who are recruited in the formal school system, who in turn, are subsequently trained. This concept of Para-teachers questions the very concept of professionalism in teacher education. This concept of Para- teachers is antithetical to the issue of supply of qualified and committed teachers to offer quality education to students as envisaged in Right to Education Act as well as in the National Knowledge Commission (NKC, 2007). Quality concerns about the quality of teacher education are expressed by the National Curriculum Framework (NCF) 2005 prepared by the National Council of Educational Research and Training (NCERT) as below:

- The transaction of teacher education curriculum leads to inactive knowledge in student teachers which is accepted without question and reflection.
- There is no integration of disciplinary knowledge and training in pedagogy.
- There is no opportunity for teachers to reflect on their own knowledge in the light of what they learn in the classroom.
- There is no clear linkage between practical work and ground realities.
- The evaluation system is information oriented and quantitative and lacks comprehensiveness. There is no provision to evaluate the affective learning outcomes of student teachers.

One of the significant developments in teacher education, after National Policy on Education, 1986 and Programme of Action

(PoA) with its modifications in 1992, is the establishment of the National Council of Teacher Education (NCTE) in 1993 through Parliament Act No. 73 as a statutory authority. The NCTE has drafted norms and standards for various types of teacher education programmes—pre-primary, primary and secondary—both face to face and through distance mode, which were mandatorily expected in the institutions running the programmes for their recognition. Although they were comprehensively covering norms not only for the required infrastructural and instructional facilities, but also for content and processes expected in the programmes, the stress was mainly on the former. This was obviously observed at the time of granting recognition to the programmes, may be because of the ease in the assessment of infrastructural and instructional facilities which were quantitative in nature, unlike transaction processes which were more qualitative in nature. However, there have been several revisions in the norms and standards prescribed for various types of teacher education programmes, including various integrated teacher education programmes. As per the New Education Policy, 2020, it is intended to restructure NCTE as a professional standard setting body under the General Education Council. Further, they have been assigned the responsibility to develop National Professional Standards for Teachers aimed to be introduced by 2022.

The NCTE has come out with a document on National Curriculum Framework for Teacher Education (NCFTE) of 2009 keeping in mind the two significant developments particularly, the National Curriculum Framework, 2005 (NCERT, 2005) and the Right of Children to Free and Compulsory Education Act, 2009 under Article 21A of the Constitution of India as well as the fundamental tenets enshrined in the Constitution of India. However, based on the New Policy on Education, 2020, a new and comprehensive NCFTE, 2021 is proposed to be formulated by the NCTE in consultation with the NCERT. Accordingly, by 2030, the minimum degree qualification for teaching will be a 4-year integrated B.Ed. degree.

Total Quality Management: As an Approach to take Teacher Education towards Quality

Total Quality Management (TQM) is a systematic approach which utilizes four main elements: quality defined by the customer, top leadership responsibility for quality improvement, increased quality through systematic analysis of work processes, and quality improvement by continuous effort conducted throughout the organization (Gilbert, Keck, & Simpson, 2005). Lachlan & Crawford (1999) briefly review how TQM operates in the industrial context and clarify how the philosophy of TQM may be translated into the context of education. They examine one interpretation of TQM which aims at improving the quality of the production system in order to produce a quality product with "zero defects". This may imply a need to make teaching and learning process to focus exclusively on achieving good examination results. In contrast, in the second interpretation, TQM is considered as a continuous cycle of improvement in the system of production. In the context of education, this may mean a need to continually improve the quality of instruction so as to encourage students to become critical and creative thinkers in a fast-changing technological world.

The second interpretation of TQM appears to be more relevant in the context of education in general, and teacher education in particular, because of the dynamic nature of the system. Applying the concept of TQM to teacher education context, it is required to define the term 'quality', examine how effectively quality concerns are managed and addressed by top leadership and responsibility taken for ensuring them, assess the input and processes built into the teacher education system, and making efforts continuously throughout the system to improve the quality. In the context of education in general, and teacher education in particular, the term 'quality' has remained an elusive concept. The goals towards which we intend to move and the processes that we define to reach the goals get redefined/modified depending on changing contexts in society.

However, in any context of Teacher Education, the term 'quality' has to be made explicit in terms of criteria agreed upon by all the stakeholders, who internalize the same and work jointly in a collaborative manner to achieve the goals of teacher education, namely to produce competent, committed and effective professional teachers who are concerned, caring for their students facilitate the achievement of goals of the education system.

Quality Issues in Teacher Education

Teacher Education is a sub-system of education system at large. Hence, every activity in the sub-system of Teacher Education should lead to the achievement of its goals and thus leading to the achievement of the goals of the larger education system. The different issues related to the total quality management of teacher education can be examined under the following heads:

(a) Clarification of Objectives of Teacher Education.
(b) Management of Quality of Inputs—Teacher Trainees, Teachers, and Teacher Educators.
(c) Management of Content and Processes.
(d) Management of Continuing Professional Education.
(e) Monitoring and Quality Control.
(f) Upholding of Professionalism by Teachers.
(g) Management of Research Output Providing Empirical base for Activities in Teacher Education Programmes.

(a) *Clarification of Objectives of Teacher Education*

Some of the issues that can be addressed with respect to aims and objectives of teacher education programmes while ensuring their quality are given below:

(i) Identifying and ensuring clarity of objectives of teacher education programmes among stakeholders;
(ii) Identifying the knowledge, understanding and skill competencies, attitudes, interests, values, aptitude components that make teachers effective, efficient and

committed in the profession so that they can prepare young people for successful, responsible, and productive lives in the new millennium;

(iii) Building consensus among different monitoring organizations about the criteria for quality of teacher education in different dimensions and the factors that influence arriving of such consensus; and

(iv) Making teacher education curriculum competency-oriented.

In the context of teacher education, the term quality has to be made explicit in terms of criteria agreed upon by all the stakeholders who include regulating and monitoring organizations like the National Council for Teacher Education (NCTE), National Assessment and Accreditation Council (NAAC), and affiliating universities but also schools, head teachers, teachers, students, student teachers, the Government, and the community at large, who all should internalize the same and work jointly in a collaborative manner to achieve the goals of teacher education, namely to produce competent, committed and effective professional teachers who are concerned and caring for their students. Every activity in the teacher education programme should lead to the achievement of the goals.

Attempts have been made to make teacher education competency-based in the process of establishing its accountability by the NCTE (1998) and identifying teacher competencies (Lalitha, 1996). Such competencies can form the basis of teacher education. As per the National Education Policy, 2020, the professional standards to be achieved in Teacher Education are proposed to be listed by the NCTE in association with the NCERT. All these efforts can help in making teacher education Programmes more objective-based. However, expected outcomes of teacher education may include teachers/teacher trainees not only to acquire pedagogic understandings, but also pedagogic and techno-pedagogic skills, in addition to outcomes in the affective domain, like predispositions, values, and concerns. This requires the teacher trainees/teachers acquire the skills of reflection both 'in-action' and 'on-action' leading to acquiring ability to take appropriate instructional decisions on changing content, methods, and moods to facilitate student learning.

(b) *Management of Quality of Input*

Some of the major inputs for teacher education programmes include student teachers, working teachers and teacher educators.

(i) *Teacher Trainees*

The input to teacher education programmes refers to the teacher trainees who would be seeking enrolment for the same. The nature and background of the teacher trainees can influence the effectiveness of any teacher education programme. Such teacher trainees can be for regular pre-service teacher education programme or para teachers who are appointed as teachers and subsequently trained. The related quality issues that can be examined are listed below:

(i) The type of background, strengths and capabilities expected to be possessed by the students who are admitted to the teacher education programmes;
(ii) The different types of screening procedures that exist for admitting teacher trainees with required prerequisites;
(iii) The background characteristics—socio-psychological and pedagogic that para teachers possess; and
(iv) The extent to which the quality of inputs relate to the objectives of the teacher education programmes.

There are issues related to ground realities threatening to alter the norms imposed to ensure quality. Some of them are referred as below. There are two issues related to the criteria and processes of selection of teacher trainees for teacher education programmes and the nature of aspirants who would like to join teacher education programmes. The first issue is applicable only to the new entrants and not so much to the untrained teachers who are already employed as teachers requiring training through alternative modes. Although the NCTE has tried to fix the minimum eligibility criteria for admission into the teacher education programmes, there are forces especially from the private institutions trying to reduce/alter the criteria in order to fill in the sanctioned intake from financial returns point of view. Secondly, there is a great demand from graduates and post-graduates who have studied highly specialized subjects at their graduation level (which are not prescribed as school subjects) who would like to enter teacher education programmes, especially at secondary level not usually by choice, but, because they could not get the opportunities for jobs or for higher studies which they anticipated at the beginning of joining their graduation programmes. It may be noted here that sometimes the teacher recruitment norms may not match the criteria for admission related to the subjects studied at the time of entry into the teacher education programme. In some states, the recruitment rules for teacher's posts do not give much weightage to the performance of the teacher trainees at the end of teacher education programmes. However, the eligibility criteria for entry into the teacher education programme should keep in mind to what specific stage and to teach what specific subject, teacher education programme is being offered. What is more important is the eligibility criteria should raise to the level of attracting candidates who are professionally talented in terms of aptitudes and attitudes with a strong knowledge base in the content area. This, however, requires the status of teaching profession to raise to the levels of other important professions in the society, namely medicine, law, and engineering, which are attracting better talent. The other quality related issues that are posing a challenge are concerning content and processes of Teacher Education. The focus in any teacher preparation programme as different from other academic programmes is to educate the learners in content and pedagogy. However, in the twenty first century, the emphasis should be on shifting teacher preparation from pedagogical content knowledge to that of technological-pedagogical content knowledge. It needs to be examined as to what extent the new curriculum framework prepared by the NCTE in 2014 addresses to this issue. Another issue to be resolved is whether teacher preparation programmes be stage specific or subject specific or both, if so, at what stage they should be subject specific. Further, the issue to be examined is of medium of instruction in which the graduates are able to pursue teacher education programme, as this affects the leaning of teacher trainees while they pursue the teacher education programmes. This, in turn affects their use of good learning resources both in the library as well as on the internet, which is generally in English language.

(ii) *Teacher Educators*

The quality of teacher education programme is determined by the quality of teacher educators who have the responsibility to run the programme. The nature and background of the teacher educators can influence the effectiveness of any teacher education programme. The related issues that can be examined are as below:

(i) Identification of general attributes and qualifications required of teacher educators for different levels of teacher education; and
(ii) Analysis of relevance of qualifications of teacher educators for the job, at different levels of teacher education.

The NCTE has drafted new norms and standards for various teacher education programmes which came into effect from 2014. One of the issues that emerges in their effective implementation includes appointing teacher educators as per the qualifications to handle different courses within different teacher education programmes. It is likely that, sometimes, it can become difficult to find and appoint suitably qualified faculty for every prescribed course because of lack of availability and sometimes, shortage of students for certain courses during some years. This mismatch can be deterrent to the quality of teacher educators. For example, as per the regulations, a teacher educator at the secondary teacher education level is expected to possess a master's degree in the content subject and possess M.Ed./M.A.(Education) with B.Ed. as a professional degree. If there is any shortage of qualified teacher educators especially in certain methodology courses, like mathematics and science, teacher educators without having any master's degree in the concerned content area are likely to teach the methodology course. Another issue related to quality that needs to be examined is in what way the academic and professional degree programmes undergone by the teacher educators as per the requirement prescribed to become eligible for appointment, prepare them for their jobs and develop necessary competencies and skills. The issue of concern is how best can teacher educators develop the skills and competencies required for the twenty first century which they themselves do not possess, but to be developed among teacher trainees, who in turn need to develop among their learners. This necessitates a relook into the inputs given to teacher educators in their qualifying degrees, especially the professional ones for any curricular redesigning and further follow-up with continuing education.

(c) *Management of Content and Process*

The most important determinants for quality of Teacher Education are 'What and How' in Teacher Education. The expected profile of a teacher or the expected professional standards at any particular level or stage of education determines the content and processes at that level of Teacher Education.

Some of the issues that need to be examined are listed as below:

(i) Facilitating integration of theory and practice and their appropriate weightage in teacher education programmes;
(ii) Facilitating appropriate balance between internship versus institution-based models of teacher training;
(iii) Facilitating integration of content and pedagogy as well as integration of content, pedagogy and use of technology;
(iv) Strengthening community-based learning;
(v) Promoting continuous and comprehensive assessment and evaluation; and

(vi) Evolving different models of teacher education programmes, their effectiveness and implications.

The National Curriculum Framework of Teacher Education (NCFTE) proposed by the NCTE in 2009 is based on NCF 2005 of the NCERT. As mentioned in the preface of the NCFTE, the framework attempts to elaborate "the contexts, concerns and vision underscoring that teacher education and school education have a symbiotic relationship and developments in both the sectors mutually reinforce the concerns necessary for qualitative improvements of the entire spectrum of education including teacher education as well" (NCTE, 2009). This framework proposes nature of content and curriculum transaction strategies in teacher education programmes suitable to the context of the present millennium. The teacher educators' role has also been elaborated in terms of facilitators of learning of teacher trainees instead of information givers. Different activities have been suggested to strengthen theory-practice integration so that the trainees construct their own pedagogic knowledge which is realistic and has potentiality for better transfer to school situations. The teacher and teacher educators are conceived as reflective practitioners. The curriculum of teacher education is broadly dealt with under foundations of education, curriculum and pedagogy and school internship. A process-based teacher education has been proposed for practicing teachers. Continuous and comprehensive evaluation procedures for developing teachers have been proposed suggesting a need for preparing the assessing tools. Based on the NCFTE, 2009, the NCTE drafted a common curriculum framework in 2014 for implementation across the country. This formed a basis for a common curriculum preparation/revision, especially for drafting syllabi for various two-year and four-year undergraduate degree programmes in teacher education for different levels of school education as well as for two-year master's degree programmes in teacher education for teacher educators. The issue to be examined is to what extent the revised curricula have addressed to the expected concerns with respect to content and processes appropriate to the levels for which they are prepared.

Teacher Education in India has always faced the challenge of bringing about integration between theory and practice. Approaches for creating conducive learning environment to facilitate integration of theory and practice should be outcome-based which indicates what the student is capable to do, instead of objective-based which indicates what the student can do at the end of learning experience. The learning competencies acquired by the students in teacher education institution should ultimately lead to effective transfer in real situation where they ultimately teach. Different models of internship can be designed to facilitate integration of theory and practice and promote generalisability and transfer of learning in the classroom.

Professional education needs to be formally given and one cannot assume that one who has mastered the content (thinks so) can teach the same effectively. Having the subject knowledge is one thing and having the knowledge of how to teach is another, which can be acquired only through formal education. Evidence does support the view that to become an effective teacher, he/she has to be good not either in content or pedagogy, but both in content and pedagogy. Pedagogy cannot be taught without reference to any content. Pedagogy generally makes use of technology to make it more effective.

Shulman (1986,1987) observed that the emphasis on teacher's subject matter, knowledge and pedagogy were being treated as mutually exclusive. He advocated the need for their integration in teacher education programmes and he introduced the notion of pedagogical content knowledge which includes pedagogical knowledge and content knowledge. He has distinguished different types of knowledge. They include: (i) content knowledge of specific subject areas; and (ii) knowledge of general pedagogical principles including broad principles of classroom management/ organization and pedagogical content knowledge—which means how to transform subject matter content into formats that are comprehensible to learners, in the light of their specific learning needs, developmental status, or background (quoted in www.bsu.edu.cn). In other words, teacher's knowledge should include curriculum knowledge and knowledge of educational contexts. The content and processes in teacher education curriculum should facilitate integration of content and pedagogy in different educational contexts among student teachers. Thus, in any professional education programme for teachers, the student teachers are ensured of possessing adequate content knowledge in a well-structured manner, pedagogic-content knowledge, and techno-pedagogic-content knowledge. A good teacher is one who can integrate pedagogic knowledge with content knowledge. This is possible when the teacher critically reflects on and interprets the content in various ways and adapts it to learners' abilities and levels in different educational contexts.

Use of Information and Communication Technology (ICT) has become integral component of teaching content in schools. The capabilities of teachers as well as teacher trainees in the use of a variety of ICT and web resources as well as digital learning materials in handling learning situation effectively in the classrooms should be enhanced.

Ability to integrate content and pedagogy is generally fostered through both theoretical and practical components of teacher education programmes. Revised curriculum drafted as per the curriculum framework of the NCTE in 2014 has suggested guidelines for strengthening linkages between theory and practice as well as between content and pedagogy. For example, for the two-year B.Ed. programme, they have suggested the practical components which include activities that can be conducted on campus and off campus as well as during internship. Many universities have included practicing various teaching and instructional skills on campus as part of the pre-practice teaching activities. However, this curriculum slot may be used for practicing and experimenting with instructional activities that can strengthen theory-practice linkage also. Universities in some states have been employing the concept of microteaching for practicing teaching skills especially at the secondary teacher education programmes. Microteaching has been a popular technique to practice teaching skills since its inception in India during 1970s in secondary teacher training curricula and extensively researched upon (Buch,1974, 1979; NCERT, 1987, 1991; Passi & Lalitha, 1976a). Even after the implementation of revised curriculum framework, micro-teaching has become part and parcel of secondary teacher education curriculum in pedagogic courses and practiced prior to practice teaching/internship with or without its nomenclature, but at least as an idea, in many Indian Universities irrespective of whether the teacher education programme is located in teacher education colleges or at the University campus. Microteaching technique is still practiced the world-over not only in teacher education, but also used to train professionals in other disciplines like medical, dental, pharmacy, geriatric care, psychological counselling, dietic advising, business/commerce, communication and instruction (Anantha Krishnan, 1993; Ralph, 2014; Ambilli Remesh, 2013; Brown, 1975). But, it has deviated from the original model with variations in the contextual factors. The focus ranges from practicing specific teaching skills to broader objectives like improving critical thinking and problem-solving skills and from behavioural changes to perceptual changes. Variations can be observed from teach-re-teach cycle to practicing segments of lesson/activity in varied contexts designed to study the outcomes with a focus on learning how to teach through investigative approach. Such an approach provides opportunities for teacher trainees to acquire a repertoire of teaching skills/competencies to suit one's teaching style. However, it appears that microteaching technique still has a role to play in teacher education programmes, because of the emphasis on critical thinking/reflection, feedback and self-analysis given in the technique which is crucial in teacher preparation, whether or not the nomenclature of microteaching is used.

Teacher Education programme should strengthen cultural connections between teachers and their students. Pre-service teachers' prior beliefs and stereotypes, and cultural background of the students they are going to teach can lead to cultural disconnections between themselves and their students and hence can be deterrent to learning by the students. Cultural-immersion experiences given to student teachers can develop in them an ability to handle situations of cultural diversities in real classrooms. Such experiences can be provided during well-planned internship.

Education of teachers is a continuous process. A teacher in-service should have the capability to design assessment procedures not only to evaluate student learning but also to assess oneself to improve his/her own instruction. The practices of assessment in teacher education programme should go beyond lower order knowledge-based tests to measuring understanding, critical and higher order thinking, and problem-solving skills. The assessment should get linked to both formative and summative purposes. The ability to design performance tasks, activities to create scientific knowledge base through higher order thinking, and in other words, ability to be a teacher-researcher is not much focused in teacher education programmes. These abilities need to be developed among pre-service teachers which help not only in creating a pedagogic knowledge base, but also in making teachers critical and reflective in their profession.

(d) *Management of Continuing Professional Education*

The pre-service teacher education and in-service teacher education have always remained inseparable. Management of quality of teachers in schools and teacher educators in teacher education programmes is a continuous process. Teacher Education and education of teacher educators are interrelated and both are dynamic in nature. Continuing professional education is required not only for teachers and teacher educators, but also for other educational personnel who are directly involved in the monitoring school education as well as teacher education institutions. Some of the issues concerning this area that may need to be examined can be as follows:

I. *Continuing Professional Education of Teachers and Teacher Educators*

(i) Identification of needs of teachers for in-service training;
(ii) Effectiveness and appropriateness of content and methodology of induction programmes given for primary school teachers;
(iii) Identification of training needs including the need for leadership role of teachers and teacher educators, primary and secondary, for in-service teacher education, at different levels;
(iv) Appropriateness of the inputs given in the training programmes for teachers and the teacher educators, primary and secondary, for in-service teacher education, at different levels conducted by various cluster level (mainly for teachers), block level, district level, and state level organizations; and
(v) Effectiveness, appropriateness, and feasibility of the existing and alternative modes of training like, face to face, online mode, distance mode, and blended approach and their follow-up.

II. *Institutional Structures*

(i) Needed types of institutional structures for strengthening teacher training programmes;
(ii) Capabilities of the existing organizations responsible training teachers and teacher educators in terms adequacy of infrastructural facilities—land, building space; material resources including resource centre and required technology support; human resources and their competencies; and financial resources; background qualifications, experience and the training needs, and the continuity in their positions of the education personnel conducting training programmes for teachers and teacher educators; and
(iii) Methods of ensuring autonomy and accountability of the organizations conducting training programmes.

Various organizations have been established from state level to cluster level all over the country whose one of the main tasks is to offer academic and resource support for the success of various strategies and programmes being undertaken in teacher education at different levels. The structures that have already been established at different levels which are adequate to reach teachers and teacher educators at different levels of teacher education for their continued professional training. For example, SCERTs/DSERTs established at the state level have the responsibility for offering resource support, conducting training, and maintaining/monitoring quality of school education and teacher education at different levels as well as adult and non-formal education based on the NPE 1986 and its POA 1992, District Institutes of Education and Training were established in all the districts in three phases by upgrading Government Teacher Training Institutes in these districts and one of the major tasks were to conduct in-service teacher education programmes for primary school teachers. Under the World Bank-assisted flagship programme, namely District Primary Education Programme, different structures were formed at cluster level (CRCs) and block level (BRCs), supported by district level, and state level structures, wherein teacher empowerment through in-service programmes including production of curricular materials formed one of the major activities. Subsequently, Block Institutes of Teacher Education have also been established. Thus, structures have already been established at different levels which are adequate to reach teachers and teacher educators at different levels of teacher education for their continued professional training. The issues of concern are not so much related to establishment of institutional structures, rather how they need to function in continuing professional development of teachers and teacher educators. For example, it is observed that the background experience of the faculty in-charge for conducting training programmes in DIETs as inadequate and the issue gets more aggravated because of lack of their continuity in their positions (Lalitha, 1998). The training methodology is generally face to face and less participative in nature.

The training programmes for teachers or teacher educators should employ such methodologies which in turn can facilitate better transfer effects into their classrooms.

The NCF 2005 has vision about a child as a generator of knowledge, but about the teacher as a facilitator of learning and reflective practitioner. This has implications for content and processes of teacher education. The professional development programmes offered by the DIETs for primary teacher educators and orientation and refresher courses offered by National and State level institutions and the universities for professional development of secondary teacher educators should address to the above issues of preparing effective and competent teacher educators who in turn can design and conduct effective in-service teacher training programmes. Teacher educators need to be exposed to the use of various open educational resources available freely online, to the use of various web tools and technologies (like Wiki). They should be trained in technology integration in curriculum transaction which requires use of multimedia projectors, learner management systems creating truly automated virtual classrooms. They need to be trained in alternative assessment strategies like portfolio evaluation, online assessment, Rubik generators, use of many of the learner management systems for generating various assessment questions. Apart from these structures/organizations meant for continuing professional development of teacher educators at different levels of teacher education, teacher educator complexes/forums can be formulated for monthly academic enrichment meetings for sharing experiences and mutual professional enrichment on need-based issues and concerns initiated by teacher educators themselves, and to create share and collaborate mutual learning using web tools.

(e) *Monitoring and Quality Control*

One of the significant developments in teacher education, after NPE and POA with its modifications in 1992, is the establishment of NCTE in 1993 through Parliament Act No. 73 as a statutory authority. In addition, NAAC had an MOU with NCTE to carry forward the work of quality reform of teacher education. The affiliating universities have an important responsibility to monitor the quality of teacher education institutions in terms of their own norms without violating the NCTE norms. The collective efforts of these organizations through seminars, workshops sharing of experiences could bring quality reform in teacher education programmes/institutions as well as monitor and ensure their quality.

Quality management can also be thought out at an institutional level. All the philosophical (Vision and Mission), physical and human (Infrastructural facilities) dimensions, the kinds of programmes run and the way they are run, the beneficiary clientele, the management and the stakeholder community, all make an institution. It is the co-ordinate effort of these components of an institution working towards common goals based on certain broad guidelines that can facilitate monitoring quality internally by the institution.

Some of the issues that can be examined are given below:

(i) Adequacy and relevancy of the norms prescribed by the NCTE for different types of institutions and courses of teacher education;

(ii) Appropriateness of the common norms for different courses/institutions across the country in the light of allowing foreign universities to establish their educational institutions in India;

(iii) Adequacy and robustness of norms suggested for teacher education institutions/courses in responding to the changes in content-pedagogy of school education, technological developments, and changes in socio-economic conditions; and

(iv) Methods of co-ordination to be established between different monitoring bodies like university, NCTE, NAAC, UGC, State and Central Governments, and such other agencies/organizations;

(v) Extent to which the proposed concept establishment General Education Council can be useful in quality management of Teacher Education.

The main agencies that are involved in monitoring the quality of teacher programmes include the State government, the Universities and the NCTE. The NAAC has also joined hands with NCTE in accrediting teacher education institutions at secondary level as well as the teacher educator preparation programmes like the master's degree in education offered by colleges and universities. The norms have been evolved covering various issues of quality. But, they are mainly related to infrastructural aspects including qualification of the faculty, although various curriculum related aspects are also included. The curricular aspects, including content and processes are difficult to be adequately assessed by these organizations at the time of monitoring/affiliation or accreditation. Coordinated and mutually complementing efforts by these institutions can help in avoiding any duplication of efforts and thus, leading to working in proper cohesion in monitoring the quality of teacher education programmes and institutions. The curricular dimensions in terms of content and processes when addressed to make teacher education programmes competency-based, can form a basis for monitoring and evaluation of the programmes. A procedure should be evolved to evaluate the in-service teacher education programmes and create a mechanism for monitoring quality of continuous professional development of teachers. The norms and standards prescribed by the NCTE should be re-examined from the points of view of contextual realities and robust enough to absorb changes in the school and socio-economic conditions. For example, the crisis created by the pandemic has created new demands content and processes of school education and hence teacher education The restructured NCTE under the General Education Council, as proposed in the New Policy on Education, 2020, may need to keep the above points in view, especially with respect to quality management of teacher education, both pre-service and in-service.

(f) *Upholding of Professionalism by Teachers*

Profession implies possession of specialized knowledge that characterizes the profession which contributes to recognized status distinctions among the professions. The classical work of Liberman (1956) on teaching as profession in the context of United States also lists a characteristics of an occupation if it has to be considered as a profession as follows: a unique, definite and essential social service; an emphasis upon intellectual techniques in performing its service; a long period of specialized training; a broad range of autonomy for both individual practitioners and for the occupational group as a whole; accountability; service to be rendered form the basis and not the economic returns; a comprehensive self-governing organizations of practitioners and a code of ethics. The emergence of teacher professionalism in India can be observed in the post-Independence period in the form of sustained initiatives and efforts to empower teachers both through pre-service and continued professional development programmes. The quality of these programmes, however, determines the quality of teacher professionalism we have been able to establish. In recent years, the professional knowledge including pedagogical-content knowledge has emerged as an important aspect of teaching profession (Darling-Hammond & Bransford, 2005). Professionalism in teachers is emerging in India in terms of some of the key components like, initial training, having opportunities for professional upgradation, reasonable degree of autonomy, active participation of the professional organizations, existence of bodies to set and monitor standards, and remuneration fixed according to the nature of service and the importance of the contribution made to the society. But, we have to go a long way in making it a profession on par with other more established professions like medicine or engineering. Some of the issues to be examined are as follows:

(i) extent to which teaching has emerged as a profession; and

(ii) approaches to make teaching as a profession on par with professions like medicine, engineering, and law.

Teaching is considered as a profession like other professions, namely medicine, dentistry, engineering, law, management and so on. Like any other professional, a teacher is not considered eligible to practice teaching profession, unless he/she possesses the needed organized body of knowledge, understandings, skills, attitudes/dispositions, and values to become effective in his/her profession. This should be relevant to the area of specialization as well as the nature of target group to be taught by him/her. This can be acquired only through a formal rigorous training/education of reasonable duration with adequate practical/situated experience. Like in other professions, there should be opportunities for developing/enriching professional knowledge and experience through research, self-reflection, and mutual sharing of professional experience by the fraternity of professional teachers. Further, there should be opportunities for continued need-based professional training to keep updated with the developments in the field.

Any professional education on teaching should develop such qualities in student teachers which help in achievement of higher levels of learners' development (cognitive, social, and emotional) in schools. Teachers can become effective, if:

- they have their professional knowledge at appropriate level of proficiency, use this knowledge to plan instructional opportunities for students that enable them to grasp new concepts and make connections organizing conceptually the factual knowledge that facilitates its retrieval, application, and transfer;
- use assessment data to help every student achieve at high levels through formative assessment which provides information about the student, and assists in designing and adapting teaching/instruction;
- collaborate with other educators and with families/communities to assure that every student's needs can be met;
- possess management skills and create a classroom environment where productive learning can possibly occur;

- use new technological innovations effectively to motivate students and to advance their learning;
- reflect on their teaching and on their role as teachers, as reflection deepens the understanding of effective instructional practices and promotes generation of new knowledge; and
- possess certain dispositions that are essential for realizing the potential of every child.

Evidence support the view that the nature of teacher education curriculum including content, orientation, and duration influence the effectiveness of teacher learning. The first issue relates to the content and orientation of any teacher education programme. In India, most popular teacher education programmes have been generic (general), that is common for all teachers of different grade levels. For example, B.Ed programme is commonly meant for preparation of upper primary teachers, secondary teachers and senior secondary teachers and is common no matter what subjects they teach. But, teachers never teach something in general. They always teach particular things to particular groups of learners in particular settings. This implies that teacher education programmes need to be more stage-specific than generic.

Most human learning and teaching are highly specific and situated, implying low possibility of transfer and generalizability of pedagogy learnt in one subject/domain of knowledge to pedagogy of another subject/domain. Different subjects demand different instructional models. Most effective form of professional education occurs at the integration of content and pedagogy. Teachers need adequate amount of subject-specific examples, analysis and practice within their professional educational programmes to become effective subject teachers. This implies that professional education especially at secondary level has to be subject-specific (Shulman, 1986, 1987).

Any form of teacher preparation needs to be of reasonable duration that provides among time and opportunity for self-study, reflection and involved engagement with learners, the school, the classroom and pedagogy activities, along with rigorous theoretical study (NCTE, 2009).

The issue of the duration of initial teacher training has been discussed at length. Although there has been a consensus on the duration of primary teacher education programme which extends for two years, no such consensus had evolved until recently about the duration of secondary teacher education which was for duration of one year has been made into two years. Although there had been a discontent on the adequacy of the duration of one year for giving proper training, the concerns expressed for extending it to two years included the practical difficulties in terms of additional burden on the students as well as on the institution itself. However, if one-year duration had to continue, it necessitated the strengthening of internal efficiency of one-year programme itself. Secondary Education Commission (1953) and the Education Commission (1964-66) have always recommended longer duration of secondary teacher education programmes which could provide a strong base in content knowledge as well as develop knowledge and skills in content and pedagogy of teaching. They have emphasized the need for development of integrated teacher education programmes as well as for the establishment of comprehensive colleges of education. The Regional Institutes of Education of NCERT have been offering four-year integrated programme which is thought as a solution for improving the quality of teacher education from the point of view of increased duration and for integrating theory and practice. This model is being implemented in institutions including universities where other undergraduate degree programmes are run, thus, to facilitate integration of content and pedagogy. This model implies that the students should decide on the profession they would like to pursue at an early age, in the same manner as in the case of the other professions. Separate norms have been developed for four-year integrated programmes at different levels of teacher education—from pre-primary through higher secondary education. As per the NPE 2020, a four-year integrated degree in Teacher Education would be the qualifying degree for teaching by 2030. Until then the existing two-year B.Ed. will also continue.

Making Teacher Education competency-based and making the core competencies for the initial training and extending the initial training with follow-up in-service training (off campus training) for achieving the other desirable competencies could be the solution to overcome the issue of inadequacy of duration. However, alternative models can be worked out to establish linkage between pre-service and in-service teacher education so that the teacher remains a life-long learner meeting the requirements of the profession as and when they change with time. Implementing any such models of teacher preparation requires structural and resource support. Just extending the duration from one year to two years, just as such may not improve the quality of secondary teacher training, unless followed by systematic in-service teacher training.

(g) *Management of Research Output to Support Activities in Teacher Education Programmes*

Teacher Education has always been criticized for lack of empirical base underlying content and processes including theoretical and practical inputs. Thus, the challenge faced by teacher education has been lack of empirical base and at the same time, the dire need to improve teacher education, especially teacher performance.

Some of the issues that need to be examined through can be as below:

(i) Identifying ideas related to quality concerns in teacher education that need empirical base;

(ii) Identifying various research questions that need to be answered related to different types of input, infrastructural facilities available in the teacher education institution, content and processes including the teaching-learning approaches followed and in general, questions related to improving effectiveness of teacher education programmes;

(iii) Identifying issues related to different approaches to assess different types of learning outcomes in different domains in teacher education;

(iv) Identifying various methodological issues in conducting empirical studies in teacher education especially related to transfer and generalisability of the learning outcomes to real situations and approaches in resolving them;

(v) Examining the roles played by the various institutions monitoring the quality of teacher education;

(vi) Exploring different research designs to answer various research questions related to improving quality of teacher education, both quantitative and qualitative approaches as well as empirical and non-empirical approaches; and

(vii) Identifying and evolving/validating methods for the development of various competencies and teaching skills for distance as well as online education by the teacher educators in responding to the changes in content-pedagogy of school education, technological developments, and changes in socio-economic conditions.

Many research studies have been conducted in the area of teaching and teacher effectiveness in India (Buch, 1974, 1979; Jangira, 1974; Padma, 1979; NCERT, 1987; 1991; 1997). Attempts have been made to synthesize findings to determine what makes teaching effective (Navodaya Vidyalaya Samiti, 1990). The researchers in the field of teaching and teacher effectiveness are facing challenges because of the nature of the field which is dynamic as well as complex and the methodological issues involved therein. This makes it difficult to evolve knowledge that can provide a base for teacher education programmes.

For example, process related factors are not easily measurable. Some of these factors are measured through ratings which themselves are subjective. Teacher accountability cannot be linked only teaching-learning processes alone. The latter could possibly be associated with many contextual factors over which researchers do not have much control. Studies conducted in the area of 'teacher education' have employed various research methodologies which include quantitative, qualitative, and mixed approaches. The qualitative research, although provides more insights into the processes of teaching, unlike quantitative research, it fails to provide for making any generalisation and hence applicability to new situations. In spite of the difficulties faced in conducting research in the field of teaching and teacher effectiveness, the pedagogic knowledge relevant to making teaching effective is emerging through research. The content and processes of teacher education are based on both empirical knowledge as well as knowledge based on experience.

Research efforts in the direction of improving quality of teacher educators especially with respect to developing in them the needed knowledge and skill competencies, is minimal and hence need strengthening. Teacher Education is being offered not only through face to face mode but also through distance mode. Use of blended approach is becoming inevitable for both initial followed by continuing teacher education. This requires identifying and validating approaches to develop teaching skills and competencies among teacher educators. Attempts have also been made to identify teaching skills in the context of online distance learning. In a study an attempt was made to determine whether online distance educators need special skills or knowledge to teach successfully online, a popular mode of learning in higher education. It is observed that educators can greatly benefit from training to make the transition from teaching in a face-to-face setting to an online setting, even though most skills are thought to be similar and applicable across settings (Jia-Ling Lee & Atusi, 2004). The investigators have identified six essential skills, namely interaction, management, organization/instructional design, technology content knowledge, and teamwork skills and sixteen outputs.

Apart from carrying on research as a separate activity, research should be built into the processes involved in teacher education system. For example, teacher educators should be encouraged to innovate, even based on intuitive judgement, for improving teacher education, with the hope of substantiating later. 'Microteaching' emerged as one such innovation which was practiced first and only at the later stage started the process of theoretical conceptualization

(Perlberg,1985). Involvement of teacher educators in curriculum designing of teacher education programmes at respective levels is likely to improve their teaching competencies. Platforms for mutual interaction among teacher educators, both face-to-face and online, like 'teacher educator complex', WhatsApp groups, can be created for regular meetings, webinars, and video conferences of teacher educators for sharing and documenting curricular experiences, action research, sharing creative ideas and such other activities. The use of Apps for online interaction like Google meet, and such others can be explored for experience sharing activities. These activities can be managed by quality monitoring organizations. The ideas generated through such activities can be further researched upon for more generalisability and implementation. These organizations can also take the responsibility for documenting and disseminating generated research ideas and experiences among teacher educators.

Conclusion

Quality teacher education programmes are inevitable in any country intending to improve quality of education at any level. Teaching is considered as a profession like other professions, like medicine, law, and engineering and teacher education programmes at any level are considered as professional programmes. The quality of teacher education determines the quality of students entering other professions and hence the quality of other professional programmes. Because of close connection between school education and teacher education, the challenges posed at school education in terms of policy perspectives to offer quality education for all children in different societal contexts, changes in global perspectives and technological advancements, creates demands on teacher education system in the country to produce teachers at different levels with required professional competencies appropriate to the educational contexts to which they are prepared. The various quality concerns that emerge in teacher education system can be identified in a total quality management perspective and addressed in a multipronged manner. Because of the dynamic nature in the societal contexts, the education system and in turn the teacher education system remains responsive to the societal needs. Establishing a firm but adaptable and at the same time responsive teacher education system with clear goals goes a long way in development of a country like India.

REFERENCES

Ambilli Remesh. (2013). "Microteaching, an efficient technique for learning effective teaching". *Journal of Research in Medical Sciences*, February *18*(2):158-163.

Ananthakrishnan, N. (1993). "Microteaching as a vehicle of teacher training: its advantages and disadvantages". *Journal of Postgraduate Medicine*, *39*(3), 142-143. NCTE.

Brown, G. (1975). *Microteaching—A Programme of Teaching Skills*. London: Methuen.

Buch, M.B. (1974). *A Survey of Research in Education. Baroda: Centre for Advanced Study in Education*, M.S. University.

Buch, M.B. (1979). *Second Survey of Research in Education 1972-78*. Vadodara: Society for Educational Research and Development.

Government of India. (2009). *Right of Children to Free and Compulsory Education Act*. New Delhi.

Hattie, J. (October 2003). *Teachers make a difference; what is the research evidence?* Paper presented to Australian Council for Educational Research Annual Conference, Melbourne, 19-21.

James, G. Gilbert, Key L. Keck and Ronald D. Simpson (2005). *Innovative higher education*. Spring Links.

Jangira, N.K. (1974). "Teaching and Teacher Behaviour: Trend Report". In M.B. Buch (Ed.), *Survey of Research in Education*. Baroda: Centre of Advanced Study Education, M.S. University of Baroda.

Jia-Ling Lee and Atusi Hirumi (October 2004). "Analysis of essential skills and Knowledge for teaching online". In: *ERIC Number* ED485021, Published in October 2004 record non-journal type. Chicago: Association for Educational Communications and Technology,

Lalitha, M.S. (1996). *Teacher Competencies for Pre-service Elementary Teacher Education*. Drafting assigned and financed by NCTE, New Delhi.

Lalitha, M.S. (1998). *Capability Study of DIETs to Support Joint UN System Community Based Primary Education Programme in Karnataka*. Study funded by UNICEF through Government of Karnataka.

Liberman, M. (1956). *Education as a Profession*. New Jersey: Prentice Hall.

Ministry of Human Resource Development (1986). *National Policy on Education*. Government of India, New Delhi: MHRD.

Ministry of Human Resource Development (2020). *National Policy on Education*. Government of India. New Delhi: MHRD.

Ministry of Human Resource Development (1992). *Programme of Action*. New Delhi: Government of India Press.

Ministry of Education (1953). *Report of the Secondary Education Commission*. New Delhi: Government of India Press.

Ministry of Education (1966). *Report of the Education Commission* (1964-66). New Delhi: Government of India Press.

National Council for Teacher Education (1998). *Competency based and Commitment*.

National Council for Research and Training (1986). *Third Survey of Research in Education 1978-1983*. New Delhi: NCERT.

National Council for Research and Training (1991). *Fourth Survey of Research in Education 1983-1988*. New Delhi: NCERT.

National Council for Research and Training (1997). *Fifth Survey of Research in Education 1988-1992*. New Delhi: NCERT.

National Council for Research and Training (2005). *The National Curriculum Framework*. New Delhi: NCERT.

National Council for Teacher Education (2009). *The National Curriculum Framework for Teacher Education*. New Delhi: NCTE.

National Council for Teacher Education (2014). *The National Curriculum Framework for Teacher Education*. New Delhi: NCTE.

National Knowledge Commission (2007). *National Knowledge Commission: Report to the Nation 2006*. New Delhi: National Knowledge Commission.

Organisation for Economic Co-operation and Development (OECD). (2005). *Teachers Matter: Attracting, Developing and Retaining Effective Teachers*, 6th ed. Paris: OECD Publishing.

Padma, M.S. (1979). "Teaching and Teacher Behaviour—Trend Report". In M.B. Buch (Ed.), *Second Survey of Research in Education 1972-1978*. Baroda: Society for Educational Research and Development.

Passi, B.K. and Lalitha, M.S. (1976). "Microteaching: Skill-based Approach". In B.K. Passi (Ed.). *Becoming Better Teacher*. Sahitya Mudranalay, Baroda.

Perlberg, A. (1985). "Microteaching: Conceptual and Theoretical Bases". In Torsterin (Ed): *The International Encyclopaedia of Educational Research and Studies*. Pergamon Press.

Ralph, Edwin G. (July 2014). "The Effectiveness of Microteaching: Five Years' Findings". *International Journal of Humanities, Social Sciences and Education* (*IJHSSE*), *I*(7): 17-28. www.arcjounals.org

Shulman, L.S. (1986). "Those who understand: Knowledge growth in Teaching." *Educational Researcher, 15*, 4-14. (Quoted in Ball State University Conceptual Framework for Professional Education www.bsu.edu.cn)

Shulman, L.S. (1987). "Knowledge and Teaching: Foundations of the new reform". *Harvard Educational Review, 19*, 4-14. (Quoted in Ball State University Conceptual Framework for Professional Education www.bsu.edu.cn)

33

Community Participation-Oriented Activities as Measure of Quality Improvement in Distance Teacher-Training Programme

P.K. Sahoo and *Surendra Kumar*

Community participation is a concept that attempts to bring different stakeholders together for problem solving and decision making. Community participation is considered necessary to get community support for educational planning and development (Cole, 2007). Teachers are the pillars of the school. They enjoy respect due to their commitment to teaching and improving students' performance. This recognition makes them approachable and lends itself to forming trust. A teacher—role in society is to transfer knowledge that is important for the future of individuals and the society (Nick Ohlsson, 2017). A teacher in a community represents a major node of the total human social system, where culture, including the academic subjects, is transmitted and observed. The teacher models adaptive functioning in the community (Rebert Akridge, 2018). A teacher plays an important role in a community, offering students guidance and sometimes being the first adult in a child's life to show interest in their goals. Teachers help shape the community and can direct students in positive directions that they may not have pursued otherwise (Floyd William, 2017). The role of a teacher to improve the society we are a part of. His/her role is to gain valuable knowledge and impart it further to the students for making this world a better place. They encourage to do something for the betterment of their community or society within their reach (James William, 2019). So, on the basis of above discussion we can say that training of a teacher is necessary. There are more formal and non-formal institutions which are organizing pre-service and in-service training of teachers.

The Need for Distance Mode Teacher Training Programme

The need for Distance mode teacher training programme is getting more attention for teachers to equip with new knowledge and skills for them to play important role in community. In-service training can enhance the professionalism of teachers who can contribute to the organisation of community participation activities in the schools.

Distance mode teacher training programme offers one of the most promising roads to the improvement of instruction. It includes goal and content, the training process and the context. According to Ong (1993), in-service training is the totality of educational and personal experiences that contribute towards an individual being more competent and satisfied in an assigned professional role. The primary purpose of in-service training is to enable teachers to acquire new understanding and instructional skills.

In this aspect, Distance mode teacher training programme for teachers is the driving force behind much change that has occurred in the area of teaching and learning. According to Kazmi, Pervez & Mumtaz (2011), in-service training for teachers enables the teachers to be more systematic and logical in their teaching style.

According to Abdul Rashid (1996), in-service training comprises two main elements, that is the fulfilment of pupils learning needs and ensuring personal and career development of the academic staff. Studies by Ekpoh, Oswald & Victoria (2013) shows that, teachers who attend in-service training performs effectively in their work concerning knowledge of the subject, classroom management, teaching method and evaluation of students. Studies by Jahangir, Saheen & Kazmi (2012) also shows that in-service training plays a major role to improve the teacher's performance in school. According to Frederick & Stephen (2010), during the in-service training, teachers will school's management skills, evaluation techniques and master wider content areas of their subjects. For this reason, teachers and educational experts should increase their effort in fostering and implementing in-service training in schools so as to improve the effectiveness of development in schools.

The importance of Distance mode teacher training programme should be looked in various perspectives. It promotes a very flexible environment and allow teachers to adapt with the working situation and it is also one form of motivation for employees or employers and it will continue to increase creativity in teaching and learning process. It also enables teachers to acquire new understanding and instructional skills to develop their effectiveness in the classroom as well as in the society.

Studies done by Thompson (1992) shows that, after going through in-service training, there are positive changes in teachers' attitude, increased self-confidence and also follow-up with teachers' readiness in facing any various resistance situation. This shows that, training programme that is planned and implemented well will give a positive effect on students, teachers and schools.

Distance mode teacher training programme places teachers at the centre of any improvement effort and assumes that the work of the teacher and the visions that teachers have about improving their work. According to Owen, "the positive aspect concerning professional development of teachers are that the programme will make sure that learning activities are planned and concentrated on empowering effective teachers to correct policies, curriculum development, teaching and views on how to achieve high productivity and student's performance" (Owen, 1990:175). It is vital that the positive performance result from the students will bring profits to teachers themselves based on the additional recognition from colleagues at workplace and the administration. In-service training for teachers will not only bring positive effect to the teacher, but also students and school because the changes, that is expected has a close relation between teachers, students and schools.

Research Questions: This study explored the following questions:

There exists a strong need to understand and analyze the processes involved in teacher training programme through distance mode. Following different questions are raised in this contex:

1. How do both of universities trained their students for community participation activities?
2. Which activities involved for making competent to the students in community participation activities?
3. How do the students involved in training process?
4. To what extent training are effective and relevant?

In order to find answers to above kind of questions the investigator intends to analyze the process of B.Ed. programme offered by Distance Education Mode and its relevance. Keeping these points in mind, the investigator perceives that there exists a strong need to study the utility and effectiveness of processes of B.Ed. programme offered through Distance Education Mode by the open universities. Since, open distance mode B.Ed. programme integrates distance mode as well as supervised mode of development of teacher competencies, the study will be considered more meaningful to evaluate the existing processes adopted at different levels of training through different means.

Objectives of the Study

1. To explore processes adopted for development of teacher competencies regarding community participation among B.Ed. students of Open Universities.

2. To study the relevance of such processes in relation to development of teacher competencies among B.Ed. students of Open Universities as per perception, statements of the teacher, counsellors and the mentors.
3. To study the effectiveness of the nature and organisation of various kinds of activities involved in development of teacher competencies regarding community participation among B.Ed. students of Open Universities as per perception of the students, counsellors and the mentors.

Hypotheses

The hypothesis of the study in the context of objectives read as:

1. The response patterns of B.Ed. trainees and the university background are not independent from each other.
2. The response patterns of counsellors and the university background are not independent from each other.

Population and Sample

Data/Open University	IGNOU	UPRTOU	Total
Study Centres	6	6	12
Trainees	6 × 50 =300	6 × 50 =300	600
Counsellors	6 × 5 =30	6 × 5 =30	60
Mentors	50	50	100

Tools

In order to collect data, the researcher used questionnaire, interview schedule and observation schedule constructed by himself:

1. Questionnaire for trainees
2. Questionnaire for counsellors
3. Interview schedule for counsellors
4. Interview schedule for mentors.

Analysis Procedures

The chi-square (χ^2) test as well as percentages have been used for analysis of quantitative data. The open responses as well as observation data were analysed qualitatively.

Response of B.Ed. Trainees about Organisation of Activities Related to Community Participation: University-wise

Table 33.1: χ^2 test of independence of trainees' response about activities and help for resolving problems related organisation of community participation activities during the workshops and university background

Response of B.Ed. trainees about organisation of activities related to community participation during workshops			
Univiversity	Yes	No	Total
IGNOU	245 (81.67)	55 (18.33)	300 (100.00)
UPRTOU	256 (85.33)	44 (14.67)	300 (100.00)
Total	**501 (83.5)**	**99 (16.5)**	**600 (100.00)**

It can be observed from Table 33.1 that 85 per cent trainees of UPRTOU and 82 per cent trainees of IGNOU stated that activities related to community participation had been organised during workshops.

Response of Trainees about Organisation of Activities Related to Community Participation during Workshop: University-wise

It can be noticed from Table 33.2 that the calculated χ^2 value of independence between the response pattern of B.Ed. trainees and the university background in relation to the conduction of varied activities to community participation workshop is found 4.39. The obtained χ^2 value is less than the Table value (7.81) at 0.05 level of significance with df: 3. The observed value is not found significant. Hence, it is clear that the response pattern of B.Ed. trainees and the university background are found to be independent from each other in relation to the conduction of varied activities related to community participation.

Table 33.2: University wise response of B.Ed. trainees about community participation

Response of B.Ed. trainees about organisation of activities related to community participation during workshops						
University	**i (Health education)**	**ii (Comm-unity work)**	**iii (i & ii)**	**iv (Noth-ing)**	**Total**	**χ^2 Value**
IGNOU	25 (8.33)	34 (11.33)	186 (62.00)	55 (18.33)	300 (100.00)	4.39 N.S.
UPRTOU	35 (11.67)	44 (14.67)	177 (59.00)	44 (14.67)	300 (100.00)	
Total	**60 (10.00)**	**78 (13.00)**	**363 (60.5)**	**99 (16.5)**	**600 (100.00)**	

Notes: Figures in parentheses indicates percentages. N.S.: Not Significant.

It can be observed that according to 61 per cent B.Ed. trainees of IGNOU and UPRTOU, community work related to health education and survey was conducted. Further 13 per cent B.Ed. trainees of IGNOU and UPRTOU considered that only community work and survey were conducted.

Response of B.Ed. Trainees about Assistance Provider for Solving Problems Faced Related to Community Participation: University-wise

It can be noticed from Table 33.3 that the calculated χ^2 value of independence between the response of B.Ed. trainees and the university background in relation to the person who solve problems during community work is found 12.17, which is greater than the Table value (7.81) at 0.05 level of significance with df: 3. Thus, the calculated χ^2 value is found to be significant. Hence, it is clear that the response pattern of B.Ed. trainees and the university background are not found independent from each other in relation to the person who solved problems during community work.

Table 33.3: University wise response of B.Ed. trainees about assistance providers for solving problems

Response of B.Ed. trainees about assistance providers for solving problems faced during organisation of community participation activities in the workshops						
University	**i (Only mentor)**	**ii (Only peer trainees)**	**iii (i & ii)**	**iv (None)**	**Total**	**χ^2 Value**
IGNOU	62 (20.67)	46 (15.33)	177 (59.00)	15 (5.00)	300 (100.00)	12.17*
UPRTOU	45 (15.00)	41 (13.67)	210 (70.00)	4 (1.33)	300 (100.00)	
Total	**107 (17.83)**	**87 (14.5)**	**387 (64.5)**	**19 (3.17)**	**600 (100.00)**	

Notes: Figures in parentheses indicates percentages. *Indicates significant at .01 level.

It can be observed that according to 70 per cent B.Ed. trainees of UPRTOU, the problems encountered during community work were resolved with the help of mentors and peer trainees, whereas only 59 per cent B.Ed. trainees of IGNOU considered the same.

Interview with Mentors about Organised Activities by B.Ed. Trainees Related to Health Education, Social and Community Work at their Own School Level

The selected mentors of IGNOU as well as UPRTOU stated that the B.Ed. trainees organised rallies for public awareness, cleaning the school and making plantation. They organized sports and cultural programmes and educational tours.

Interview with Mentors about Process of Organisation of Activities by B.Ed. Trainees Related to Health Education, Social and Community Work

The selected mentors of both the universities stated that B.Ed. trainees organised health education, social and community works with the help of students and teachers of their school. The B.Ed. trainees prepared poster by students on the topic "For good health".

They organised educational tours, community works, plantation programmes and cultural programmes.

Interview with Mentors about Problems Faced by B.Ed. Trainees During Organisation of Activities Related to Health Education, Social and Community Works in their Own School

The selected mentors of both the universities informed that various problems were faced by B.Ed. trainees during organisation of activities related to health education, social and community work, i.e. indiscipline among students, non-cooperation of students and problem of controlling of students during the tour etc.

Interview with Mentors about their Help to B.Ed. Trainees in Organisation of Activities Related to Health Education, Social and Community Work

The selected mentors stated that they helped B.Ed. trainees in organisation of health education, social and community activities. They helped them in maintaining discipline among students.

Response of Counsellors about Organisation of Activities Related to Community Participation during Workshop: University-wise

Table 33.4: χ^2 test of independence of counsellor's response about organisation of activities related to community participation during the workshops and university background

Response of counsellors about organisation of activities related to community participation								
University	**i (Health education related)**	**ii (Community work and survey)**	**iii (i & ii)**	**iv (Group project)**	**v (Group discussion)**	**vi (None)**	**Total**	**χ^2 Value**
IGNOU	7 (23.33)	6 (20.00)	10 (33.33)	1 (3.33)	1 (3.33)	5 (16.67)	30 (100.00)	
UPRTOU	6 (20.00)	1 (3.33)	23 (76.67)	0 (0.00)	0 (0.00)	0 (0.00)	30 (100.00)	15.77*
Total	**13 (21.67)**	7 (11.67)	**33 (55.00)**	**1 (1.67)**	**1 (1.67)**	**5 (8.33)**	**60 (100.00)**	

Notes: Figures in parentheses indicate percentages. *Indicates significant at .01 level.

It can be noticed from Table 33.4 that the calculated χ^2 value of independence between response patterns of counsellors and the university background in relation to the activities performed related to community participation is found 15.77, which is greater than the Table value (11.07) at 0.05 level of significance with df: 5. Thus, the obtained χ^2 value is found to be significant. Hence, it is clear that the response pattern of counsellors and the university background are not found to be independent from each other in relation to the activities performed related to community participation.

It can be observed that 77 per cent counsellors of UPRTOU mentioned that activities related to health education, community work and survey was conducted during workshops, whereas only 33 per cent counsellors of IGNOU mentioned the same. About 23 per cent counsellors of IGNOU and 20 per cent counsellors of UPRTOU mentioned that only activities related to health education were conducted during workshops.

Response of Counsellors about Training Provided by Themselves to B.Ed. Trainees for Organisation of Activities Related to Community Participation: University-wise

Table 33.5: University wise response of counsellors about types of training

Response of counsellors about types of training provided for organisation of activities related to community participation						
University	**i (By providing detailed knowledge)**	**ii (By organizing Activities)**	**iii (i&ii)**	**iv (None)**	**Total**	**χ^2 Value**
IGNOU	6 (20.00)	9 (30.00)	10 (33.33)	5 (16.67)	30 (100.00)	10.45*
UPRTOU	4 (13.33)	5 (16.67)	21 (70.00)	0 (0.00)	30 (100.00)	
Total	**10 (16.67)**	**14 (23.33)**	**31 (51.67)**	**5 (8.33)**	**60 (100.00)**	

Notes: Figures in parentheses indicate percentages. *Indicates significant at .05 level.

It can be noticed from Table 33.5 that the calculated χ^2 value of independence between the response patterns of counsellors and the university background in relation to the training provided for organizing activities related to community participation is found 10.45, which is greater than the Table value (7.81) at .05 level of significance with df: 3. Thus, the obtained χ^2 value is found to be significant. Hence, it is clear that the response pattern of counsellors and the university background in relation to the training provided for organizing activities related to community participation are not found to be independent from each other.

It can be observed that 70 per cent counsellors of UPRTOU and merely 33 per cent counsellors of IGNOU mentioned that they provided theoretical knowledge regarding organization and implementation of activities related to community participation during the workshops.

Interview with Counsellors about Organisation of Activities related to Social Work and Community Survey during Workshops

The selected counsellors of both the universities stated only survey work and educational tour were organised during workshops. The trainees submitted report of educational tour organised by themselves at their own schools.

Interview with Counsellors about Process Adopted for making Competent to B.Ed. Trainees in Activities of Health Education

The selected counsellors of both the universities made clear that there was no provision of separate session for conducting activities related to health education, but it was included in school based activates for some credits for the development of abovementioned activities. The B.Ed. trainees were made aware of first aid.

Response of B.Ed. Trainees about Relevance of Training given to them for Development of Competency of Community Participation: University-wise

It can be noticed from Table 33.6 that the calculated χ^2 value of independence between the response patterns of B.Ed. trainees and the university background in relation to the relevance of training provided for the development of competency related to community participation activities is found 0.80, which is less than the Table value (5.99) at .05 level of significance with df: 2. Thus, the obtained χ^2 value is not found to be significant. Hence, it is clear that the response pattern of B.Ed. trainees and the university background in relation to the relevance of training provided for the development of competency related to community participation activities are found to be independent from each other.

Table 33.6: χ^2 test of independence of trainees' response about relevance of training process for development of community participation skill and university background

Response of B.Ed. trainees about relevance of training for development of competency of community participation						
Statements	**University**	**Max. Agree**	**Least Agree**	**Disagree**	**Total**	**χ^2 Values**
Community work conducted during workshops is related to surrounding environment of your school.	IGNOU	214 (71.33)	65 (21.67)	21 (7.00)	300 (100.00)	0.80 N.S.
	UPRTOU	215 (71.67)	69 (23.00)	16 (5.33)	300 (100.00)	
	Total	**429 (71.50)**	**134 (22.33)**	**37 (6.17)**	**600 (100.00)**	

Notes: Figures in parentheses indicate percentages. N.S.: Not significant.

It can be observed that 72 per cent B.Ed. trainees of IGNOU and UPRTOU considered training provided for the development of competency about organisation and implementation activities regarding to community participation related to local environment to their school as more relevant.

Response of Counsellors about Relevance of Training given to B.Ed. Trainees for Development of Competency of Community Participation: University-wise

It can be noticed from Table 33.7 that the calculated χ^2 value of independence between the response pattern of counsellors and the university background in relation to the relevance of training given to B.Ed. trainees for development of competency in activities related to community participation is found 3.70, which is less than the Table value (5.99) at .05 level of significance with df: 2. Thus, the obtained χ^2 value is not found to be significant. Hence, it is clear that the response pattern of counsellors and the university background in relation to the relevance of training given to B.Ed. trainees for development of competency in activities related to community participation are found to be independent from each other.

Table 33.7: χ^2 test of independence of counsellor's response about relevance of process adopted for development of competency of community participation and university background

Response of counsellors about relevance of training for development of competency of community participation						
Statement	**University**	**Highly Agree**	**Agree**	**Disagree**	**Total**	**χ^2 Value**
Community work conducted by you related to surrounding environment of B.Ed. trainee's school	IGNOU	17 (56.67)	10 (33.33)	3 (10.00)	30 (100.00)	3.70 N.S.
	UPRTOU	16 (53.33)	14 (46.67)	0 (0.00)	30 (100.00)	
	Total	**33 (55.00)**	**24 (40.00)**	**3 (5.00)**	**60 (100.00)**	

Notes: Figures in parentheses indicate percentages. N.S.: Not significant.

It can be observed that 55 per cent counsellors of IGNOU and UPRTOU considered training provided for the development of competency in activities related to community participation related to local environment of their school as more relevant, and 45 per cent counsellors of IGNOU and UPRTOU did not consider such activities relevant.

Response of B.Ed. Trainees about Effectiveness of Training Provided to them for Development of Competency of Community Participation in B.Ed. Trainees: University-wise

It can be noticed from Table 33.8 that the calculated χ^2 values of independence between the response patterns of B.Ed. trainees and the university background in relation to the effectiveness of training provided for reducing pollution and maintaining hygienic environment in and around school are found 11.34 and 11.70

respectively, which is greater than the Table value (5.99) at .05 level of significance with df: 2. Thus, the obtained χ^2 values are found to be significant. Hence, it is clear that the response pattern of B.Ed. trainees and the university background in relation to the effectiveness of training provided for reducing pollution and maintaining hygienic environment in and around school are not found to be independent from each other.

Table 33.8: χ^2 test of independence on trainees' response about effectiveness of process adopted for development of competency of community participation and university background, skill-wise

Benefits of training for development of competency of community participation						
Developments of skills	**University**	**More extent**	**Some extent**	**Least**	**Total**	**χ^2 Values**
1. Development of reduce pollution by Plantation	IGNOU	233 (77.67)	52 (17.33)	15 (5.00)	300 (100.00)	11.34*
	UPRTOU	250 (83.33)	26 (8.67)	24 (8.00)	300 (100.00)	
	Total	**483 (80.50)**	**78 (13.00)**	**39 (6.50)**	**600 (100.00)**	
2. Development of cleanness arrangement near school	IGNOU	221 (73.67)	63 (21.00)	16 (5.33)	300 (100.00)	11.70*
	UPRTOU	230 (76.67)	38 (12.67)	32 (10.67)	300 (100.00)	
	Total	**451 (75.17)**	**101 (16.83)**	**48 (8.00)**	**600 (100.00)**	
3. Development of enrich participation of students in Pulse Polio Programme	IGNOU	212 (70.67)	69 (23.00)	19 (6.33)	300 (100.00)	5.66 N.S.
	UPRTOU	218 (72.67)	51 (17.00)	31 (10.33)	300 (100.00)	
	Total	**430 (71.67)**	**120 (20.00)**	**50 (8.33)**	**600 (100.00)**	
3. Development of motivate students and guardians for the success of adult education?	IGNOU	236 (78.67)	39 (13.00)	25 (8.33)	300 (100.00)	3.00 N.S.
	UPRTOU	225 (75.00)	37 (12.33)	38 (12.67)	300 (100.00)	
	Total	**461 (76.83)**	**76 (12.67)**	**63 (10.50)**	**600 (100.00)**	

Notes: Figures in parentheses indicate percentages. N.S.: Not significant.
* Indicates significant at .01 level.

It can be observed that majority of B.Ed. trainees (77 to 83%) of UPRTOU mentioned training provided for the development of skills in community participation as effective on following items:

(i) Reducing pollution *via* tree plantation (83.33%).
(ii) Arranging hygienic conditions in and around school (76.67%).

While 74 to 78 per cent B.Ed. trainees of IGNOU mentioned training provided for the development of skills in community participation as effective on following items:

(i) Reducing pollution *via* tree plantation (77.67%).
(ii) Arranging hygienic conditions in and around school (73.67%).

It can be noticed from Table 33.8 that the calculated χ^2 values of independence between the response pattern of B.Ed. trainees and the university background in relation to the effectiveness of training provided for increasing participation of students in pulse polio programme and motivating students and guardians for developing skills for adult education programme are found 5.66 and 3.00 respectively, which are less than the Table value (5.99) at .05 level of significance with df: 2. Thus, the obtained χ^2 values are found not significant. Hence, it is clear that the response pattern of B.Ed. trainees and the university background in relation to the above-mentioned community participation programme are found to be independent from each other.

It can be observed that 72 to 77 per cent B.Ed. trainees of IGNOU and UPRTOU considered training provided for the development of skills for community participation effective on following items:

(i) Motivating students and guardians for adult education (76.83%).
(ii) Increasing participation of students in pulse polio programme (71.67%).

Response of Counsellors about Effectiveness of Training Provided for Development of Competency of Community Participation among B.Ed. Trainees: University-wise

Table 33.9: χ^2 test of independence on counsellor's response about effectiveness of process adopted for development of competency of community participation and university background, skill-wise

Benefits of training process for development of competency of community participation among B.Ed. trainees						
Developments of skills	**University**	**More extent**	**Some extent**	**Least**	**Total**	**χ^2 Values**
1. Reducing pollution by plantation	IGNOU	23 (76.67)	4 (13.33)	3 (10.00)	30 (100.00)	4.36 N.S.
	UPRTOU	22 (73.33)	8 (26.67)	0 (0.00)	30 (100.00)	
	Total	**45 (75.00)**	**12 (20.00)**	**3 (5.00)**	**60 (100.00)**	
2. Cleanness arrangement near school	IGNOU	23 (76.67)	4 (13.33)	3 (10.00)	30 (100.00)	4.36 N.S.
	UPRTOU	22 (73.33)	8 (26.67)	0 (0.00)	30 (100.00)	
	Total	**45 (75.00)**	**12 (20.00)**	**3 (5.00)**	**60 (100.00)**	
3. Enriching participation of students in Pulse Polio Programme	IGNOU	18 (60.00)	10 (33.33)	2 (6.67)	30 (100.00)	9.51*
	UPRTOU	28 (93.33)	2 (6.67)	0 (0.00)	30 (100.00)	
	Total	**46 (76.67)**	**12 (20.00)**	**2 (3.33)**	**60 (100.00)**	
4. Motivating students and guardians for the success of adult education	IGNOU	21 (70.00)	6 (20.00)	3 (10.00)	30 (100.00)	4.02 N.S.
	UPRTOU	20 (66.67)	10 (33.33)	0 (0.00)	30 (100.00)	
	Total	**41 (68.33)**	**16 (26.67)**	**3 (5.00)**	**60 (100.00)**	

Notes: Figures in parentheses indicate percentages. N.S.: Not significant.
*Indicates significant at .01 level.

It can be noticed from Table 33.9 that the calculated χ^2 values of independence between the response pattern of counsellors and the university background in relation to the effectiveness of training provided for development of competency for reducing pollution *via* tree plantation, arranging hygienic conditions in and around school, motivating students and guardians for adult education are found 4.36, 4.36 and 4.02 respectively which is less than the Table value (5.99) at .05 level of significance with df: 2. Thus, the obtained χ^2 values are not found significant. Hence, it is clear that the response pattern of counsellors and the university background in relation to the above-mentioned skills for community participation are found to be independent from each other.

It can be observed that 68 to 75 per cent counsellors of IGNOU and UPRTOU mentioned training provided for the development of skills for enhancing community participation as effective on the following items:

(i) Reducing pollution *via* tree plantation (75.00%).
(ii) Arranging hygienic conditions in and around school (75.00%).
(iii) Motivating students and guardians for success of adult education programme (68.33%).

It can be noticed from Table 33.9 that the calculated χ^2 value of independence between the response pattern of counsellors and the university background in relation to the effectiveness of training given for enhancing student participation in Pulse Polio programme is 9.51, which is greater than the Table value (5.99) at .05 level of significance with df: 2. Thus, the obtained χ^2 value is found significant. Hence, it is clear that the response pattern of counsellors and the university background in relation to the effectiveness of training provided for enhancing student's participation in Pulse Polio programme are not found to be independent from each other.

It can be observed that majority of counsellors (93%) of UPRTOU and 60 per cent counsellors of IGNOU considered training provided for the development of skills in community participation for enhancing participation of trainees for Pulse Polio programme as effective.

Conclusion

In this study majority of trainees of both the open universities agreed that activities of community participation were organized during workshops. Trainees told that activities related to health education and community survey were organised during workshops. Trainees also stated that mentors and peer trainees helped them for reducing problems which occur during organisation of activities related to community participation.

Mentors of B.Ed. trainees of both the universities told that B.Ed. trainees conducted many activities, i.e. rallies for public awareness, making plantation, organisation of sports, cultural programmes and educational tour. Mentors also stated that B.Ed. trainees conducted health education activities, social and community works with the help of students and teachers of their schools. Mentors stated that they provide help to trainees in organization of activities related to community participation and maintaining discipline of students. The selected counsellors of both the open universities stated only survey and educational tour were organised during workshops. Counsellors told that trainees submitted the report of educational tour which is organised by themselves at their own school level and they were provided feedback and grades also. Majority of trainees and counsellors of both the open universities considered that process of making trainees competent in community participation activities as relevant and effective.

REFERENCES

Abdul Rashid Hj. Mohamad (1996). "Staff Development: Creating a Learning Culture", *Jurnal Pendidikan Gerak*, Bil. 8, MPPP.

Alice Ong Char Yee (1993). "Teacher Improvement Through Staff Development: Problems and Issues", *Prosiding Seminar Nasional Ke-3: Pengurusan Pendidikan*, Institut Aminuddin Baki.

Aytaged Sisay Zeleke (2012). "Continuous Professional Development Program for Higher Education Academics in Ethiopia : Views, Perceived needed Competencies and Organization in Focus", *Greener Journal of Educational Research, 2*(3).

Ekpoh,V.I., Oswald, A. & Victoria (2013). "Staff Development Programmes and Secondary School Teachers' Job Perfomance in Uyo Metropolis, Nigeria", *Journal of Education & Practice, 14*(12).

Frederick, B.J.A. & Stephen, O.O. (2010). "Teachers' Perceptions of Staff Development Programmes As It Relates to Teachers' Effectiveness : A Study of Rural Primary Schools' in Kenya", *Educational Research & Review, 5*(1).

Hacer Hande Vysal (2012). "Evaluation of An In-Service Training Program for Primary School Language Teachers in Turkey", *Australian Journal of Teacher Education, 37*(7).

Jahangir, S.F., Saheen, N. & Kazmi, S.F. (2012). "In-Service Training: A Contributory Factor Influencing Teachers' Performance", *International Journal of Academic Research in Progressive Education and Development, 1.*

Kazmi, S.F., Pervez, T., Mumtaz, S. (2011). "In-Service Teacher Training in Pakistan Schools and Total Quality Management", *Interdisciplinary Journal of Contemporary Research in Business*, March Edition 2011.

Kumar, S. (2011). *A Study of Processes of B.Ed. Programmes in Open Universities*, Unpublished Ph.D. Thesis, University of Allahabad, Allahabad, UP, India.

Matnoh @ Indi B. Minan (1995). *Programme Perkembangan Staf Dalam Mempertingkatkan Ilmu Pengetahuan Guru*, Thesis M.Sc. Universiti Utara Malaysia.

Nick Blanchard, P. & James W. Thacker (1999). *Effective Training: Systems, Strategies & Practices*, New Jersey: Prentice Hall.

Omar Che Mohd Zulkifli Che (2014). "The Need for In-Service Training for Teachers and It's Effectiveness in School", *International Journal for Innovation Education and Research, 2*(11), www.ijier.net

Owen, J.M. (1990). "Perspectives From Down Under" in Joyce, B. (ed.), *School Culture Through Staff Development*, Alexandria: American Schools Curriculum Development.

Pusat Perkembangan Kurikulum, Kementerian Pendidikan Malaysia (1992). *Pukal Latihan Kurikulum Baru Sekolah Menengah (KBSM)*. Kuala Lumpur: Dewan Bahasa dan Pustaka.

Ronald, W. Rebore (2004). *Human Resource Administration in Education: A Management Approach*, USA: Pearson Education, Inc.

Syed Makhdoom, Khalid Mehmood & Istiaq Hussain (2011). "In-service Training of Secondary Level Teachers: A Follow Up of Teachers' Performance in Comparative Perspective", *Journal of Education and Practice*, *2*(11&12).

Thompson, J.T. (1992), "Developing and Implementing an In-Service Program Designed to Change Teacher Attitude Towards Mainstream Learning Disabled Students at the Secondary Level", *Research Report*, Nova University.

34

Yogic Activities for Quality Enhancement in Primary Education

B.S. Gupta

Now-a-days the education, which students are getting in the schools and colleges are only developing the brain of the student. Syllabus builds in the schools has nothing to do with the real needs of the society. Values are going down and all round development is lacking, unemployment has spread all over the country. This chapter will focus on these things to make the education relevant to society and to make the students ready, alert, mature, useful and self-dependant.

The *Yog-Sutras* acknowledge the personality of Godhead in an oblique way, but only as helper whom the advancing *yogi* can utilize. Though brief, the *Yoga Sutras* are an enormously influential work on *yoga* Philosophy and practice. Primary aim of *Yoga* is to control the desires and aspirations of man and to understand the true nature of the soul. Eight aspects of *Yoga-Yama, Niyam, Asan, Pranayam, Pratyahar, Dharana, Dhyan* and *Samadhi*. These eight aspects help one to remove ignorance and awaken wisdom. The peak of the *Yoga* is detachment for all attributes (*Dharmas*). God is the Supreme Being. Meditation is meant to have a glimpse of self. To familiarize the students with the eight aspects of *Yoga* will be helpful. Trained teachers in *Yoga* should be appointed in schools.The aim of *Yoga* is to control one's desires and aspirations. *Yoga* strives to understand the real nature of soul. This can be best understood by controlling one's desires and aspirations. The state of *Yoga* can be achieved only be controlling one's desires and lusts. Just as we cannot see the true image of a thing in disturbed water, similarly when the mind is instable and out of control, we cannot perceive God. *Yoga* meditation is necessary to get a glimpse of God.

Intelligence is the intellectual power of child, which is marked by complex cognitive feats and high levels of motivation and self-awareness. Intelligence enables students to remember descriptions of things and use those descriptions in future behaviours. It is a cognitive process. It gives children the cognitive abilities to learn, form concepts, understand, and reason, including the capacities to recognize patterns, comprehend ideas, plan, solve problems, and use language to communicate. Intelligence enables students to experience and think.

Literature reviews are secondary sources, and as such, do not report any new or original experimental work. Satischandra Chatterjee (1994) found that *yoga* is essentially and predominantly the path of knowledge. John David (1914) observed that the *Samadhi* techniques are directly borrowed from the Buddhists with just the inclusion of the mystical and divine interpretations of mental absorption. Ganganath Jha (1907) observed that the *Yogabhashya* is a commentary on the *yoga sutras* of Patanjali which has been attributed in the discourse of the tradition to Vyasa. Ramdev (2004) observed that by regular practice of *Pranayama,* one gets a feeling of calmness of mind as a result of excess of oxygen to the brain cells.

Yoga is the practical path of realization. It maintains gradual control over body, senses, mind, intellect and ego so that the pure self may be realized. The realization of the pure self requires the cognition that the self is beyond the body, mind, intellect and ego. It is beyond space and time liberated, eternal and beyond sins, disease, miseries and death. The realization of this truth is the self-realization. The *Samkhya* philosophy emphasizes the attainment of knowledge by means of study, concentration and mediation. The *yoga* presents a practical path for the realization of the self. It tells us the way of following which the self can be realized.

Objectives

1. To study the effect of *Yogic* activities on Intelligence of boys at primary level.
2. To study the effect of *Yogic* activities on Intelligence of girls at primary level.
3. To study the effect of *Yogic* activities on Intelligence of students at primary level.

Hypotheses

1. There is no significant difference in Intelligence of boys of experimental and control groups.
2. There is no significant difference in Intelligence of girls of experimental and control groups.
3. There is no significant difference in Intelligence of students of experimental and control groups.

Research Method

The Quasi-experimental method of research has been used in the study.

Population and Sample

The population for the present study consists of all students of class Vth of Prayagraj. The present study consisted of 50 students for Experimental group and 50 students of control group from Devprayag School of Prayagraj.

Tools Used

Coloured Progressive Matrices were used to collect the data in the present study designed for children aged 5 to 11 years-of-age. This test contains sets A and B from the standard matrices, with a further set of 12 items inserted between the two, as set AB. Most items are presented on a coloured background to make the test visually stimulating for participants. However, the very last few items in set B are presented as black-on-white.

Statistics Used

In order to find out the significance of difference in gain score of pre- and post-t-test was used. This was achieved using SPSS version 17.0 statistical package.

Analysis and Interpretation

1. *To Study the Effect of Yogic Activities on Intelligence of Boys at Primary Level*

Table 34.1: Mean, SD and t-ratio of gain score of Intelligence of boys of experimental and control groups

Groups	N	Mean	S.D.	Std. Error	t-ratio
Experimental	25	7.450	2.450	.490	4.917*
Control	25	3.841	2.730	.546	

*Significant at .05 level of significance.

From Table 34.1, it is clear that the calculated value of t-ratio 4.917 is greater than the Table value of t-ratio at .05 level of significance. Therefore, the null hypothesis is rejected at .05 level of significance that "There is no significant difference in Intelligence of boys of experimental and control groups" and the research hypothesis is accepted that "There is significant difference in Intelligence of boys of experimental and control groups." Hence, it is stated that there is significant difference in Intelligence of boys of experimental and control groups.

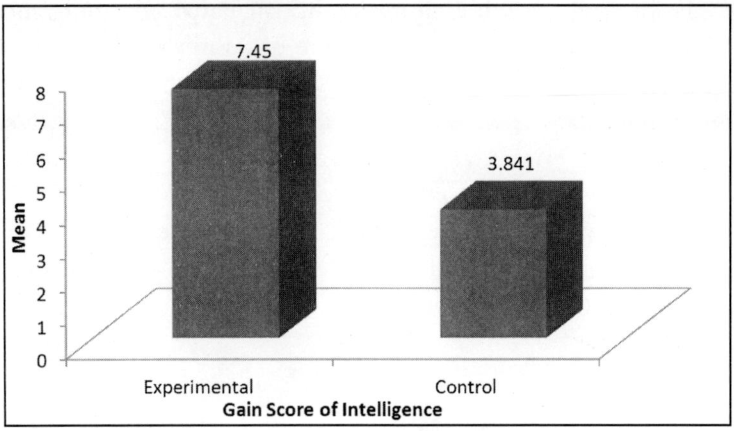

Fig. 34.1: Mean of gain score of Intelligence of boys of experimental and control groups

It is observed from Table 34.1 that the Mean of gain score of Intelligence of boys of experimental group is 7.450 and the Mean of gain score of Intelligence of boys of control group is 3.841. It indicates that there exists significant difference in Mean of gain score of Intelligence of boys of experimental and control groups. From the observation of mean difference of Mean of gain score of Intelligence of boys of experimental and control groups, it is stated that *Yogic* activities are more effective to enhance the intelligence of boy's experimental group than the boys of control group.

2. *To Study the Effect of Yogic Activities on Intelligence of Girls at Primary Level*

Table 34.2: Mean, SD and t-ratio of gain score of Intelligence of Girls of experimental and control groups

Group	N	Mean	S.D.	Std. Error	t-ratio
Experimental	25	7.050	2.621	.524	3.395*
Control	25	4.630	2.413	.482	

* Significant at .05 level of significance.

From Table 34.2, it is clear that the calculated value of t-ratio 3.395 is greater than the Table value of t-ratio at .05 level of significance. Therefore, the null hypothesis is rejected at .05 level of significance that "There is no significant difference in Intelligence of Girls of experimental and control groups" and the research hypothesis is accepted that "There is significant difference in Intelligence of Girls of experimental and control groups." Hence, it is stated that there is significant difference in Intelligence of Girls of experimental and control groups.

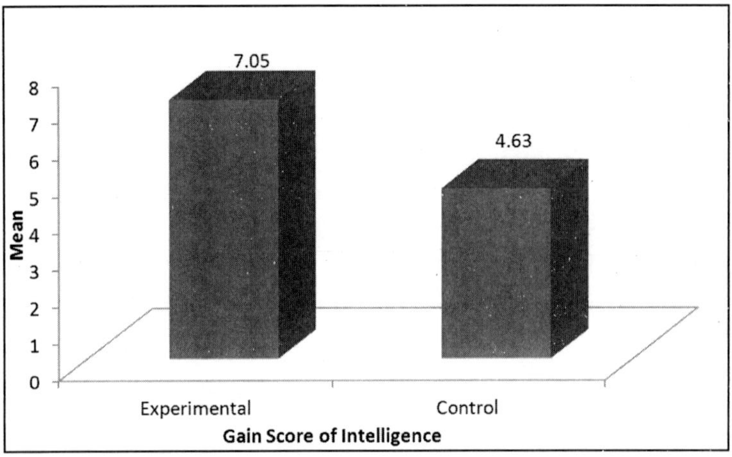

Fig. 34.2: Mean of gain score of Intelligence of Girls of experimental and control groups

It is observed from Table 34.2 that the Mean of gain score of Intelligence of Girls of experimental group is 7.050 and the Mean of gain score of Intelligence of Girls of control group is 4.630. It indicates that there exists significant difference in Mean of gain score of Intelligence of Girls of experimental and control groups. From the observation of mean difference of Mean of gain score of Intelligence of Girls of experimental and control groups, it is stated that *Yogic* activities are more effective to enhance the intelligence of girl's experimental group than the girls of control group.

3. *To Study the Effect of Yogic Activities on Intelligence of Students at Primary Level*

Table 34.3: Mean, SD and t-ratio of gain score of Intelligence of Students of experimental and control groups

Group	N	Mean	S.D.	Std. Error	t-ratio
Experimental	50	7.250	2.519	.356	5.908*
Control	50	4.235	2.581	.365	

* Significant at .05 level of significance.

From Table 34.3, it is clear that the calculated value of t-ratio 5.908 is greater than the Table value of t-ratio at .05 level of significance. Therefore, the null hypothesis is rejected at .05 level of significance that "There is no significant difference in Intelligence of Students of experimental and control groups" and the research hypothesis is accepted that "There is significant difference in Intelligence of Students of experimental and control groups." Hence, it is stated that there is significant difference in Intelligence of Students of experimental and control groups.

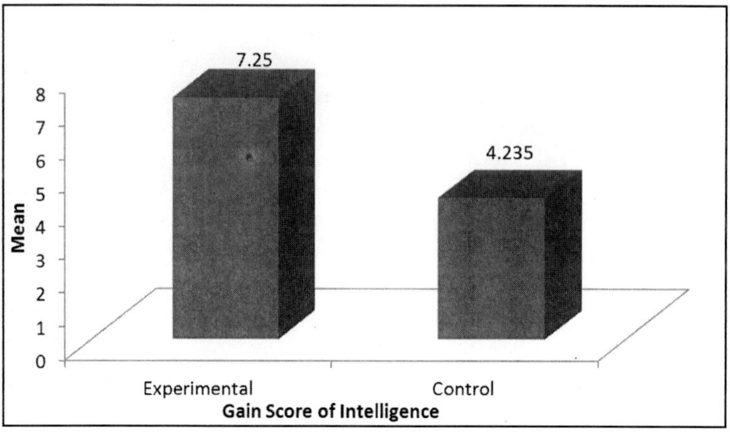

Fig. 34.3: Mean of gain score of Intelligence of Students of experimental and control groups

It is observed from Table 34.3 that the Mean of gain score of Intelligence of Students of experimental group is 7.250 and the Mean of gain score of Intelligence of Students of control group is 4.235. It indicates that there exists significant difference in Mean of gain score of Intelligence of Students of experimental and control groups. From the observation of mean difference of Mean of gain score of Intelligence of Students of experimental and control groups, it is stated that *Yogic* activities are more effective to enhance the intelligence of students of experimental group than the Students of control group.

Implications

Patanjali has advocated different postures which are very much helpful in the control of mind as well as of vital elements in the body. They also help in removing the suffering due to cold and heat. As a matter of fact Posture is the control of the body. It also keeps the body free from disease and makes it strong. By it one can control the different external as well as internal organs in the body. Thus, Patanjali *Yoga* made the valuable insight the mental control requires and in the discipline of the body as well.

REFERENCES

Chatterjee, Satishchandra (1994). *An Introduction to Indian Philosophy,* Patna: Pustak Bhandar.

David, John (1914). *The Yog System of Patanjali with Commentary Yogabhasya Attributed to Veda Vyasa and Tattva Vaicharadi* by Vachaspati Misra, Harvard: University Press.

Gupta, B.S. (2019). *Effect of Yogic Activities on Memory at Primary level Students*, D.Phil. in Education. Prayagraj: University of Allahabad.

Henry, E. Garrett (2005). *Statistics in Psychology and Education*, New Delhi: Paragon International Publishers.

Jha, Ganganath (1907). *The Yoga Darshan: The Sutras of Patanjali with the Bhasya of Vyasa,* Bombay: Theosophical Publication Fund.

Karlinger, F.N. (2007). *Foundations of Behavioural Research*, New Delhi: Surjeet Publications.

Ramdev (2004). *Yog Sadhana Evam Yog Chikitsha Rahasa,* Haridwar: Divya Prakashak, Divya Yog Mandir Trust.

35

Resource Management and Challenges in Teacher Education Programme

Ashok Dansana and *Gulsan Behera*

A lot of planning and resources have been spent for improving the quality of Teacher Education. New technologies have been introduced in the field of education, still our teacher-education could not raise unto the expected level. It is lacking behind somewhere in realizing its purpose. Its scope has broadened and its objectives have become focused during the last thirty five years, but Teacher Education could not realize its objective fully. In science and technology the world has become interdependent and is turning gradually into a global village. But educational programmes for teachers or teacher-education has not made full use of their development skill. The teachers with the knowledge of latest technological advancement are not being produced who are expected to use these upcoming techniques.

Developing Creativity

No doubt Bloom in his lifetime revised the objectives of higher mental order by placing creativity at the top because development of creativity is very essential for the all-round development of human being. But, we have forgotten that knowledge cannot be delivered, it has to be created. It means that we should emphasis on creativity.

Working of Teacher-Education Institutions

The National Council for Teacher Education (NCTE) is a regulatory body which controls the functioning of these institutions and prevent them from becoming commercial institutions, but because the country is so diverse with innumerable institutions, it sometimes get difficult to monitor all the institutions. Some unscrupulous institutions have become simply money making centre and produce certified but incompetent teachers which is a matter of great concern because incompetency of teachers can harm the system of education.

Globalization and Erosion of Values

Due to globalization and advancement of science and technology world has become closer. Access to all kinds of information is very easy. The facility of internet has reached every nook and corner of the country. Every transaction is going to be online. But there are several deviations particularly of young students who are prone to malpractices. It is said that "our inclination towards bad is more than our inclination towards good." In this sense mobile culture, internet, face book and twitter etc. have polluted young minds. This led to the erosion of values.

Developing Life Skills

Life skills are certain skills which are essential for personal development and growth. These skills enable man to deal with the life's difficulties and adversities more effectively. These skills are: (a) Thinking Skills, (b) Self-Awareness, Problem Solving, Creative Thinking, Decision making and Critical thinking, (c) Social Skills—Interpersonal relations, effective communication and empathy, and (d) Emotional Skills—Stress management. Main issue is that teacher-education is memory based, i.e. there is no active involvement of students, so we are lacking in the development of life skills among the students, which are essential for all-round development of students.

Realisation of Constitutional Goals

India is a democratic society and there are four founding pillars of this democratic society as are mentioned in our Constitution. These are Equality of Status and Opportunity. Liberty of thought, expression, faith, belief and worship, fraternity assuring the dignity of the individual and unity and integrity of the nation and Justice—Social, economic and political. These concepts incorporated in the Constitution are essential for national development. There are various social problems that today our nation is confronting. These are population explosion, unemployment, diversity and communal tension. Teacher can safeguard students against these social problems if they are sensitive towards these issues.

Structure of Teacher-Education Programme

Lot of stress is given on Teacher Education course in India, unfortunately still there are several loopholes in the system.

Curriculum

Curriculum of Teacher Education porgramme in India has been criticized much. Some educationists feel that it does not fully address the need of contemporary Indian Schools and society and it does not contain relevant contents for teachers who have to impart quality education in schools.

Quality Concern: Quality in education relates to the quality of the work undertaken by a teacher, which has significantly effect upon his or her pupils. Teacher Education has not come upto the requisite standards. Teachers are not able to think critically and solve the issues related to teaching methods, content, organisations etc. more knowledge of theoretical principles is emphasized and teachers are not able to these principles in actual classroom situations.

Time Duration: One year duration of Teacher Education programme has been an issue of much long debate. The Teacher

Education curriculum which includes theory and practical and internship in actual schools require much more time for its effective implementation. National Curriculum Framework (1998) also recommends for two year duration of Teacher Education programme but could not be implemented. So, there is a need to extend the time period of present teacher-education programme. There are problems of quality perception, quality scaling and quality differentiation in Teacher Education. There is a significant variance between expected and actual quality. Alas, this gap is widening. This is exemplified by the successive entrance tests for higher level, be it Graduate, Post-Graduate or Doctoral Level. There has to be adequate focus on all the systemic parameters—input, process and output. The degeneration of quality of Teacher Education can be attributed more to the private sector. Unless the Teacher Education norms are observed sincerely by the society, nobody can help. Overgrowing establishment has overgrown enrolment in most of the Teacher Education programmes. But, at the same time, there is uneven distribution of the Teacher Education institutions. Teacher Education regulations, norms and standards though latest visited during 2009, have further scope for perfection. There is a need to have demand and supply estimates. Blanket " NO" and even blanket " YES" can be grossly harmful in the public interest. Teacher Education for preparing humane and professional teachers needs to be holistic. Along with content and methodology, there is a need to integrate emotional competencies, such as self-awareness and self-management, social sensitivity and social management. There is a need to integrate life skills, such as self-awareness, empathy, interpersonal relationship, effective communication, critical thinking, creative thinking, decision making, problem solving, and coping up with emotions and stress. But now the situation is different and such type of teachers are precious and rare. The term skill has become a misnomer, particularly, in education. All the skills, such as life skills, techno-pedagogic skills, techno-savvy skills, info-savvy skills, emotional skills, human development skills, spiritual skills need to be integrated in Teacher Education.

There is little parity amongst various modes of education, such as distance mode, e-mode, and face to face mode. Distance mode is diluted, e-mode is in infancy, whereas, the face to face mode is stagnant. There is no network amongst the various modes of Teacher Education. These are functioning more or less in isolation. Teacher Education has not been in a position to come out of school education. It has made very little contribution to higher education. Educationists have been overobsessed with school education intensively for complexity, enormity, and the large number of the schools and students, but this is at the cost of neglecting higher education. Teacher Education is a discipline which educates the progressive generations on what has gone by, where we are, where we want to go, and what we like to create, observing healthy, meaningful and long life. Innovations in Teacher Education are very rare. It may be attributed to various factors. Novel ideas do not incubate because of the adverse external conditions. There are wide gaps between the visionaries and actors. The twenty first Century is highly complex. The return on investment, be it public sector or corporate, is measured in terms of material returns than in terms of human development. Human beings are most neglected. There is more focus on GNP than on HDI. In this ICT and digital age machines are most respected, whereas, men are most neglected. What to talk of the knowledge poor, even in the knowledge rich societies, gross injustice is rampant. There are demand and supply imbalances in Teacher Education. Appreciable attempts have been made for manpower planning. But, the manpower planning still needs to be done more scientifically. It is expected that the various State Governments play an active role in manpower planning. The various laboratories of Teacher Education institutions, namely Science Lab, Psychology Lab, Guidance & Counselling Lab, Educational Technology Lab, Computer Lab, and Language Lab are either not there or are mostly in very bad stage. The field reality is still worse. All the laboratories ought to be fully functional and innovative to address the problems. Some of the distance and open universities have become over activists in the context of Teacher Education. These have a notion that they can open their Teacher Education extension centres anywhere. To give birth to infinite is their right, but who will rear their babies. Such distance and open universities have resulted into the dilution of Teacher Education. There are questions on recognition of Teacher Education institutions. There are questions on inputs and processes of Teacher Education. There are questions even on Accreditation of Teacher Education institutions. Escola Normal of Goa was much better established during Portuguese period than the most recent modern Teacher Education institutions in India. Nalanda was having a much better profile and grade than the highest graded modern universities.

Rationale of the Study

The rationale behind selecting the Self-Financed Teacher Education Institutes is that as we all know India has one of the biggest higher education systems in the world. Teacher Education is a part of it. Teacher Education means programmes of education and research which equip an individual to teach at schools. The role of teacher has been changing from time to time. In this context, the Teacher Education programme is undergoing changes nationally as well as internationally. Today, Education is a service industry—a part of globalization process under the umbrella of General Agreement on Trade in Services (GATS). It was during the 1820s when a few private academics began offering a medium of teacher training. However, during the past decades it is observed that there has been an exponential increase in self-financed colleges. So, it increases the availability and access to Teacher Education with high fees. In this view various educationists have also argued for establishing private institution has been to make money. Despite the high fees, the private colleges have been able to attract a huge crowd. This shows the private entrepreneur succeeds against all odds! In the view of this consideration, the researcher wishes to attempt this study and investigate into the factual realities of self-financed Teacher Education colleges. There are many studies conducted on self-financing Teacher Education programme by different researchers. Darji (2015) conducted a study on Innovative practice in Teacher Education institution of Gujarat state and found that to consider the all-round development of pupil teaches and properly facilitated ICT integration and bridge the gaps between school education and Teacher Education. Raman (2018) conducted a study on analysis of causes of stress and its management technique adopted by college teachers with reference to self-financing colleges in Chennai city and found many respondents were stressful and facing physical problems due to work stress. Chaudhary (2013) conducted a study on demographic and academic variables as correlates of job satisfaction of self-financed institution teachers and to found self-financed teachers have moderate degree of job satisfaction and teachers who have more educational qualification have lower job satisfaction. Pritam (2018) conducted a study on privatization and quality in Teacher Education: A study on policies and practices and to found the quality parameters such as manpower resources, ICT and infrastructure, professional development were compromised. Ranjan (2010) conducted a study on self-financed English medium Teacher Education institutions of Gujarat to find out these institutions have adequate infrastructure facilities and interactive teaching-learning in the class rooms. Gorain (2017) study on views of teacher educators towards two year B.Ed. programme of West Bengal to find out no significance difference between views of teacher educators teaching in private and government institutions, male and female teachers towards Two-Year B.Ed programme. Barman (2015) conducted a study on teaching effectiveness of teacher educators in different types of B.Ed. colleges in West Bengal, India to find out there exist moderate level of teaching effectiveness and government aided B.Ed. college teachers are more effective than self-financed B.Ed. college teachers. Shete (2017) conducted a study on working conditions of teachers in self-financing courses in higher education institutions in Mumbai to find out majority of women and very young teachers were teaching in self-financing course. Barua (2015) conducted study on quality of public and private funded B.Ed. programme in north region based on perception of teacher trainees with regard to learning enhancement to find out there was no significant difference in perception of male and female teacher trainees of Public-Funded Institutions with respect to key areas in the factors 'Learning Enhancement'. Dutta (2018) conducted a study on privatization of secondary Teacher Education programme in West Bengal to find out not only the infrastructural set up but available facilities and equipments are far below than the expectations. Sasikumar (2017) conducted a study on professional commitment of teacher educators working in B.Ed. colleges to find there is no significance difference in professional commitment between male and female, urban and rural teacher educators. The above reviews on related studies have been conducted on perception of teacher educators towards teaching education programme by government aidded and private funded institution but few studies had laid stress on self-financing Teacher Education programme which is newly introduced in government autonomous colleges affiliated by state university. Despite so many researches carried out in the area of Teacher Education including self-financing, it was found that there is lack of studies in Odisha especially in the context of the perception of teacher educators towards self-financing Teacher Education programme. Besides the fact, the growing interest and concern over the programme by the stakeholders, the parents and practitioners, felt need of taking views of teacher educators on the availability of resources, needs, satisfaction of students as well as job security and management supports to the teacher educators. It's a new term used in Educational sphere for encouraging some courses to be available for the students by their demand through the self-financing mode where the students are provided all course fee and the government should not take any responsibility of financing but it perform to verify on NCTE norms and issued certificate to the students. It should be run on Universities, Government autonomous colleges or Government aided colleges. Self-financing Teacher Education programme in Odisha introduced in 2016 in 9 colleges. Now in 2020, the number of self-financing

Teacher Education programmes running in government colleges and universities is 20. It should be more effective and enhanced due to the increasing number of Students and demand of Teacher Education among them. Government does not establish adequate number of institutions so it is a way to mixing of financing from students and authority and academic support from government to be encouraged Teacher Education programme in Odisha.

Objectives of the Study

1. To study the perception of teacher educators and student teachers on self-financing Teacher Education programme on availability and utilization of resources.
2. To study the perception of teacher educators and student teachers on the nature of teaching-learning process in self-financing Teacher Education programme in Odisha.

Methodology

The population of the present study consists of all teacher educators and student teachers of self-financing Teacher Education programme in Odisha. The accessible population was the teacher educators and student teachers of S.C.S. Autonomous College, Puri, Shailabala Womens' Autonomous College, Cuttack, Fakir Mohan Autonomous College, Balasore, Rama Devi University, Bhubaneswar. The investigator randomly selected four self-financing Teacher Education programmes in the state of Odisha. Further, from all four Teacher Education programme the researcher collected data from 20 teacher educators, 4 from each institution and 80 student teachers where 20 from each Teacher Education programme. One structured questionnaire schedule was prepared by the researcher with the guidance of the supervisor and administered to collect data from Teacher Educators and Student Teachers on utilisation of available resources and teaching-learning process of the self-financing Teacher Education programme. Questionnaire schedule was developed based on the availability of resources with its utilization and the teaching-learning process existed in institution. After developing the tools by the investigator, it was finalized taking the guidance and suggestion of supervisor.

Procedure of Data Collection and Analysis

In the present study for getting relevant information, the researcher collected data from respondents, i.e. 20 Teacher Educators and 80 Student Teachers from 4 self-financing Teacher Education programme. For collecting information from the respondents, the researcher randomly selected S.C.S. Autonomous College, Puri, Shailabala Womens' Autonomous College, Cuttack, Fakir Mohan Autonomous College, Balasore, Ramadevi University, Bhubaneswar. The data was collected by the investigator personally by visiting the research sites through the employment of adequate tools and techniques. At first, the researcher made convince the principal of the institution and with the permission of principal the researcher administered the tools for data collection from the respondents. To analyze the data, firstly the researcher organized the data, then it was categorized, classified and finally, analyzed and discussed the data along with the discussion of previous studies of related literature by using appropriate content analysis of quantitative technique.

Major Findings

Major findings are grouped here in two categories—one is on availability and utilization of resources in self-financing Teacher Education institutions and other one is on teaching-learning process in those institutions.

(a) *Availability and Utilization of Resources*

67.88 per cent student teachers and 79.50 per cent teacher educators agree with proper utilisation of available resources there. However, remaining 32.12 per cent of student teachers and (20.50%) of teacher educators did not agree upon proper utilisation of available resources in the self-financing Teacher Education programme. Whereas 78.75 per cent of student teachers and 80 per cent of teacher educators reveal that the Teacher Education Institutions provide all kinds of necessary resource supports. However, remaining 21.25 per cent of student teachers and 20 per cent of teacher educators do not agree on it. In other words, they disagree on the availability of necessary resource supports. 72.50 per cent of student teachers and 80 per cent of teacher educators appreciate the Teacher Education programme whereas remaining 27.50 per cent of student teachers and 20 per cent of teacher educators do not accept that the resources used in considerable extent. In this study, it is revealed that 75 per cent of student teachers and 90 per cent of teacher educators express their agreement on teacher educators that they perform task for the fullest development of the students but remaining 25 per cent of student teachers do not agree with it. On academic support facilities of self-financing Teacher Education programme, 65 per cent of student teachers and 20 per cent of teacher educators appreciate it. But remaining 35 per cent of student teachers and 20 per cent of teacher educators agree that there are no appropriate academic support facilities in these institutions. In self-financing mode student teachers are charged with all course fee. On behalf of this 61.25 per cent of student teachers and 25 per cent of teacher educators appreciate that the course fee proportionately give benefit in the self-financing Teacher Education programme whereas remaining 39.75 per cent of student teachers and 25 per cent of teacher educators do not agree upon it. On the matter of sufficient staff support services, 77.50 per cent student teachers and 85 per cent of teacher educators agree on there were adequate and sufficient staff support services whereas remaining 22.50 per cent of student teachers and 15 per cent of teacher educators consider that there was no sufficient staff support services in self-financing Teacher Education programme. On the matter of organization of field trips and study tour for the knowledge exploration for the students, 39 per cent of student teachers and 55 per cent of teacher educators agree it. By this action, the student teachers as well as teacher educators get more practical knowledge.

Teaching-Learning Process

For the Teaching-Learning Process of the self-financing Teacher Education programme in Odisha, the student teachers and teacher educators mostly revealed that 73.75 per cent of student teachers and 87 per cent of teacher educators appreciate the teaching-learning process of the institutions. In this study, it is revealed that 82.50 per cent of student teachers and 95 per cent of teacher educators agree that the teacher educators orient students to acquire teaching-learning skills. However, remaining 17.50 per cent of student teachers and 5 per cent of teacher educators do not agree on it. On the matter of needs and interests of the students of self-financing Teacher Education programmeit is revealed that 73.75 per cent of student teachers and 85 per cent teacher educators agree the students are supported whereas remaining 26.25 per cent of student teachers and 15 per cent of teacher educators do not agree on that fact. In self-financing Teacher Education programme concern on that the teacher educators follow adequate methods of teaching or not. Accordingly, 71.25 per cent of student teachers and 95 per cent of teacher educators appreciate that they follow adequate methods of teaching but remaining 28.75 per cent of student teachers express their disagreement on it. On the matter of progress of student teachers by the teacher educators get maintained well or not by this study 75 per cent of student teachers and 90 per cent of teacher educators agree that students, progress is ensured in self-financing Teacher Education programme but remaining 25 per cent of student teachers and 10 per cent of teacher educators do not agree on this matter. In this study, it is revealed that 66.25 per cent of the student teachers and 75 per cent of teacher educators appreciate that there is appropriate student support services in self-financing Teacher Education programme but remaining 33.75 per cent of student teachers and 25 per cent of teacher educators replied that student support services should be more effective and enhanced. On the occasion of organization seminar, workshops and internship programme for the development of the student teachers as well as teacher educators, 83.75 per cent of students and 95 per cent of teachers consider that it is mostly fruitful whereas remaining 16.25 per cent students do not consider the same.

REFERENCES

Al-Yousef, H. (2009). "They Know Nothing about University—Neither of them Went: The Effect of Parents' Level of Education on their Involvement in their Daughters' Higher Education Choices", *Compare: A Journal of Comparative and International Education, 39*(6): 783-98.

Ancheh, K.S.B., Krishnan, A. & Nurtjahja, O. (2007). "Evaluative criteria for selection of private universities and colleges in Malaysia", *Journal of International Management Studies, 2*(1): 1-11.

Anderson, P. (1999). "Factors influencing student choice in higher education", *Perspectives: Policy and Practice in Higher Education, 3*(4): 128-31.

Bagley, William C. (1908). *Classroom Management*. London: Macmillan & Co. Ltd.

Ball, S.J. (2007). *Education plc: Understanding Private Sector Participation in Public Sector Education*. New York: Routledge.

Barman, P. (2015). "Teaching Effectiveness of Teacher Educator in Different Types of B.Ed Colleges in West Bengal, India." *American Journal of Education Research, 3*(11).

Barun S. (2005). "A study on Quality of Public and privet Funded B.Ed. programme in Northern Region Based on Perception of Teacher Trainees with Regard to Learning Enhancement." *Journal of Education and Practices, 6*(21).

Chaudhary, M.V. (2013). "Demographic and Academic Variables as Correlated of Job Satisfaction of Set Finance Institution Teacher." *Scholary Research Journal for Interdisciplinary Studies, 2*(14).

Goel, D. & Goel, C. (2012). "Teacher Education Scenario in India: Current Problems & Concerns." *MIER Journal of Educational Studies, Trends & Practices, 2*(2): 231-42.

Gorain, R. (2017). "View of the Teacher Education Towards Two Year B.Ed. Programme of W.B." *International Journal of Interdisciplinary & Multidisciplinary Studies* (*IJIMS*), *4*(2).

Government of India (2010). All India Educational Survey (AIES), NCERT, New Delhi. DISE-2010-11 Report, National University of Educational Planning and Administration, New Delhi, Documents of Ministry of Education.

Kumar, R. & Mohalik, R. (2017). "Perception of Teacher Educators Towards Professional Development." *International Journal of Innovative Studies in Sociology and Humanities* (*IJISSH*), *2*(8).

Pritam, B.P. (2018). "Privatization and Quality in Teacher Education: A Study of Policy & Practices." *International Journal of Education & Applied Social Science, 9*(3).

Sahoo, P.K. and Sharma, P. (2018). "Student Teachers' Perception Towards Curriculum Reform in Teacher Education Programme in Odisha." *Educational Quest: An Int. J. of Education and Applied Social Science, 9*(1): 1-11.

Wang, J. *et al.* (2016). "Teaching and Teacher Education: A Kaleidoscope of Notions." *Journal of Teacher Education, 62*(4).

36

Inclusive Teacher Education

S.K. Panda

The inclusive Teacher Education has now become the need of the hour. The design and practice of current teacher education programme is based on certain assumption, which impede the progress of ideas and the professional and personal growth of the teacher (Aggarwal, 2010). In this regard, teacher educators need to be committed and dedicated professionals who can sincerely and efficiently implement the teacher education programmes and transact the curriculum. Teacher Education institutions have the duties and responsibilities, for realizing the aims and objectives set for Teacher Education. As mentioned in the Programme of Action (PoA) 1986, the University in cooperation with National Council for Teacher Education (NCTE) will exercise responsibility for academic aspects including conduct of examinations, award of degrees and ensuring quality of teacher education institutions. Thus, pre-service, in-service and continuing education should be a continuous and comprehensive teacher education programmes which in order to be effective and meaningful. Teacher Education programme at the secondary stage, like at all other stages, will include theory, practice teaching in schools and practical work in the light of context, concerns, profile of teachers and general and specific objectives.

The most critical aspect of the teacher education curriculum is its transaction. Teaching is a profession and teacher education is a process of professional preparation of teachers. The teacher must now be equipped not only to teach but also to understand the students, their parents and the community so that children will be regular in schools and learn. In addition, the NCF 2005 requires a teacher to be a facilitator of children's learning in a manner that the children are helped to construct their knowledge. It also opens out possibilities for the teacher to participate in the construction of syllabus, textbooks and teaching-learning materials. Such roles demand that teachers be equipped with a better understanding of curriculum, subject content and pedagogy on the one hand and community and teacher education institutions structures and management on the other.

Presently in India, total universities are 935 (50 Central Universities, 409 State Universities, 127 Deemed to Be Universities and 349 Private Universities) as on 1st February, 2020 (UGC, 2020) and 621 autonomous colleges (170 Government colleges and 451 Non-Government colleges) as on 8 September 2017. About 200 universities offered either MA (Education) programme or M.Ed. programme or both. Even some universities are offering B.Ed. (both regular and open mode), BA-B.Ed, B.Sc-B.Ed and B.Ed.-M.Ed. integrated programmes. Out of total number of Teacher Training Institutions in India, 95 per cent are managed by private entrepreneurs and rest by public sector. Teacher Education is not a mechanical activity of training information transmission and teacher educators are not training information dispensers. Currently in India, there are different teacher education programmes running at various level and for each programme, curriculum are different from one programme to another programme. These teacher education programmes are:

Diploma Programmes

The Diploma Programmes for Teacher Education includes:

- Diploma in Early Childhood Education programme leading to Diploma in Pre-School Education (DPSE).
- Elementary Teacher Education Programme leading to Diploma in Elementary Education (D.El.Ed.).
- Diploma in Physical Education Programme leading to Diploma in Physical Education (D.P.Ed.).
- Diploma in Elementary Education Programme through Open and Distance Learning System leading to Diploma in Elementary Education (D.El.Ed.).
- Diploma in Arts Education (Visual Arts) programme leading to Diploma in Arts Education (Visual Arts).
- Diploma in Arts Education (Performing Arts) programme leading to Diploma in Arts Education (Performing Arts).

Bachelor Programmes

The Bachelor Programmes for Teacher Education includes:

- Bachelor of Elementary Teacher Education Programme leading to Bachelor of Elementary Education (B.El.Ed.) Degree.
- Bachelor of Education Programme leading to Bachelor of Education (B.Ed.) Degree.
- Bachelor of Physical Education Programme leading to Bachelor of Physical Education (B.P.Ed.) Degree.
- Bachelor of Education Programme through Open and Distance Learning System leading to Bachelor of Education (B.Ed.) Degree.
- Bachelor of Education Programme 3-year (Part Time) leading to Bachelor of Education (B.Ed) Degree.

Master Programmes

The Master Programmes for Teacher Education includes:

- Master of Education Programme leading to Master of Education (M.Ed.) Degree.
- Master of Physical Education Programme leading to Master of Physical Education (M.P.Ed.) Degree.

Integrated Programmes

- Four-year Integrated Programme leading to B.A.B.Ed./ B.Sc.B.Ed. Degree.
- Three-year Integrated Programme leading to B.Ed.-M.Ed. Degree.

Teacher educators need to be looked at as crucial mediating agents through whom curriculum is transacted. Textbooks by themselves do not help in developing knowledge and understanding. Learning is not confined to the four walls of the classroom. We need to connect knowledge to life outside the school and enrich the curriculum by making it less textbook-oriented (NCFTE 2009):

- The NCF 2005 has described the current concerns of teacher education as follows: Experiences in the practice of teacher education indicate that knowledge is treated as 'given', embedded in the curriculum and accepted without question; there is no engagement with the curriculum.
- Curriculum, syllabi and textbooks are never critically examined by the student teacher or the regular teacher.
- Language proficiency of the teacher needs to be enhanced, but existing programmes do not recognize the centrality of language in the curriculum.
- Teacher Education programmes provide little scope for student teachers to reflect on their experiences.
- Disciplinary knowledge is viewed as independent of professional training in Pedagogy.
- Repeated 'practice' in the teaching of a specified number of isolated lessons is considered as sufficient condition for professional development.

- It is assumed that links between learning theories and models and teaching methods are automatically formed in the understanding developed by student teachers.
- There is no opportunity for teachers to examine their own biases and beliefs and reflect on their own experiences as part of classroom discourse and enquiry.
- Theory courses have no clear articulation with practical work and ground realities.
- The evaluation system followed in teacher education programmes is too information-oriented, excessively quantitative and lacks comprehensiveness.
- Apart from conceptual and pedagogical aspects, the programme needs to develop certain attitudes, dispositions, habits and interests in a teacher.
- The present evaluation protocol has no place for evaluation of these aspects.

The above observations provide distinct pointers for addressing issues on the different aspects of teacher education curriculum reform. The NCTE and the NCERT over the past few decades have addressed the review of teacher education curriculum in the light of changing educational scenario and brought out a series of frameworks. These frameworks provide guidelines on development of teacher education programmes incorporating current concerns as well as national and global developments. The pioneering effort of designing a curriculum framework for teacher education was made by the non-statutory NCTE, way back in 1978. That Teacher Education Curriculum—A Framework (1978) responded to the implications of the national educational policy and priorities as a result of the implementation of the Report of Education Commission (1964-66) and made recommendations for the restructuring of teacher education programmes and their content. That was reviewed in 1988. Subsequently, it was followed by the development of a model curriculum by the University Grants Commission (UGC) curriculum development centre in 1990. After the NCTE became a statutory body in 1995, it brought out

Curriculum Framework for Quality Teacher Education in 1998. Another framework, *Teacher Education for Future* was brought out by the NCERT to support the NCF for School Education (2000). Two attempts were made by the NCTE to develop draft curriculum framework (the first in 2005 and the second in 2006). The latter incorporated the substantial inputs provided by the NCERT in the context of the adoption of the NCF (2005) for School Education. Two more draft frameworks, one in 2007 and the other in 2008 have since been added. For various reasons, related action on the ground in respect of these documents did not take place. The present document represents a continuation of these curriculum renewal efforts. It has given due consideration to the earlier frameworks, particularly to the 2006 document, tried to consolidate the work that has been accomplished thus far and presents by and large an updated and upgraded version of a new National Curriculum Framework for Teacher Education (NCFTE). The modalities to be employed for organizing activities other than teaching for all-round capacity building and empowerment of a teacher trainee will involve joint supervision by the teacher educators and school teacher. The transaction modes, for example for motivating adults for making them literate can be through mass participation, folk songs, street plays etc. It is expected that a student teacher undertakes several practical activities which facilitate instruction as also those that relate to management.

The transaction mode of the community related practical work may include interaction between school teacher and intending teachers and members of the community a component of assessment, evaluation and remediation has been added. Internship programme shall be enriched to provide all the experiences that a teacher needs. For the purpose of transaction, a course may be divided into units and then the modular approach may be followed. Pupil-teacher may be encouraged to pursue independent and group studies. Multiple approaches should be adopted for the purpose of evaluating achievement for the theoretical content. It shall be continuous as well as annual, internal as well as external.

The objectives of Teacher Education Institutions for newly admitted pupil teachers should be:

- To orient the incoming students to the nature, scope and significance of their training programme.
- To orient them according to the needs and responsibilities of the teacher education institutions.
- To orient them according to the specific course choice available in the respective programme.
- To develop among them closeness and familiarity with their classmates and advisors.

This course should be organized for a period of one week or two week depending upon the needs of the students. The Syllabus for the entire programme has to be developed in advance and to be circulated among the pupil-teachers.

Responsibility of Teacher Education Institutions

This is the twenty-first century—a digital age in which information is incessantly created, knowledge is expanding exponentially, and the rapid advancement of ICT is bringing us various tools for flexible access to, and management of, this vast pool of information and knowledge. Today students need to master these new skills and knowledge, and they need to understand the use of ICT which is essential to workplace productivity. Students also need more than core subjects to cope with the demands of the modern day. They need critical thinking and problem-solving skills, the ability to communicate and collaborate with others, to manage information/ knowledge in a variety of forms and media, and effectively utilize new tools for learning.

Teacher Education Institutions have a key role in the social competitiveness challenge, either by offering high-quality training, appropriated to labour market and to the socio-economic environment needs (specific to each region/country), either by the preparation of professionals who can address the real needs of public or private organizations, through the ability to mobilize their scientific/technical knowledge to any situation, at the right time and with discernment. In this new teaching and learning paradigm, the individual also takes an increasingly important role and responsibility in managing its own career, but he must be prepared and advised during its bachelor's/academic studies, with teaching methodologies that drag out their ability to be a proactive element on the inclusive society building. Qualified people have to be prepared to find a job or to create business/professional opportunities, where they can be entrepreneurial and become a proactive element on the organizational positioning. Generally, people look for organizations that can meet their career motivations and needs, but organizations, otherwise, are looking for workers that are able to bring any competitive advantage. Learners should become active participants in the educational process. From this proposition, it clearly follows that in learning from their own experience, students become, in a sense, their own teachers. The changed role of the learner has, in turn, implications for that of the teacher. Instead of the source of knowledge, teachers become facilitators of the learning process; that is, their role is to create the set of conditions under which students can best learn from their experiences. Furthermore, teachers can fulfil this role only by becoming learners themselves, and a primary source of their learning must be their students. In a simpler way, teachers who learn to become better teachers, and learners who teach to become better learners. In this sense, the learning process, according to present demands, must necessarily be seen as a collaborative process of sharing and interaction, where all players feel really motivated to participate. In teacher education institutions, teacher has to hand on his knowledge through interactive methodologies and be able to interact simultaneously with different shapes and speeds of learning. Student, in return, must be motivated to accept the theoretical and conceptual knowledge to be able to solve and manage any situation (theoretical or real, in academic or professional context). All this interaction between teacher educator and pupil-teacher is seen as a team work, where the empowerment is a constant reality, and where all members share values and principles in an ethic and good governance basis, promoting best practices and citizenship deepening itself.

Teaching Practice: a Teacher-training Requirement

Teaching practice is an integral component of teacher training. It grants student teachers experience in the actual teaching and learning environment. During teaching practice, a pupil-teacher is given the opportunity to try the art of teaching before actually getting into the real world of the teaching profession. Pupil-teachers also know the value of teaching practice. They perceive it as 'the crux of their preparation for the teaching profession' since it provides for the 'real interface' between studenthood and membership of the profession. As a result, teaching practice creates a mixture of anticipation, anxiety, excitement and apprehension in the student teachers. The term teaching practice represents the range of experiences to which student teachers are exposed when they work in classrooms and schools. Teaching practice is a challenging but important part of teacher training, especially in developing countries such as India, where the effectiveness of the teaching practice can be diminished or eroded by a range of challenges, such as geographical distance, low and uneven levels of teacher expertise, a wide-ranging lack of resources as well as a lack of discipline among a wide cross-section of learners and educators. These challenges, if not addressed, may affect student teachers' performance during teaching practice and may in the long run affect their perception of the teaching profession. Teaching practice is meant to provide for the authentic context within which student teachers are exposed to experience the complexities and richness of the reality of being a teacher. This process allows the student teacher an opportunity to establish whether the right career choice has been made or not.

Teaching practice is a form of work-integrated learning that is described as a period of time when students are working in the relevant industry to receive specific in-service training in order to apply theory in practice. It is an integral component of teacher training in order to achieve the standards required for qualified teacher status. A student teacher is required to do teaching practice in at least two teaching subjects. Teaching practice can be conducted in a number of forms depending on the institution. Some institutions send student teachers to go for teaching practice once a day each week; others do this over a semester; while others send student teachers in a two-to six-weeks' block. On the other hand, student teachers could have doubts about their ability to cope with unfamiliar situations, controlling and managing learners or establishing a working relationship with the mentor or supervisor. It is such mixed feelings that can contribute to the making or breaking of a student teacher. Towards the end of teaching practice, the pupil-teachers were asked about their experiences during teaching practice and whether these experiences may have influenced their perception of the teaching profession.

For integrating of different components of teacher education curriculum, we should give importance on particular things which are given below:

1. *Maintain Good Communication Skills among Pupil-teachers*

A successful pupil-teacher is one that is able to build a rapport with his/her peers, one that can easily connect with his peers. Open and clear communication is the key to develop a healthy friendly learning atmosphere during teaching practice.

2. *Engagement in Different Activities*

There is nothing as challenging as getting students engaged. Today's students are multitasked and can hardly maintain a long concentration. They can easily get bored and therefore, disconnected. There are many ways of fighting off this problem: Using interesting educational games and activities, using technology and multimedia resources and finally, make the teaching student-centred and try your maximum to relate what you teach to students' immediate environment.

3. *Clear and Precise Instructions*

At present students are digitally focused with short attention span. Several of the problems some teacher-educators face due to ambiguous and unclear instructions. Cut off on the clutter and be to the point.

4. *Positive Feedback*

"Good job, excellent" are simple words that might not mean anything to the teacher but they mean the whole world to students. Publicly praise positive behaviour and show the students that their achievements are celebrated by the teacher as well.

5. *Involve Students in Decision Making*

Students tend to do great when they feel they are trusted and that they are real parts in the learning/teaching operation. Use voting and polling to investigate about a certain topic or classroom assignment. Try from time to time to give them the wheel and let them lead.

6. *Use Peer Learning*

Peer learning is a form of 'cooperative learning that enhances the value of student-student interaction and results in various advantageous learning outcomes.'

7. *Love Your Subject/Job*

The best way to get students interested in your subject is to love it so much that your passion for the field shows in your attitude. Students positively respond to authenticity. And as Abraham Lincoln once said "Love the job you do and you will never have to work a day".

Preparation of Lesson

For the preparation of lesson, pupil-teachers must know the subject, the relevant books and audio visual aids, which he/she is going to teach, because already prepared lessons give confidence to the teacher. Student teachers and supervisor can reform the teaching-learning process after its evaluation.

Evaluation of Teaching Practice

In order to evaluate the teaching practice supervisor observes the pupil-teacher while teaching in the classroom. Supervisor evaluates/observes the punctuality, lesson planning, teaching methods, use of audio visual aids, adequacy of audio visual aids, pitch of voice, dress, start and end of lesson, interest of the students, discipline of class, use of black/white board, students' notebooks and objectives of the lesson.

Before evaluating teaching practice we should keep in mind the following points which are given as under:

- To provide the prospective teachers with an opportunity of establishing an appropriate teacher-pupil relationship.
- To provide an opportunity for evaluating the student potential as a teacher and suitability for the teaching profession.
- To develop personal relationship with others: administrators, teachers, parents and students.
- To provide the future teacher with practical experience in school to overcome the problems of discipline and enable him/her to develop method of control.
- To provide with an opportunity to put theories into practice and to develop a deeper understanding of educational principles and their implication for learning.
- To enable the student teachers effectively to plan and prepare lessons.
- To develop skill in the use of fundamental procedures, techniques and methods of teaching.
- To develop desirable professional interests, attitudes and ideas relative to teaching profession.
- To enable student teachers to acquire desirable characteristics/traits of a teacher and to display appropriate behaviour.

- To provide student teachers with an opportunity to have teaching evaluated and to gain from the benefits of constructive criticism.
- To provide an opportunity for self-evaluation and to discover own strengths and weaknesses.
- To develop skills in future teachers related to teaching like fluent speaking, meaningful reading, using blackboard and other teaching material.
- To provide an opportunity to liaise with school environment, its functioning and with community and its resources.
- To provide for the exchange of ideas and methods between practicing school and teacher training institution, by teacher training institutions' staff and students, perceiving new ideas, material and equipment in use in practicing schools and introducing new ideas, material and equipments into the school.

Participation in Other Routine Works of School

Teaching in the classroom is not only the objective of teaching practice, but also to provide training in all activities/work which student teachers are going to perform in future during their job. For this purpose they have to spend whole day in school as teacher. They have to participate in all the activities of school, e.g. preparation of timetable, preparation and maintenance of different registers, evaluation of class work and home work, arrangement of tutorial groups, sports/games, morning assembly, co-curricular activities, duty during recess, duty as day master, duty before and after school timing, decoration of classroom, preparation and maintenance of attendance board, news board, information board, look after and arrangements of Audio Visual Aids room, science laboratories and library.

How to deal with students' parents, officers of the school, school employees and guests are also the part of teaching practice. Duties as invigilators, preparation of question papers for examinations, evaluation of answer scripts and compilation of results is also part of teaching practice.

Supervisor's duty is not only to evaluate the lessons of teaching practice, but by using his/her all the abilities to make this experience (All the stages of teaching practice) result oriented. He/she should have meeting and conversion with teacher educators, experienced teachers of the institution, educationists, concerned school head teachers and other teachers. Demonstration should be arranged before the departure of student teachers to the practicing schools in order to aware the pupil-teachers about the preparation of lesson plans and other assigned activities. During teaching practice, it is the duty of supervisors to supervise their lessons, other assigned activities, guidance and counselling as well as provide the student teachers with feedback and to enable them so that they can criticize and reform themselves. During the teaching, practice pupil-teachers should not be criticized in front of the practicing school staff and students.

Teaching practice is doing nothing to teaching other than *ad hoc* basis. The schools where teaching practice is conducted are doing nothing but only bearing it and not taking active part in the preparation of teachers of future. The administration and teachers of practicing schools are not aware with the information and evaluation techniques, which are used during teaching practice. They are not fully aware about the importance of teaching practice for student teachers and future generations. It is a fact that pupil-teachers are not perfect teachers, practicing school teachers cannot give them full authorities but they can trust on them.

Suggestions to Improve Teaching Practice

Here are some suggestions to improve the teaching practice:

(a) In teacher training institutions teaching methods were not only teach but also practically demonstrated by the teacher educators.

(b) The duration of teaching practice should be increased up to 20 weeks at least, so that practical training should be given for a quarter of the year.

(c) Teaching practice should not be consisted of classroom teaching only. Other aspects like attendance of students, collection of fee, calculation of fee, preparation of registers, conduct of morning assembly, conduct of co-curricular activities, preparation of question papers, marking of answer scripts, compilation of results, solution of students' problems and meetings with students' parents should be included.

(d) Student teachers are not given marks only for model lessons and all the aspects of teaching practice should be included in evaluation.

(f) In order to make the evaluation of teaching practice more effective, appropriateness of lesson, teaching methods, teaching aids, practical organization of lesson, interest of students and teachers and students' answers should be included in evaluation.

(g) It should be encouraged that pupil-teachers make audio visual aids by themselves and student teachers should be given/provided guidance after every lesson.

(h) In order to make teaching practice more effective, it is also proposed that pupil-teachers should watch the lessons of experienced teachers for one week and write evaluation report about them and supervisors should provide guidelines to student teachers in the light of this evaluation report.

(i) It should be ensured that pupil-teachers keep the sequence of lessons in such a way, so that they can teach all types of lessons and use different teaching methods.

(j) Prior to teaching practice pupil-teachers should practice in their fellows in order to build more confidence in them.

(k) During teaching practice, pupil-teachers should be given projects, which cover all the aspects of teaching practice, (i.e. preparation of teaching kit, planning for decoration of classrooms, betterment of environment and provision of facilities).

(l) During practice teaching prospective teachers should be made habitual of preparing daily lesson plan.

(m) Practice teaching should be more realistic and suited to the actual classroom situations.

Teaching practice is an activity, which can play an important role in the preparation of teachers. Its effectiveness is necessary for the nation. It is a milestone for professional adolescence. It is a combination of personality, professional skills, knowledge and training, which is fuel for an endless journey. Now it is the duty/ responsibility of teacher educators and teachers of practicing schools to make this fuel/expenditure endless.

Conclusion

Before planning a teacher education programme, we should keep in mind the course objectives, duration, resource requirements, and budget. For designing a inclusive teacher education programme, the minimum requirements are: assessment of training needs, formulation of training curriculum, preparation of course material and for organising the same, the minimum requirements are: common problems faced by a teacher educator and guidelines for communication, arrangement, preparation, facilitating participation and collecting feedback and evaluation.

REFERENCES

Aggarwal, Pradeep (2010). *Teacher Education.* New Delhi: Saurabh Publishing House.

Feuer, Michael J., Floden, Robert E., Chudowsky, Naomi and Ahn, Judie (2013). *Evaluation of Teacher Preparation Programme.* Retrieved From www.naeducation/.org on 28.09.2015.

Gijjar, Aijaj Ahmed (2009). *Teaching Practice: Concept, Stages, Objectives & Suggestions.* Retrieved from http://www.articlesbase.com/. on 27.09.2015.

Hansen, Ronald E. (1995). "Five Principles for Guiding Curriculum Development Practice: The Case of Technological Teacher Education", *Journal of Industrial Teacher Education.* Retrieved from www.google.com on 25.07.2015.

Kiggundu, Edith and Nayimuli, Samuel (2009). "Teaching Practice: A make or Break Phase for Student Teachers." *South African Journal of Education, 29*: 345-58.

Laksmi, T.K.S., Rama, K. and Hendrikz Johan (2007). *An Anthology of 'Best Practices' in Teacher Education.* Bangalore: NAAC.

Laohajaratsang, Thanomporn (2011). *Changing Roles of the Teacher Educational Institutions (TEIs) in integrating ICT in Teacher Education: Experiences of Chiang Mai University in UNESCO's Facilitating Effective ICT-Pedagogy Integration Project and Next-Generation of Teachers Project.* Retrieved from www.unescobkk.org on 18.10.2015.

Malhotra, S.P. (2015). *Teacher Educators can Only Improve Teacher Quality.* Retrieved from www.aiaer.net on 27.09.2015.

Mohanty, Jagannath (2003). *Teacher Education.* New Delhi: Deep and Deep Publication.

NCERT (2015). *National Focus Group on Teacher Education for Curriculum Renewal.* Retrieved from www.teindia.nic.in on 24.07.2015.

NCTE (2009). *National Curriculum Framework for Teacher Education.* New Delhi: NCTE.

NCTE (2014). *Norms and Standards.* Retrieved from http://ncte-india.org on 15.08.2018.

Santos, P., Guedes, A. and Fonseca, M. (2012). "The Role of Teaching Institutions to Prepare and Promote Social Entrepreneurs." *ACRN Journal of Entrepreneurship Perspectives, 1*(1): 161-67.

Sharma, Sashi Prabha (2012). *Teacher Education.* New Delhi: Kaniska Publishers.

Singh Priya (2015). "Curriculum Design and Transaction in Teacher Education: Present and Future." *Scholarly Research Journal for Interdisciplinary.* Retrieved From www.srjis.com on 23.07.2015.

UGC (2020). *Consolidated Universities.* Retrieved from www.ugc.ac.in on 23.04.2020.

Yadav, S.K. (2013). *Preparing Teacher Educators: M.Ed. Curriculum Review and Reconstruction.* Retrieved from www.ncert.nic.in on 22.07.2015.

37

Preparation of Teachers through ODL Mode

Issues and Challenges

Subhash Chandra and *Manju Kumari*

The need to recruit and train teachers is the main challenge before our educational system. UNESCO estimates that some 10 million teachers must be recruited and trained in less than a decade. They will be needed to replace the large numbers of teachers due to retire in many countries; complete the drive to universal primary schooling, particularly in Africa and South Asia; and address the challenge of secondary schooling (UNESCO, 2008). Without preparation of enough qualified teachers, it is impossible to fulfil the aim of quality education for all by 2015. But, it is not possible only with the classical teacher education mode. ODL can be a better way to fulfil the demand of preparation of quality teachers. There are too many limitations of these conventional teacher education colleges; like Pressure of budget, seat limitations, availability of infrastructure, old methods of teaching, necessity to attend classes, rigid in rules and regulations etc. So, open distance learning can be better alternative of teacher education. The current 3D virtual world is also facilitating the

ODL mode of teacher education. But the development of this approach depends on the availability of infrastructure and positive mindset of people towards it. In the present chapter we will discuss about the various issues and challenges of ODL mode teacher training programmes, which are important for the proliferation of programmes, and to maintain and upgrade the quality of different ODL mode teacher training programmes.

Distance learning and its relationship to emerging computer technologies have together offered many promises to the field of education. In practice, however, the combination often falls short of what it attempts to accomplish. Some of the shortcomings are due to problems with the technology; others have more to do with administration, instructional methods, or students. Despite the problems, many users like technologies such as compressed video and see continued growth in the area. This chapter will examine some of the current research and thought on the promises, problems, and the future possibilities in modern distance learning, particularly types that are delivered *via* electronic means.

History of Distance Learning

Before any discussion of distance learning, we need to look at the way the term has been defined in the past and how it is currently defined in the literature. The term can be used to describe any of a number of instructional situations. Although it is thought of as a new term, distance learning has been around for well over 100 years. One of the earlier forms of distance learning was done through correspondence courses started in Europe. This stayed the primary means of distance learning until the middle of this century when instructional radio and television became more popular (Imel, 1996). As technology has changed, so has the definition of distance learning. Videotaped lectures have been a standard in university and professional courses for the last two decades (Moore & Lockee, 1998). Audiotapes and lessons sent through the mail have been used in correspondence courses to teach subject, such as foreign language for quite some time (Teaster & Blieszner, 1999). Today, the Internet and compressed video have taken distance learning in new directions, allowing distance learning to occur in real time. Live video instruction is the most popular and fastest growing delivery mode in the United States (Ostendorf, 1997).

Definitions of Distance Learning

With the history of distance learning encompassing so many different learning environments, we need to find a definition that fits in all situations. There have been many definitions put forward in modern literature. Greenberg (1998) defines contemporary distance learning as "a planned teaching/learning experience that uses a wide spectrum of technologies to reach learners at a distance and is designed to encourage learner interaction and certification of learning" (p. 36). Teaster and Blieszner (1999) say "the term distance learning has been applied to many instructional methods: however, its primary distinction is that the teacher and the learner are separate in space and possibly time" (p. 741). Desmond Keegan (1995) gives the most thorough definition. He says that distance education and training result from the technological separation of teacher and learner which frees the student from the necessity of travelling to "a fixed place, at a fixed time, to meet a fixed person, in order to be trained" (p. 7). From these definitions we can see that the student and teacher are separated by space, but not necessarily by time. This would include compressed video, which is delivered in real time. As stated earlier, this type of live video instruction is the fastest growing means of distance learning today. Because of this, much of the discussion here will be dedicated to the promises and problems of this technology.

The Promises of Distance Learning

Many of the promises of distance learning are financial in nature. Universities hope to save money by delivering education to students that are unable to attend classes because of time or distance. The theory is that class size increases while the overhead remains the same. In a 2001 article by Burton Bollag and Martha Ann

Overland, they say that developing countries are turning to state run distance education programmes to take the place of ever increasing enrolments and a lack of physical building space. Places such as Beijing, Jakarta, and South American countries such as Brazil and Argentina have all begun to use distance-learning techniques to reach those that would by any other means be unreachable. Bollag and Overland say countries like China are moving from "elite to mass education", and that "traditional universities cannot meet the demand" (p. A29). China uses a radio and television delivery system to serve 1.5 million students, two-thirds of which are in a degree programme.

In Australia, Curtin University uses compressed video conferencing to reach remote students in Western Australia, and to enhance classes in Business Studies by connecting with students in Singapore. Other examples, can be found in the UK and Norway, where several sites have been linked together (Keegan, 1995). Of course, there is also wide use in the United States, both in the public and private sectors. It should be obvious by these examples and by the definition of distance learning, that it can meet the promise to deliver classes to a geographically broad and diverse population. Not only that, but the need seems to be strong for such programmes. According to the American Council on Education, the number of students in distance learning doubled from 1995 to 1998 totalling 1.6 million (Devarics, 2001). Another market forecast says that by the year 2002 there will be 2.2 million students in distance education programme, a full 15 per cent of all US college students (Rochester *et al.*, 1999, cited in Dibiase, 2000). Many Universities are feeling the pressure to control their costs, improve quality of instruction, focus on customer needs, and respond to the competitive pressures (Horgan, 1998: 1). Distance learning technologies have the potential to assist in solving these problems. In 1994, Basom and Sherritt surveyed higher education administrators and state politicians to find out what they thought would be the major problems facing American higher education in the next millennium. The answers they most often received were: "meeting increased demands at a time of decreased resources, increasing or maintaining access, using technology more efficiently, and sharing resources across state lines so that colleges would not have to be all things to all people" (p. 4). Distance learning seems to address all of these issues. Administrators hope that distance learning methods will help make higher education more cost-effective (Dibiase, 2000). This type of answer may be seen as a quick fix for many administrators. If not approached seriously, however, the distance programmes can quickly become second rate.

The convenience of time and space is a big promise made by distance learning. Students do not have to physically be with the instructor in space and, depending on the method used, they do not have to be together in time as well. This is a great advantage for non-traditional students who cannot attend at regular times. Satellite campuses such as the ones Arkansas State University have recently opened are drawing out a "hidden market" of adult students in small towns and recent high school graduates who don't want to go away to a bigger city to get an education. The satellite campuses could conceivably help the school's enrolment to grow tenfold (Savoye, 2001).

Problems of Distance Learning

Despite the promises and obvious advantages to distance learning, there are problems that need to be resolved. These problems include the quality of instruction, hidden costs, misuse of technology, and the attitudes of instructors, students, and administrators. Each one of these has an effect on the overall quality of distance learning as a product. In many ways, each of these issues relates to the others. We will examine each of these issues separately.

Quality of Instruction

The first issue is the quality of instruction that is given through distance learning programmes. Much of the quality of instruction depends on the attitude of the administration and the instructor. Data collected in a 1999 study by Elliot Inman and Michael Kerwin showed instructors had conflicting attitudes about teaching distance education. They report that after teaching one course, the majority of instructors were willing to teach another, but that they rated the quality of the course as only equal or lower quality than other classes taught on campus. Many times it seems that the administration believes the technology itself will improve the quality of the class. Palloff and Pratt (2000) remind us that "technology does not teach students; effective teachers do"(p. 4). They make the point that the issue is not technology itself, but how it is used in the design and delivery of courses. Too often instructors do not design their lessons to take advantage of the technology presented. This affects the quality of the instruction. Research suggests that the effectiveness of distance learning is based on preparation; the instructor understands the needs of the students, and an understanding of the target population (Omoregie, 1997). Sherritt (1996) found in her survey of higher education administrators that many of the decision makers view distance programmes as second rate, a "necessary but deficient form of education" (p. 2). She writes that this attitude also was found in academic departments that "have no strong mandates to adjust their curriculum and instruction to fit distance learning beyond cursory cooperation" (p. 2). There are no rewards for doing so and the effort takes away from research time. Sherrit also cites a study by Caffarella *et al.* done in 1992, which found off campus instructors to be "a demoralized bunch, perceiving poor working conditions, isolation, personal and professional deprivation" (p. 3). This attitude hardly seems conducive to an effective learning environment for the students. If the administration and instructors are lacking in true commitment, it is bound to have a negative influence on the entire distance learning experience.

Cost-Effectiveness

The second issue is the true cost and the cost-effectiveness of distance learning programmes. Are they actually cost-efficient? A study by Phelps *et al.* (1991) found that "the potential cost-effectiveness of using online technologies in distance education is still uncertain" (p. 303). The study further showed that the concepts of costs and effectiveness are not as simple as they first appear. Atkinson (1983, cited in Ng, 2000) notes, "it is possible for a programme to be efficient but not cost-effective if the outputs which are actually produced do not contribute to the programme objectives: that is it may be efficient at doing the wrong things" (p. 306). Ng also comments on the cost of human capital. He states, "Human capital and the costs of conversion are expenses that can easily be underestimated" (p. 306). Ng notes that the cost of online courses is affected by how they are implemented: as an enhancement or as the primary teaching medium. If it is implemented as a primary teaching medium, it is considerably more expensive. The teaching purpose of the different approaches needs to be taken into account. If this is not factored in by administration, there may be costs that are not apparent at first glance. Caffarella *et al.* (1992) found in a study at the University of Northern Colorado that when electronic distance delivery costs were compared with those of instructor travel directly to the site, the least costly alternative was the live instruction with the instructor travelling to the remote site compressing the class into fewer weeks. This alternative was one-third of the cost of any other alternative. Starting a compressed video distance-learning programme is not cheap. Southern Arkansas University, Magnolia, decided to try compressed video as an alternative to other methods. The start-up equipment for the unit was approximately $80,000. Establishment of a permanent T-1 telephone line was another $1,200 per month (Weber, 1996). These costs are start-up only and do not reflect any of the human capital costs as discussed earlier. Carr (2001) discusses a report by the California State University System that looked at cost savings in distance learning programmes. The report found that only in really large courses with many sections would cost savings be possible. Courses in excess of 500 students would benefit from this setup, while it was still more cost-effective to teach smaller groups in a traditional setting. The startup costs, maintenance costs, and personnel costs should also be factored in to arrive at a true cost for a distance-learning programme. The minimum number of staff required for delivery of a compressed video class would be one instructor and two technicians, one at each site. This means a minimum of three people is needed to deliver the same class as one instructor does in a traditional setting. The costs associated with training technicians and instructors should not be overlooked. For effective distance education to take place, the staff delivering the instruction should be well trained.

Misuse of Technology

Besides the cost of the technology, there is the possibility of not utilizing all its potential. Some of these problems arise from a lack of training, some from the instructor's attitude about using the technology, and still others by hardware problems. It seems to be self-evident that instructors need to be trained to use distance learning technology, but too often they are not. Once again, it appears that administration may feel that the technology itself will improve the course. Advancement in technology does not lead to effective distance education. The best distance education practices depend on creative, well-informed instructors (Greenberg, 1998). Bates (1995) suggests that newer technologies are not inherently better than old ones and many of the lessons learned from the application of older technologies will still apply to any newer technology. Again, the instructor should be trained to take advantage of both their experience and being able to adapt that experience to the new environment of distance learning. The instructors must be trained "not only to use technology, but also to shift the way in which they organize and deliver material" (Palloff & Pratt, 2000: 3).

The Role of the Technicians

One overlooked factor in the success or failure of distance learning programmes is the role that the technicians play in distance learning. Of course, they play a large role in the technical delivery, but little is known about the non-technical activities of the technicians that could have an influence on the instructional process. In a 1995 study, Olenski *et al.*, found that technicians could indirectly influence the learning environment by "orientating participants to the technology, reducing the anxiety of the participants" (including the instructor), "and by advising the instructor on instructional techniques"(p. 3). This type of role, if viewed negatively by the instructor, can have a huge impact on the quality of the presentation, yet many times the instructor and the technicians do not meet until the initial class meeting. Olenski also found that the technicians felt the instructors were given inadequate orientation to the equipment and really could not operate it until they had hands on experience. The technicians also saw a difference in the instructors who could adapt their styles to the technology, and those who could not. Those who adapted were, in the opinion of the technicians, superior in conducting the classes. So we see not only does the instructor need to adapt to the educational environment, they must also adapt to another person in the room that can help or hinder the delivery of the lesson. Much of the outcome depends on the attitude of the instructor.

Problems with Equipment

Equipment and hardware malfunctions can be a great detriment to the effectiveness of distance learning. When a problem occurs in a class everything comes to a standstill and the learning environment is interrupted. If there are too many instances, the entire course can be affected. For instance, if an overhead projector goes out during an instructor's presentation, an alternate way of delivering that information can easily be found. However, if a compressed video presentation has problems, the entire class must be stopped until the problem is resolved. If the instructor goes ahead with the lesson, one site will miss out on that information. Carter (2001) did a study of students taking courses by compressed video in the Mississippi Gulf Coast Community College programme. One of the questions he asked pertained to the equipment and technology operating correctly. His results from three groups spread over the different sites showed that only 42 per cent agreed with the statement that the equipment and technology operated correctly. A programme studied by Teaster and Bliesner (1999) found that unanticipated technical problems with the system shortened the class time and discussion that negatively affected the overall quality of the presentation. In one presentation, the connection was lost twice prior to the students arriving and ten times during the actual instructional session. During this particular session there was never more than a four-minute period before the connection to one of the sites was lost. This may be an extreme example, but according to the instructor involved in the presentation, the course experience was "better, but similar to past experiences" (p. 743). At Southern Arkansas University, Magnolia, they discovered that using compressed video as a single medium of delivering distance education was not as effective as was first hoped. Because of this they developed a different concept of an "electronic classroom" that did not rely on just one mode of delivery (Weber, 1996). Their experience was that compressed video had connection problems and did not work well broadcasting information delivered by lecturer. The failure of the hardware can be a very frustrating thing for all involved in distance learning. For the instructor, it means they can be well prepared for the class only to have a bad connection or camera failure cause the entire lesson to go bad. For the technician, the frustration and inability to keep the class running smoothly may affect the instructor's view of their competency, causing friction. For the student, an inability to get a flow to the class and feel like progress is being made can hinder the learning process. Those students used to the traditional face-to-face instruction and who do not have a tolerance for ambiguity will have a difficult time.

Attitudes towards Distance Learning

Despite problems with hardware that may or may not get worked out with new advances in technology, we must come back to instructors and their attitudes towards teaching in a distance-learning environment as a major potential roadblock to effective distance education. As in any educational situation, the instructor can set the tone for learning in the educational environment. That instructor must be properly trained and motivated to be effective. An instructor must have technological skills and confidence to use all of the various electronic devices in order to be truly effective in the electronic classroom. Instructors must also change the manner in which information is delivered. While lecture does not work well, multimedia presentations are successful (Weber, 1996). Of course, this means more preparation time for the instructor and the motivation must be there (Walcott, 1994, cited in Carter, 2000), found in a study of adult distance learning that "to effectively bridge the gaps between classroom and distance teaching, faculty need to look at the distance teaching from the students' point of view" (p. 249). The faculty must also be aware of getting instructional materials, handouts, tests, and other class items to both sites simultaneously. It is important for the instructors to develop a sense of community between the sites, achieve maximum participation, and get the participants to buy into the process. The idea of learning as a collaborative process is very important when students are separated by distance. According to research by Palloff and Pratt (2000), "collaborative learning processes assist students to achieve deeper level of knowledge generation through the creation of shared goals, shared exploration, and a shared process of meaning making" (p. 6). It is up to the instructor to be aware of this in the distance learning environment and to encourage collaborative learning and a sense of community among the students.

Another important consideration for the instructor is their view regarding the goal of distance education. There are two main thoughts on this. Schlosser and Anderson (1994, cited in Imel, 1998) put this thought forward in a review of distance education literature. They submit that the goal of distance education in the United States is "to offer the distance student an experience as much like that of traditional, face-to-face instruction as possible" (p. 3). This would mean that distance learning pedagogy would not differ much from that used in an ordinary classroom. Bates (1995) has a different idea. He suggests that instead of using technology to replicate traditional methods, it should be used to improve instruction. Holmberg (1989) also discusses these two schools of thought and concludes that distance education as a mode of education in its own right has very different consequences (than viewing it as a substitute for face-to-face instruction). The instructor must decide which attitude they will adapt because it has a profound impact on their approach to instruction.

Instructors also have adaptations they need to make to the technology. An instructor used to visual cues may find it difficult to adapt to a situation such as compressed video. The students at the remote site are not always in clear view of the instructor. West (1994) calls adapting to the lack of visual cues a major adaptation for the instructor. Part of this can be alleviated by good communication with the technician, but as we have seen earlier, that communication is not always present. McKnight (2000) contends that proximity and eye contact are important factors in education that are limited in the distance learning environment. She says that we inherently recognize the connection these provide, but in the distance learning environment they are "both severely and sometimes permanently compromised" (p. 2). She asserts that professors are unable to observe the emotions of the students and cannot detect "moments of anxiety", thereby limiting their ability to respond to student needs. This puts a burden on the instructor and causes the students to respond differently than they might in a traditional classroom setting. As we saw earlier, creating a community is an important factor for the instructor to have an effective class. The instructor must do all he can to overcome the limits of the technology and involve the students in an environment of interaction, which can work to create the feeling of a true class (Hiltz & Wellman, 1997).

Instructors' Concerns

Instructors have other concerns about distance learning, primarily how it will change their role in education. Clark (1993) found in a national survey of attitudes of higher education faculty that there was a moderately positive attitude about distance learning in general, but moderately negative attitudes about their own use of it. Writing about geography educators, Gober (1998) worries that if they rely too much on distance-learning techniques, the discipline would "risk losing our collective soul in the rush to convenience, cost-effectiveness, and accountability" (p. 130). Instructors worry about putting their course materials online because once there, the knowledge and course design skill in that material is out of their possession. This puts the administration in a position to hire less skilled, and cheaper workers to deliver the technologically pre-packaged course (Noble, 1998 cited in Dibiase, 2000). Instructors are not always convinced that administration is behind distance learning. The rewards are not always there for the good distance-learning instructor. "Tenure and promotion usually does not recognize excellent off campus teaching which, in fact, takes valuable time from research agendas" (Sherritt, 1996: 4). This puts the instructors behind when trying to publish to get their department recognized. The increased amount of time necessary to adequately prepare for distance learning takes away from the activities they will be evaluated on, such as grant writing and publishing. Many of the instructors concerns are valid and should be addressed by administration as distance learning becomes more common, as is predicted to happen.

Student Concerns

Finally, there are the students and their concerns with distance learning classes. Not all students are suited to this type of learning and not all subjects are best taught *via* this medium. More mature students are the most likely to find success with distance learning. The successful student needs to have a number of characteristics such as tolerance for ambiguity, a need for autonomy, and an ability to be flexible (Threkeld & Brzoska, 1994). Hardy and Boaz (1997) found that "compared to most face-to-face learning environments, distance learning requires students to be more focused, better time managers, and to be able to work independently and with group members" (p. 43). Many distance learners are different from traditional undergraduates in that they are already in professions. They have well defined goals and are more motivated (Dibiase, 2000). As we saw earlier, distance education students need to feel a part of a community. Greenburg (1998) describes this as a virtual learning community.

Students in these communities often feel less pressure to perform individually, and more pressure to collaborate and be part of the team (Kantor, 1998 cited in Greenberg, 1998). Being involved in a collaborative learning process is an important part of forming the foundation of a learning community. When this is not encouraged, participation is generally low and dialog is absent (Palloff & Pratt, 2000). Students also need the attention of the instructors. This may be truer in a distance situation than in a traditional classroom. In a situation where eye contact and proximity are limited, students cannot be disciplined nor affirmed by eye contact and body language (McKnight, 2000). Students may also have a difficult time reading the reactions of the remote location class members. This lack of interaction can cause problems when there is a dissenting opinion that cannot be picked up on with non-verbal cues, and is misperceived as a verbal attack. This type of miscommunication can cause the community problems as the class progresses. It is fair to say that compressed video can magnify the strength and weaknesses of the instructor. Students are prone to pick up on a lack of organization and direction and respond with apathy and absenteeism (West, 1994).

Conclusion

What may we conclude from the promises and problems of distance learning? Are there possibilities for improvement in the future? The technology will undoubtedly keep improving and the price will drop, as technology is prone to do once it comes into general use. Already we see improvement in the delivery systems of compressed video and computer assisted instruction. Despite student problems with distance learning, studies indicate they are relatively satisfied with what they are receiving. A study of students at Indiana University of Pennsylvania found 75 per cent were very satisfied with the instruction they received and 90 per cent rating the technology as satisfactory (Ferguson & Wijekumar, 2000). Another study by Harner *et al.* (2000) was done on a distance learning accounting course at the University of Connecticut. They found that 57.5 per cent would take another such course. Two other findings were generally favourable and included comments on how the course could be improved. The first suggested the instructors needed to be comfortable with the medium, and that the students needed to have more guidance on how to fully take advantage of the presentation (Teaster & Blieszner, 1999). The second showed that students were highly satisfied with the instructors and the course, but that direct interaction with the instructor played no role in the students' satisfaction (Inman & Kerwin, 1999).

It would seem one element that needs immediate improvement is with instructors. The literature indicates a need for instructors to adapt their teaching methods to the distance learning format. Keegan (1995) shows many excellent ways that instructors can better prepare for the classroom including multimedia use, speaking voice, and even font size considerations. Instructors also need to realize that the technician is an integral part of the experience of distance learning and treat them as such. Many times opinions and communication between the technician and the instructor are not shared either because the technician's role is unclear, or there is a shared perception of a difference in status between the two (Olenski *et al.*, 1995). Instructors must be motivated to prepare adequately for classes. Part of the responsibility for motivation must lie with the administration and their support of the programme. "Because teaching a distance learning class involves a new role for instructors and administrators who must provide them time, tools, and the training to meet these new responsibilities" (Inman & Kerwin, 1999: 586). Administration needs to train and educate instructors on this role and how to meet the challenges. Sherritt (1996) found in her survey of higher education administrators that "for whatever reasons, higher education administrators and politicians understand the need for technology. But, lacking the heart for distance education, they cannot bring themselves to support it with adequate personnel, simple supplies, and a reasonable operating budget" (p. 4). This sort of attitude from administration can do nothing but trickle down into the instructors and the students. Administrators need to carefully weigh their goals and objectives when taking on a distance education programme.

Despite the need for improvement, the future of distance learning seems bright. Increasing number of students enrolling in distance learning classes underscore the need for "comprehensive and thoughtful evolution of distance education if it is to become the educational model of the future" (Harnar, *et al.*, 2000: 37). Despite the cost, coordination, and training that must be put into a programme, it has "great potential to deliver and receive educational programmes to and from remote sites" (Weber, 1996: 219). Perhaps Keegan (1995) puts it best when he says "the challenge is to design cost-effective and educationally-effective systems for use in the new millennium of the new technologies that permit for the first time in history (electronic) teaching of students face-to-face at a distance" (p. 53). Thus, with all ifs and buts ODL mode TE Programmes have their own strength and implications.

REFERENCES

Basom, M. & Sherritt, C. (1992). *Higher Education Problems in the twenty-first Century: A Survey of Higher Education Administrators and Politicians.* Paper presented at the Annual Conference for International Higher Education Administrators, Nice, France.

Bates, T. (1995). *Technology: Open Learning and Distance Education.* New York: Routledge.

Bollag, B. & Overland, M.A. (2001). "Developing Countries Turn to Distance Education." *Chronicle of Higher Education, 47*(40): 29-31.

Caffarella, E. *et al.* (1992). *An Analysis of the Cost Effectiveness of Various Electronic Alternatives for Delivering Distance Education Compared to the Travel Costs for Live Instruction.* Greeley, Colorado: University of Northern Colorado, Western Institution for Higher Learning. (ERIC Document Reproduction Service No. ED 380 127).

Carr, S. (2001). "Union Publishes Guide Citing High Cost of Distance Education." *Chronicle of Higher Education, 47*(35): 39-41.

Carter, A. (2001). "Interactive Distance Education: Implications for the Adult Learner." *International Journal of Instructional Media, 28*(3): 249-61.

Christensen, E. *et al.* (2001). "Receptivity to Distance Learning: The Effect of Technology, Reputation, Constraints, and Learning Preferences." *Journal of Research on Computing in Education, 33*(3): 263-76.

Clark, T. (1993). "Attitudes of Higher Education Faculty Toward Distance Education: A National Survey." *The American Journal of Distance Education, 7*: 19-33.

Dervarics, C. (2001). "Support Builds For Distance Learning." *Community College Week, 14*(1): 3-5.

Dibiase, D. (2000). "Is Distance Education a Faustian Bargain?" *Journal of Geography in Higher Education, 24*(1): 130-36.

Ferguson, L. & Wijekumar, K. (2000). "Effective Design and Use of Web-Based Distance Learning Environments." *Professional Safety, 45*(12): 28-33.

Gober, P. (1998). "Distance Learning and Geography's Soul." *AAG Newsletter, 33*(5): 1-2.

Greenberg, G. (1998). "Distance Education Technologies: Best Practices for K-12 Settings." *IEEE Technology and Society Magazine* (Winter) 36-40.

Harner, M. *et al.* (2000). "Measuring the Effect of Distance Education on the Learning Experience: Teaching Accounting via Picturetel". *International Journal of Instructional Media, 27*(1): 37-50.

Hiltz, S.R. & Wellman, B. (1997). "A Synchronous Learning Network as a Virtual Classroom." *Communications of the ACM, 40*(9): 44-49.

Holmberg, B. (1989). "The Concept, Basic Character, and Development Potentials of Distance Education." *Distance Education, 10*(1): 127-35.

Horgan, B. (1998). *Transforming Higher Education Using Information Technology: First Steps* (On-Line). Available: http://microsoft.com/education/hed/vision.html

Imel, S. (1998). *Myths and realities of distance learning. Columbus, Ohio: ERIC Clearinghouse on Adult, Career, and Vocational Education*. Ohio State University. (Eric Document Reproduction Service No. ED 414 446).

Inman, E. & Kerwin, M. (1999). "Instructor and Student Attitudes Toward Distance Learning." *Community College Journal of Research & Practice, 23*(6): 581-92.

Keegan, D. (1995). *Distance Education Technology for the New Millennium: Compressed Video Teaching. ZIFF Papiere*. Hagen, Germany: Institute for Research into Distance Education (Eric Document Reproduction Service No. ED 389 931).

McKnight, M. (2000). *Distance Education: Expressing Emotions in Video-Based Classes*. Paper presented at the Annual meeting of the Conference on College Composition and Communication, Minneapolis, Minnesota. (Eric Document Reproduction Service No. ED 441 270).

Moore, D.R. & Lockee, B.B. (1998). *A Taxonomy of Bandwidth: Considerations and Principles to Guide Practice in the Design and Delivery of Distance Education*. Unpublished manuscript: Portland State University.

Ng, K. (2000). *Costs and Effectiveness of Online Courses in Distance Education. Open Learning, 15*(3), 301-08.

Olesinski, R. *et al.* (1995). *The Operating Technician's Role in Video Distance Learning*. Paper Presented at the Instructional Technology SIG, San Francisco, California. (Eric Document Reproduction Service No. ED 387 123).

Omoregie, M. (1997). *Distance Learning: An Effective Educational Delivery System*. (Information Analysis 1070), (ERIC Document Reproduction Service No. ED 418 683).

Ostendorf, V.A. (1997). *Teaching by Television. Teaching and Learning at A Distance: What It Takes to Effectively Design, Deliver and Evaluate Programmes, 71*: 51-57.

Palloff, R. & Pratt, K. (2000). *Making the Transition: Helping Teachers to Teach Online*. Paper presented at Educause: Thinking it through. Nashville,Tennessee. (Eric Document Reproduction Service No. ED 452 806).

Phelps, R.H. *et al.* (1991). "Effectiveness and Costs of Distance Education Using Computer-Mediated Communication." *American Journal of Distance Education, 5*(3): 7-19.

Savoye, C. (2001). "Distance Learning with a Twist-real Campuses." *Christian Science Monitor*, pp. 15, 21.

Schlosser, C.A. & Anderson, M.L. (1994). *Distance Education: A Review of the Literature*. Washington DC: Association for Educational Communications and Technology. (Eric Document Reproduction Service No. ED 382 159).

Sherritt, C. (1996). A Fundamental Problem with Distance Programmes in Higher Education. (Opinion Paper No. 120). *Viewpoints* (Eric Document Reproduction Service No. ED 389 906).

Teaster, P. & Blieszner, R. (1999). "Promises and Pitfalls of the Interactive Television Approach to Teaching Adult Development and Aging". *Educational Gerontology, 25*(8): 741-54.

Threlkeld, R. & Brezoska, K. (1994). "Research in Distance Education". In Willis, B. (ed.) *Distance Education Strategies and Tools*. Englewood Cliffs: Educational Technology Publications.

Weber, J. (1996). *The Compressed Video Experience*. Paper presented at Summer Conference of the Association of Small Computer Users. North Myrtle Beach, South Carolina. (Eric Document Reproduction Service No. ED 405 838).

West, G. (1994). "Teaching and Learning Adaptations in the Use of Interactive Compressed Video." *The Journal, 21*(9): 71-74.

38

Assessing Need Level Research Competencies in Relation to Ph.D. Coursework

B.C. Das and *Debajani Sahoo*

The aim of this study was to identify the research competencies needed by education research scholars upon completion of their Ph.D. coursework. The sample consisted of 100 education research scholars, and data collection was conducted through a questionnaire. The collected data were analysed using percentage analysis and chi-square tests of independence. The research competencies were evaluated across five dimensions: research review, proposal writing, and research methodology, usage of ICT, and research publication and ethics. Results indicated no significant association between different research competencies and the gender of the research scholars. However, scholars reported varying levels of need, with the majority expressing a need for additional competencies. The coursework is designed to identify and address these competency needs.

Coursework is instrumental in shaping the academic journey of research scholars, providing them with essential knowledge, research skills, and networking opportunities crucial for their research endeavours. Effective management of coursework and research demands, including prioritization, communication, time management, and peer support, is essential for navigating the academic path successfully. A study was conducted on the research competency of post-graduate students. The results reveals that there were various research knowledge, skills and attitudes possessed by the post-graduate students which forms their premise of their research competence (Afolabi *et al.,* 2022). A study was carried out on research competence of teacher education students in Eastern Samar State University main campus. The study revealed that the common problem encountered by the respondents six research competence of post-graduate students in the conduct of research is the lack of time/class schedule which does not allow the conduct of research (Caliwan-Fuentes, 2017). The level of competencies required during Ph.D. coursework varies depending on the programme and field of study. High-level intellectual curiosity and critical thinking skills are key competencies needed during Ph.D. coursework, alongside proficiency in research review, proposal writing, and research methodology, usage of ICT, and research publication and ethics.

Objective and Methodology

The objective of this study was to investigate the association between different levels of research competencies and the gender of research scholars' post-completion of Ph.D. coursework in education. The hypothesis tested was that there exists no significant association between these variables. A descriptive design was employed, focusing on 100 education Ph.D. research scholars selected purposively. Data were collected through a questionnaire and analysed using percentage and chi-square tests of independence.

Analysis and Interpretation of Data

The different need level competencies of the research scholars described with five dimensions including competencies related to (i) Research Review, (ii) Proposal Writing, (iii) Research

Methodology, (iv) Usage of ICT, and (v) Research Publication and Ethics. The need of the research scholars develop during the coursework in relation to their gender are analysed and interpreted in the following heads.

Competencies Related to Research Review

Need level competencies among the female and male research scholars have been comparatively analysed and interpreted dimension-wise on the basis of different levels such as Need More Additional Competency (NMAC), Need Some Additional Competency (NSAC) and Need No Additional Competency (NNAC) respectively. On the aspect of the research review, it is evident from Table 38.1 and related figures that there exit no significant association between the need of the research scholars related to research review and their gender.

Table 38.1: Chi-square test of Independence between the need of the Research Scholars related to Research Review and Gender

Review of related Literature	**Need Level of Competencies**			χ^2	**df**	**'P' Value**
	NMAC	**NSAC**	**NNAC**			
Female	32 (69.6)	10 (21.7)	04 (8.7)	1.198	2	.549 NS
Male	33 (61.1)	17 (35.5)	04 (7.4)			
Total	**65 (65.0)**	**27 (27.0)**	**08 (8.0)**			

Note: NS—Not Significant.

It is evident from Table 38.1 and Fig. 38.1 that majority (65%) of the research scholars were needed more additional competencies as compared to need some additional competencies (27%) and need no additional competencies (8%) in research review. Further, with regards to their gender, it is observed that more female research scholars were needed more additional competencies in research review as compared to their male counterparts. In contrast to

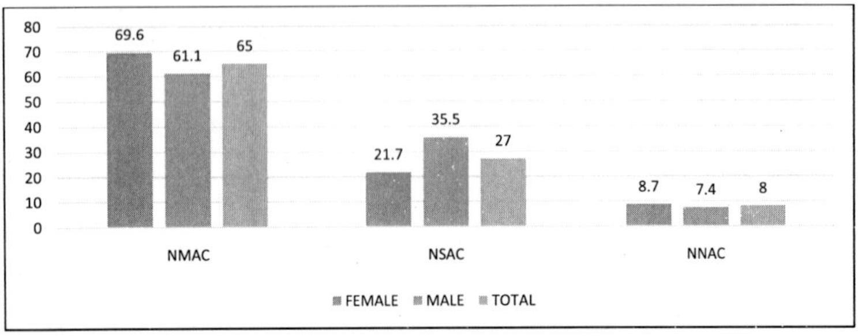

Notes: NMAC—Need More Additional Competency, NSAC—Need Some Additional Competency, NNAC—Need No Additional Competency.

Fig. 38.1: Need level competencies of the Research Scholars in relation to research review and gender

this, more male research scholars were needed some additional competencies (35.5) as compared to their female counterparts (21.7%). It is also show that female research scholars (8.7%) were needed no additional competencies in relation to research review as compared to their male counterpart (7.4%). It is also observed from Table 38.1 and Fig. 38.1 there exist no significant association between the differentneed levels of research competencies in reviewing the research related literature with the gender of the research scholars.

Competencies Related to Proposal Writing

The need related to proposal writing among the female and male research scholars have been comparatively analysed and interpreted dimension-wise in Table 38.2 and Fig. 38.2.

It is observed from Table 38.2 and Fig. 38.2 that majority (58%) of the research scholars were needed more additional competencies as compared to need some additional competencies (34%) and need no additional competencies (8%) in proposal writing. Further, with regard to their gender, it shows that female research scholars (58.7%) were needed more additional competencies than their male counter parts (57.4%). In contrast to this more male research scholars (11.1) were needed no additional competencies as compared to their female counter part (4.3%). It is also showed that

Table 38.2: Chi-square test of Independence between the need of the Research Scholars related to Proposal Writing and Gender.

Proposal Writing	Need Level of Competencies			χ^2	df	'P' Value
	NMAC	NSAC	NNAC			
Female	27 (58.7)	17 (37.0)	02 (4.3)	1.646	2	439 NS
Male	31 (57.4)	17 (31.5)	06 (11.1)			
Total	**58 (58.0)**	**34 (34.0)**	**08 (8.0)**			

Note: NS—Not Significant.

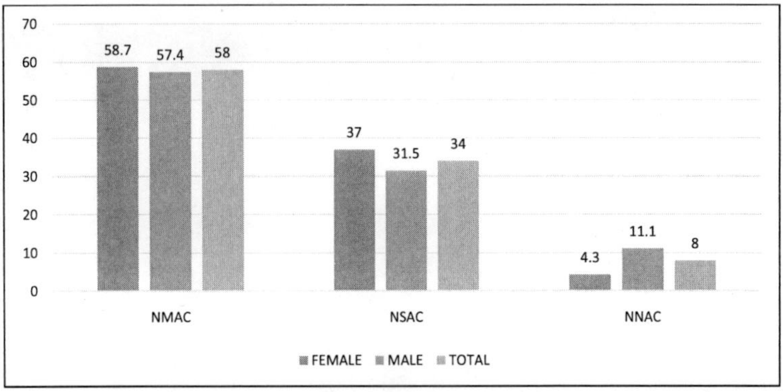

Notes: NMAC—Need More Additional Competency, NSAC—Need Some Additional Competency, NNAC—Need No Additional Competency.

Fig. 38.2: Need level of competencies of the Research Scholars in relation to proposal writing and gender

the female research scholars (37%) were needed some additional competencies in relation to proposal writing as compared to their male counterpart. It revealed from Table 38.2 that there exist no significant association between the different need levels of research competencies in writing proposal with the gender of the research scholars.

Competencies Related to Research Methodology

Table 38.3: Chi-square test of Independence between the need of the Research Scholars related to Research Methodology and Gender

Research Methodology	Need Level of Competencies			χ^2	df	'P' Value
	NMAC	NSAC	NNAC			
Female	31 (67.4)	14 (30.4)	1 (2.2)	.928	2	.629 NS
Male	33 (61.1)	18 (33.3)	3 (5.6)			
Total	**64 (64.0)**	**32 (32.0)**	**4 (4.0)**			

Note: NS—Not Significant

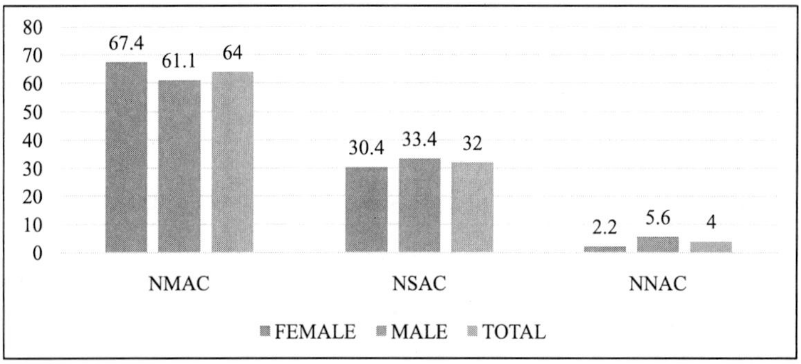

Notes: NMAC—Need More Additional Competency, NSAC—Need Some Additional Competency, NNAC—Need No Additional Competency.

Fig. 38.3: Need level competencies of the Research Scholars in relation to research methodology and gender.

It is evident from Table 38.3 and Fig. 38.3 majority (64%) of the research scholars were needed more additional competencies as compared to the need some additional competencies (32%) and need no additional competencies (4%) in relation to Research Methodology. Further in relation to gender, it showed that majority of the female research scholars (67.4%) were needed more additional competencies as compared to their male counterpart (61.1%). It is also observed that male research scholars (33.4% and 5.6%) were needed some additional competencies and need no additional competencies than their female counter part (30.4% and 2.2%) respectively in relation to Research Methodology. It is revealed from the Table that there exist no significant association between the different need levels of research competencies in research methodology with the gender of the research scholars.

Competencies Related to Usage of ICT

The need related to research methodology among the female and male research scholar have been comparatively analysed and interpreted dimension-wise in Table 38.4 and Fig. 38.4.

Table 38.4: Chi-square test of Independence between the need of the Research Scholars related to Usage of ICT and Gender

Usage of ICT	Need Level of Competencies			χ^2	df	'P' Value
	NMAC	NSAC	NNAC			
Female	33 (71.7)	11 (23.9)	2 (4.3)	3.432	2	.180 NS
Male	29 (53.7)	21 (38.9)	4 (7.4)			
Total	**62 (62.0)**	**32 (32.0)**	**6 (6.0)**			

Note: NS—Not Significant.

It is evident from Table 38.4 and Fig. 38.4 that the majority (62%) research scholars were needed more additional competencies as compare to the need some additional competencies (32%) and need no additional competencies (6%) in relation to Usage of ICT. Further, with regard to gender, the female research scholars (71.7%) were needed more additional competencies as compared to their male counterpart (53.7%). In contrast to this, the male research scholars (38.9% and 7.4%) were needed some additional competencies and no additional competencies in relation to Usage of ICT. It is also observed that there exists no significant association

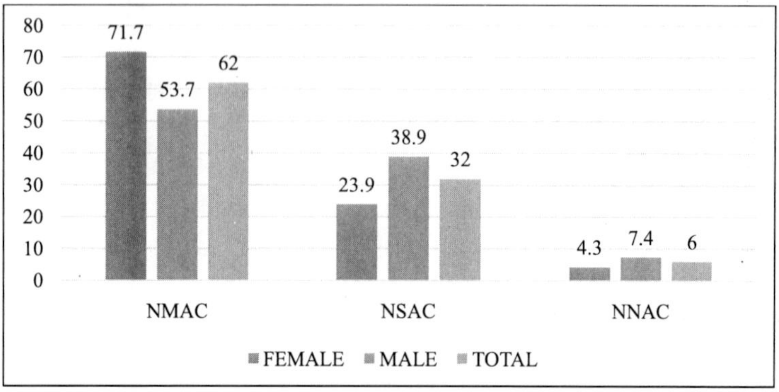

Notes: NMAC—Need More Additional Competency, NSAC—Need Some Additional Competency, NNAC—Need No Additional Competency.

Fig. 38.4: Need level competencies of the Research Scholars in relation to Usage of ICT and gender

between the different need levels of research competencies in using ICT in research with the gender of the research scholars.

Competencies Rrelated to Research Publication and Ethics

The need related to research publication and ethics among the female and male research scholars have been comparatively analysed and interpreted dimension-wise in the following table and graph.

Table 38.5: Chi-square test of Independence between the need of the Research Scholars related to Research Publication and Ethics and Gender

Research Publication Ethics	**Need Level of Competencies**		χ^2	**df**	**'P' Value**
	NMAC	**NSAC**			
Female	36 (78.3)	10 (21.7)	.239	2	.625 NS
Male	40 (74.1)	14 (25.9)			
Total	**76 (76.0)**	**24 (24.0)**			

Notes: The column NNAC was deleted because of no responses.
NS—Not Significant.

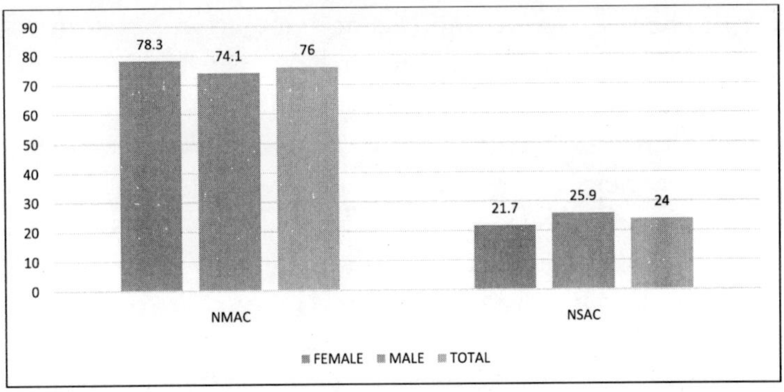

Notes: NMAC—Need More Additional Competency, NSAC—Need Some Additional Competency, NNAC—Need No Additional Competency.

Fig 38.5: Need level of research competencies of the Research Scholars in relation to Research Publication and Ethics and gender

It is observed from Table 38.5 and Fig. 38.5 that the majority (76%) of the research scholars were needed some additional competencies as compared to need more additional competencies (24%). Further with regard gender, it is evident from Table 38.5 that the female scholars (78.3%) were needed more additional competencies as compared to their male counter parts (74.1%). In contrast to this it is observed that the male research scholars (25.9%) were needed some additional competencies than their female counterparts (21.7%). It is also observed that there exist no significant association between the different need levels of research competencies in relation to research publication and ethics with the gender of the research scholars.

Major Findings

1. There exists no significant association between the different need levels of research competencies in reviewing the research related literature with the gender of the research scholars.
2. There exists no significant association between the different need levels of research competencies in writing proposal with the gender of the research scholars.

3. There exists no significant association between the different need levels of research competencies in research methodology with the gender of the research scholars.
4. There exists no significant association between the different need levels of research competencies in using ICT in research with the gender of the research scholars.
5. There exists no significant association between the different need levels of research competencies in research publication ethics with the gender of the research scholars.

Conclusion and Implications

The research scholars need more additional competencies and some additional competencies in reviewing the research related literature, proposal writing, research methodology, usage of ICT and research publication ethics. Coursework play a crucial role in the Ph.D. programme. During a Ph.D. coursework, the level of need and competencies required are essential for success in the programme. For the advancement of Ph.D. coursework to check the need level competencies is essential.

Most of the research scholars required to develop their need level competencies even after completion of their Ph.D. coursework through different activities related to the research review, proposal writing, research methodology, usage of ICT and research publication and ethics.

Ph.D. coursework is very essential for the development of research competencies among the research scholars. Even after the completion of the Ph.D. coursework there is need to develop some competencies among the research scholars. Different activities like workshop on tools development and validation of tool, seminars on proposal writing and conferences need to be organised in order to develop research competencies among the research scholars.

REFERENCES

Afolabi, O.E., Afolabi, O.E. and Aragbaye, M.O. (2022). "Research Competence of Postgraduate Students in Library Schools in South-West, Nigeria", *Library Philosophy and Practice (e-journal) 7181.* http://digitalcommons.unl.edu/libphiprac/7181

Das, B.K. and Das, B.C. (2022). "Need Assessment of Technological Pedagogical and Content Knowledge (TPACK) Among Pre-Service Teachers", *Excellence in Education,* A multidisciplinary International Peer reviewed/Refereed Journal, APH Publishing Corporation.

UGC (2009). *UGC Regulations on Minimum Standards and Procedures for the Award of M.Phil./Ph.D. Degree Regulation, 2009 and Clarification on Guidelines for Admission in Ph.D.* Retrieved from www.ugc.in/oldpdf/regulations/mphilphdclarification.pdf

UGC (2009). The Gazette of India on "Minimum Standards and Procedures for Awards of M.Phil./Ph.D. Degree Regulations". University Grants Commission, New Delhi, *The Times of India* (4 May 2011)

Caliwan–Fuentes, H. (2017). *Research Competence of Teacher Education Students in Eastern Samar State University Main Campus,* (*e-journal*). http://uruea.org/siteadmin/upload/DIR0117524.pdf

Index